SEX
in the
USSR

SEX in the USSR

by
MIKHAIL STERN, M.D.
with
AUGUST STERN, Ph.D.

Edited and Translated
from the French by
Mark Howson and Cary Ryan

NYT
Times
BOOKS

Published by TIMES BOOKS, a division of
Quadrangle/The New York Times Book Co., Inc.
Three Park Avenue, New York, N.Y. 10016

Published simultaneously in Canada by
Fitzhenry & Whiteside, Ltd., Toronto.

First published in France in 1979
by Editions Albin Michel, Paris.

Library of Congress Cataloging in Publication Data

Stern, Mikhail, 1918-
Sex in the USSR

Translation of La vie sexuelle en U.R.S.S.
Includes index.
1. Sex customs—Russia. 2. Family—Russia.
I. Howson, Mark. II. Ryan, Cary. III. Title.
HQ18.R9S5713 306.7'0947 80-5149
ISBN 0-8129-0942-9

Manufactured in the United States of America.

CONTENTS

Contents

INTRODUCTION
The Land Where Sex Is Forbidden

THE SUBJECT of this book is sex in the Soviet Union, by which I mean a number of things: how we make love; what we say to our wives and lovers and what they say to us; how and why we get married and divorced; why we commit rapes, and tell lies, and how we search for the truth; how we perceive the sexual reality of the West; the normal and pathological sexual behavior of free men and women, and of men and women in prisons and camps; the emotions of young people in their first encounters with sex . . . Does women's liberation exist in the Soviet Union? What about homosexuality? And those discreet country weekends enjoyed by the chiefs of the Kremlin, which we never read about in *Pravda*. . . .

The Soviet Union today is a secret world, a vast forbidden realm. When a foreign visitor lands at Sheremyetovo Airport outside Moscow, he may expect that he is about to set off on the discovery of a new country. But in the overwhelming majority of cases these expectations will remain unfulfilled, since his trip has been carefully planned in advance and will hold few surprises for him. He will be shown around Red Square, the Kremlin, and the historic places of Leningrad; a visit will be arranged to a model factory or a collective farm, a visit which has been anticipated by a painstakingly prepared itinerary. When he tries to make personal contact with the Soviet people—not just the faithful Intourist guide but the man in the street—he usually discovers, if he is shrewd enough to perceive it, an undertone of fear, tension, and uneasiness that is enough to freeze even the sincerest of smiles. In a country where the lie is regarded as an essential safeguard of national security, where every effort is made to present reality in the guise of an earthly paradise, and where every citizen is obliged to make a public profession of the official creed—everyone is busily concealing something from someone else. Thus our traveler will leave the Soviet Union without really having learned anything about the country—about the everyday existence of its citizens or their private thoughts.

One has only to consider this contrast: on one track the elegant and comfortable train called the Red Arrow runs between Moscow and Leningrad, and foreign visitors always ride first class. On another track I rode for fourteen days on the transit train that took me from the Vinnitsa prison to the forced-labor camp at Kharkov; ten prisoners were crammed into the filth, the stench, and the suffocating heat of a single compartment. I have chosen this deliberately shocking image to convey some small idea of the great chasm that divides the sunlit official landscape from the darker, hidden reality.

This division is the essence of Soviet reality. The split personality—the unresolvable contradiction between the Russians' publicly expressed attitudes and their behavior in private—even more than the absence of political and individual freedom, is what is destroying them, their bodies as well as their souls.

Nowhere are the somatic side-effects of this national schizophrenia more apparent than in the sex lives of ordinary people. Stalinist ideology officially banished sex from Soviet territory. The "Soviet man" was meant to be a sort of superman of irreproachable morals whose amorous activities, reduced to a chaste minimum, were only intended to strengthen the "Red Soviet family" and the socialist economy. When a woman made an appearance in the official iconography, she was always brandishing either a rifle or a sickle, and if she should make so bold as to uncover a breast, you could be certain that such immodesty could only serve the greater good of suckling a future Young Pioneer of the socialist motherland.

This essential feature of the regime, one which I cannot stress too strongly, is still very much alive in the Soviet Union, although it has been severely tested by the passage of time. And this may help to explain why there is more information available today in the Soviet Union about life in the camps than there is about the sexual behavior of ordinary men and women.

Of course, the prohibitions and the taboos which surround everything that has to do with sex are not an invention of the Soviet government; many countries have experienced this and many still do. But what is peculiar to Soviet society is the irksome and painful awareness of a moral overseer constantly looking over your shoulder, a nervous tic that has become ingrained in the character of *Homo sovieticus.* This moral standard has been imposed from on high and, in contrast to all traditional systems of morality, does not correspond to any sort of human reality. It constitutes a brutal interference on the part of the regime in the most private aspects of human existence. In the totalitarian state imagined by Orwell in *1984* the exercise of sexual freedom is considered to be a challenge to the established order; I have no doubt whatsoever that Communism has always striven toward this "ideal" state.

Quite simply then, the subject of this book is the sexual behavior of the Soviet people; I had no intention of writing either a political polemic or a medical treatise. I wished simply to express my views as an endocrinologist and sex therapist on the socio-sexual anomalies created by the Soviet way of life, and to describe my experience of thirty years as a medical practitioner. I do not claim to have produced a comprehensive sociological study—which would be impossible for reasons I will explain—but I will present all the evidence which I have been able to gather, even touching on such taboo subjects as homosexuality and certain practices indulged in by the great men of the regime in the seclusion of their dachas. Anyone who undertook such a project in the Soviet Union could be confident of being awarded a prominent place on the KGB blacklist of known and suspected dissidents. Censorship is so stringent that any kind of objective research into the subject would be impossible.

Numerous studies of male and female sexuality have appeared in the West in the past few years, *The Hite Report* and Pietropinto and Simenauer's *Beyond the Male Myth,* to name only two. From the official Soviet standpoint, such works simply confirm the moral disintegration of the "decadent" West, already so far advanced that only lurid accounts of sexual perversion are capable of exciting any interest. It goes without saying that sexology has no legitimate status in the Soviet Union. The word *sexologist* itself scarcely exists, except as an article of intellectual contraband that has occasionally been displayed during the rare outbreaks of liberalism in the last decades. Neither the scientific discipline of sexology nor the clinical practice of sex therapy exists in the USSR, so that the Soviet citizen who seeks professional help for some sexual problem is obliged to consult a psychiatrist, an endocrinologist, a urologist or gynecologist, or a specialist in venereal diseases. As the prevalence of sexual disorders in the Soviet Union is appalling, any practicing sexologist brave enough to hang out his shingle would soon have all the patients he could cope with and no competition at all.

Those doctors who do attempt to meet this need are like advance scouts in enemy territory, lonely Quixotes battling the taboos promulgated by the regime and the moral prejudices and horrifying ignorance of the vast majority of the Soviet population. They must rely entirely on their own practical experience and personal resources, for there is little information to be found in the orthodox medical canons of a country which claims to lead the world in the quality and efficiency of its health services.

Had the reader been present at my consultations, I have no doubt that he would have found them somewhat perplexing. For even if he were fluent in Russian, he would have heard little but the endless repetition of the word *it*. *It* can mean the penis, the vagina, intercourse, pregnancy, masturbation, orgasm, or any one of a number of other things for which there are no precise equivalents in colloquial Russian. The accuracy of the doctor's diagnosis and the success of his treatment depend entirely on his ability to interpret correctly all these various *it*'s—or the lack thereof. Very often the subject does not even come up during the medical consultation itself; I cannot recall how many times a patient came to see me on the pretext of seeking treatment for a glandular problem of some sort and then, at the end of the visit, suddenly found the courage to add in a worried voice, "Doctor, I have a little problem I want to ask you about. . . ."

Despite these handicaps, the task of the "clandestine" sex therapist is made easier by the fact that in the Soviet Union the doctor is invested with an important social role which transcends his strictly medical responsibilities. Formerly when Russians wished to confess their sins, ask for advice, or simply talk about their problems, they would go to see the priest. Now that the Orthodox Church has been effectively suppressed, all priests are suspected of collaborating with the police, and people no longer know whom to confide in. Often it is the doctor who takes on the responsibility of receiving such confidences and thus of curing his patients' souls as well as their bodies. The doctor's office is probably one of the last remaining islets of humanity which is sheltered from the rigors of the Communist regime, a kind of confessional where people will talk willingly about personal problems they would never discuss anywhere else.The doctor enjoys the confidence of the people, and he often comes to know things that even the KGB has not found out yet.

This is the ambiguous state of sex therapy in the USSR—a semi-clandestine trade which consists of equal measures of pure medicine, psychotherapy, and simple, friendly conversation. My own experience as an endocrinologist and sex therapist fits precisely into this general pattern, and the greater part of the book is based on data that I have collected in the course of my medical practice. As a doctor I have always worked among the "masses" (as they still say in Russia), and my patients were of all ages, from the very young to the very old, and came from all strata of the population, ranging from simple farmers to government ministers and KGB generals. It would be difficult to calculate just how many patients I treated in the course of thirty years. The clinic I directed in Vinnitsa was legally required to receive thirty to thirty-five patients a day, but in practice the number was usually twice as great. There were even periods in which I had to examine a hundred patients a day. During the terrible famine of 1947, I sometimes saw two hundred.

Although during most of my medical career in the U.S.S.R. I lived and worked in the Ukraine, I have seen or treated patients from all over the Soviet Union—from Norilsk and Vorkuta in the far north, Baku on the Caspian Sea, and Vladivostok on the Pacific; from Leningrad, Moscow, Odessa, Kiev, Minsk, Yerevan; from "open" cities such as Tashkent, Novosibirsk, and Ivanovo, and "closed" cities such as Gorky, Sverdlovsk, and Perm, which foreigners are not permitted to visit. The ethnic diversity of my patients is no less remarkable: I have treated Ukrainians, Jews, Russians, Georgians, Czechs, Poles, Buddhist Buryats, Muslim Azerbaijanis, Christian Armenians—the entire mosaic of Soviet nationalities, atheists and believers alike—and in the process have acquired a rather broadly based clinical background.

Vinnitsa is a typical Soviet city. There is a saying that France is not Paris; there is all the more reason for saying that the USSR is not Moscow or Leningrad. The real Russia is the small city, and consequently I believe that my essentially provincial background is more representative of Soviet reality than any experience I might have gained in Moscow or Leningrad—even though these commonly serve as reference points for Westerners and Russians alike, who too often tend to extrapolate from their observations of what are, after all, only showcases arranged by the Soviets for the benefit of the Western world.

Vinnitsa is interesting for other reasons as well. During World War II it was the headquarters of the Soviet general staff; when Vinnitsa was occupied by the Germans, it was Hitler's personal headquarters during his tours of the Eastern Front. The pleasant summer climate has made it a gathering place for all sorts of highly placed personnages—generals, Party VIPs, and other representatives of the privileged classes. One street in the older section of the city is occupied almost entirely by retired generals. It sometimes happened that VIPs would send for me or visit me in my consulting room, and so it was that I had the honor of receiving the Party First Secretary for the Vinnitsa region—in other words, the grand panjandrum of our part of the country.

In my thirty years of practice I have observed all sorts of sexual and hormonal anomalies, witnessed incredible human tragedies, and gained an insight into the secret destinies of some extraordinary men and women. The most common problems I encountered were sexual immaturity, impotence, premature ejaculation, and frigidity. Some of my patients came to see me of their own accord; others came unwillingly—impotent husbands whose wives had finally convinced them to talk to a doctor, or children whose parents had caught them masturbating. Some were brought to me by despair; some had had their lives destroyed by a pathological phobia. Some were already aware that they were suffering from an abnormal condition; others discovered it in the course of the consultation. Some became my patients by proxy, after their families had come to ask for my help, and there were even some modest souls who could only consult with me over the telephone. There were patients who came to my house for private consultations who would not have dared to visit the clinic at all—for the most part homosexuals, men and women who had contracted venereal diseases, women from Kiev who wanted their abortions performed in secret to avoid the "disgrace," and impotent men who wanted to be treated privately for their equally "disgraceful" affliction. Whenever I felt that one of my clinic patients was unable to speak frankly about his problems, I would suggest a private consultation, and a great many patients became much less reticent when they visited me in my home. I also received a number of referrals from colleagues in Kiev, Moscow, and Kharkov; one woman, a lesbian, came all the way from Leningrad to see me. And I sometimes traveled to other cities to treat members of the Party elite as well as ordinary people.

However, I am compelled to cite all these thousands of cases from memory: when I left the USSR, I was only able to take with me some notes, letters, and photographs, for all my files had been confiscated by the police. If this seems surprising, you should bear in mind that in a totalitarian society memory plays a much more important role than it does elsewhere. In the West no one—except perhaps spies and criminals—hesitates to commit his experiences to writing, but in the USSR, where the written word can all too easily become the pretext for house searches, confiscation, and prosecution, names and facts *must* be entrusted to memory—and as a result Russians have developed extraordinary powers of retention. In the Soviet Union the written page is never truly the property of its author. Nadezhda Mandelstam, the widow of the poet Osip Mandelstam, set herself the difficult task of learning hundreds of his poems by heart—the only possible way of preserving his works from almost certain oblivion. In the circumstances, it is understandable that all Soviet dissident writing has a "remembered" quality, an autobiographical flavor, and my book is no exception to the rule.

As I have said, the book is based primarily, though not exclusively, on my own experience. I have also relied on information gathered from others whom I encountered in the course of my medical practice—chance acquaintances, friends, and colleagues—and from "special" patients—Party dignitaries and their wives, government ministers, officers on leave, officials of the KGB, of Intourist, of the office of the People's Prosecutor, and reporters for *Pravda*. As everyone knows, information in virtually every sector of Soviet society is "classified," in the sense that it remains in the possession of a small, closed group and does not circulate freely. News travels by word of mouth, and the anecdote takes the place of the local newspaper. My profession has allowed me to share in the confidences of some of the best informed people in the USSR; moreover, as a physician and former Party member, I had access to certain confidential documents which never fall into the hands of ordinary mortals.

I have also made use of Soviet sociological works—or at least of the few intriguing facts that have somehow slipped through the censor's net—and articles that have appeared in the Soviet press on both medical and general topics, which sometimes allow the experienced eye to read between the lines, as well as several Western sociological and historical studies which I have been able to consult since leaving the USSR.*

And last but not least, I would like to acknowledge my final source—the fifteen hundred inmates of ITK-12, the "correctional labor colony" outside Kharkov where I spent my last three years in the Soviet Union and where I discovered an important new aspect of Soviet sexuality. To be sure, a concentration camp is not a research laboratory, and the inmate is more concerned with his own survival than with observing the sexual behavior of his companions in misfortune. But there too the respect which is accorded the medical profession won me a special position as confidant, privileged observer, and consulting specialist among my fellow inmates. Now that I have awakened from the nightmare, I am astonished by how vividly the names, the tales of violence, murder, and suicide, the tragic and tragicomic events, the faces of the living and the dead, remain engraved on my memory.

It was there, in the camp, that I finally understood something that I had never really grasped as a free man—that there is a real connection between the bloody outbreaks of terror that have periodically stained the pages of Soviet history and the profound abnormalities of Soviet sexual life. I understood then that the totalitarian regime which came into power in 1917 was directly responsible for certain pathological phenomena which are in fact peculiar to that regime and which have become appallingly common in Russia today. In a way, then, this book is not just the product of my own experiences as a doctor and as a dissident; to some degree it also reflects the experience of thousands of patients whom I was able to speak with and sometimes help. The fact that I have lived under a totalitarian regime for most of my life—and for three years behind barbed wire—has stamped my own political beliefs with an indelible imprint, for which I make no apologies and of which there will be ample evidence in this book.

* Perhaps the most important of these was I. Kurganov's *Women and Communism* (in Russian), New York, 1968.

The two years that I have spent outside Soviet Russia have allowed me to measure the vast cultural distance that separates the Western and the Soviet worlds. Notwithstanding the culpability of the Soviet system and the particular character of the Russian people, the backwardness of Soviet medicine and the incredible naiveté of the Soviet citizen with regard to any problem that involves sexuality would truly astonish many Westerners. I should also point out that even today the terminology that is current in the USSR is much less precise than in the West. We often hear of the universal language of medicine, and in fact the UNESCO convention on uniform medical terminology has been adopted by virtually every country in the world, including the USSR. This normalized terminology, however, has not been applied to sexual matters in the USSR, and for reasons that are scarcely fortuitous. For example, the terms *impotence* and *frigidity* can describe a number of different states which Western medicine defines more analytically than we do (for example, premature ejaculation and anorgasmia). *Gratification, pleasure,* and *orgasm* are a few of the many terms which are used indifferently in the absence of any consensus as to their specific meanings.

In this book I have deliberately used the current Russian terminology, since it does have some evidential value in itself. I ask the reader to indulge me in this, since my purpose is to give as detailed an account as I can of Soviet sexuality, and there is no more demanding task than that of expressing the evidence of experience in precise terms.

I am fully aware that this book contains many faults, contradictions, and naive oversimplifications, but I hope that at least it will have the effect of stimulating further enquiries into the subject of Soviet sexuality.

I

SEXUALITY
and the
SOVIET REGIME

It may seem odd to begin a book about sexuality with a discussion of the problems of a political regime. What possible connection can there be between the workings of a government—preoccupied with politics, economics, and foreign affairs—and the most intimate aspects of human existence? Could it be that the author has succumbed to his anticommunist obsession and begun to look for commissars under every bed?

I will answer with a story drawn from my own clinical experience, one which has always seemed to have a horrifying symbolic significance.

The tale begins in 1937 in the Ukraine. Elena and Andrei were newly married and eager to begin sampling the pleasures of their new life together—an emotion as old as mankind itself and one which transcends political and ideological divisions.

Yet, at that time, the country was in the midst of the Great Purge of 1937, the height of the prewar Stalinist terror. Millions of innocent people were being sentenced without trial, sent to prisons or the camps, condemned to death on the most implausible pretexts. Fear was everywhere—in the log huts in the countryside and in the Tsarist mansions of the great cities; in the working class districts and in the villas of the Party elite.

Can a condemned man still be in love? Yes—and perhaps his love is even more intense than the complacent executioner's. No one in those days wished to die; everyone clung passionately to life, to its simplest pleasures and its maddest hopes. And everyone expected that arrest was more or less imminent, but they gritted their teeth and went on with their lives all the same. At night, after all the annoyances of a long working day, they would go to bed exhausted and begin the interminable wait for the midnight knock on the door, asking themselves if this would be the last night they would spend in their own beds.

The NKVD preferred to operate at night. For those who drew a twenty-five year sentence to the camps or a bullet in the back of the neck, it was of no great importance whether they were in bed or in the middle of dinner when the knock finally came. But the nocturnal visits of the NKVD had a horribly traumatic effect on the survivors; it would be difficult to overestimate the significance of the damage done. During those years the entire population was mute with fear, and this fear not only had a disastrous psychological effect on millions of people but also caused serious sexual problems for a great many. Imagine if you will an errant husband trying to make love while his wife is pounding on the door; perhaps he can think up a convincing excuse, or simply not open the door, or escape through the window with his lover. But with the NKVD it was no use offering excuses or trying to escape—when the knock on the door came, it had to be answered.

Andrei was finally picked up in 1938, on the night of April 20—Hitler's birthday, as he liked to recall later. He was sentenced immediately to twenty years in a camp; but in 1941, when the war broke out, he was sent to the front with a penal battalion composed of "criminals" and "enemies of the people." All his comrades were killed; he escaped with the loss of an arm, and for some obscure bureaucratic reason or perhaps simply as a fortunate result of the chaos that followed the war's end, he was allowed to return home instead of being sent back to the camp. Sexually Andrei was perfectly normal—outside his marriage with Elena. After he returned home, he could not rid himself of the terrible fear of arrest. At night the slightest sound in the street would send him into a genuine paroxysm of terror: "They're coming after me again!" Sometimes he would get up and silently walk over to the window and peer through the curtains. Seeing no one, he would return to bed, and again he would feel his throat constrict with fear. His wife showed great understanding and assured him that she still loved him, even though he had lost an arm. Her reassurances were in vain, and despite his ardor, his fears proved stronger, and he remained impotent.

I met Andrei in 1950 and he recounted for me in painful detail the six or seven occasions on which he had been able to make love to Elena in five years. Their great love had kept their marriage together, but they could not continue to live like this. Andrei was prepared to set his wife free to do as she chose, although he was still deeply attached to her. I don't think that Elena would have agreed to his unselfish proposal; she was fully prepared to sacrifice her own sexual satisfaction for the sake of their life together.

A series of hypnosis sessions was ineffective, and I began to feel very discouraged, since it seemed I could do nothing to help these people whose lives had been destroyed by the Soviet system. Simply to restore my own peace of mind, I advised Andrei to stop sleeping in the same bed with Elena for a week or two, then to try to make love to her again, but this time during the day—which is highly exotic by Soviet standards.

I don't recall how I happened to hit on this idea—perhaps I had already grasped the full significance of this "arrest complex," or perhaps it was simply intuition. But I will never forget when Elena and Andrei came to my house with a bottle of vodka and an enormous cake. They were both crying, making no attempt to hold back their tears as they embraced me. This was in 1952. In Moscow, preparations for a new wave of purges in the wake of the alleged Doctors' Plot were well underway, and it was almost as if we were crying out, "Enough! We want to remain human! We want to live! We will never turn our backs on love!"

I have not chosen arbitrarily to introduce the real subject of this book with an illustration of the effect the violence unleashed by the Soviet regime has had on the sexual lives of its people. It was the regime itself which made it necessary for me to inquire into the private lives of its most inoffensive citizens.

The twentieth century has taught us that every society, every social and political order, has imposed certain prohibitions on sexuality, rules of conduct which it compels its members to obey with a greater or lesser degree of success, and finally ideological and moral commandments which are graven on the collective conscience. Men become detached from the pure biological function of sexuality and quite often have no idea of the profound connections which exist between sexual activity, erotic love, and orgasm on the one hand, and the history of a society and of a particular people on the other. Without even stopping to consider the obvious example of Victorian England, we might take note of the fact that so-called primitive societies, once supposed to exist in a natural state of total promiscuity, in fact are bound by extremely rigid kinship systems by which incest, for example, is generally prohibited.

The Soviet system, which claims to exercise total control over the individual in all his activities and even his thoughts, is thus all the more likely to be concerned with sexuality. Lenin once wrote to his platonic friend Inessa Armand that "as far as the question of love is concerned, the entire problem lies in the *objective logic* of class relations." Whether we wish it or not, love falls under the control of the public sector. The family should be a "Communist" family and the wife should be liberated (in Soviet fashion); homosexuality has been a criminal offense since 1934.

Thus it will not be possible to understand anything about Soviet sexuality if we lose sight of the social and political backdrop against which all human relationships are played out. A brief digression into Russian social history in Tsarist times, and particularly since 1917 seems to be in order. I am not a historian, and moreover the present state of the evidence would scarcely justify as ambitious a project as *Sexuality in Russia Through the Ages.* I merely hope to point out several consistent factors which may shed some light on the sexual mores of the Russian people on the eve of the revolutionary era.

Chapter 1
A Bit of Ancient History

The regime which was created in October 1917 set out to remake Russian society according to a preestablished formula. What was the nature of this old society, and what were the sexual mores of the Russian people in prerevolutionary times?

The "Barbarians"

Western historians have begun to take an interest in the sexual practices of medieval and modern Europe. This is a relatively new subject which, as far as Russia is concerned, remains completely unexplored. Our only extant sources for the early modern period are church records and the testimony of foreign travelers. Among the earliest of these (although still comparatively late) was Adam Olearius, the ambassador of the Duchy of Holstein to Moscow in the seventeenth century. Olearius is notable for the precision and accuracy of his account of Russian life, as well as for his horrified reaction to the "barbarities" of the Russians, whom he found to be "extremely coarse: *

> They give themselves up to all sorts of indecencies and even to crimes against nature, not only with men but with animals as well.

And further on:

> In truth the Muscovites have . . . not the slightest notion of what is seemly. The postures of their dances and the boldness of their women are infallible signs of their wicked propensities. In Moscow we saw men and women emerge naked from the public baths, accosting the young folk in our party and enticing them with obscene and lascivious speeches. It is idleness, the mother of all the vices, which seems to have been bestowed on these barbarians in good measure, that leads them to these excesses—and to drunkenness, and lewdness as well, to which they give themselves up entirely after they have set to drinking.

Finally he describes the "most pious" activities of the pilgrims of Novgorod after they have spent the entire day drinking brandy:

> . . . one woman was so besotted that as she stumbled from the tent she fell down and went to sleep, quite naked, in the very middle of the street and at the height of the day. This circumstance inspired a drunken Muscovite to lay himself down beside her, and having had his pleasure with her, he went to sleep also, in plain sight of everyone. The passersby did nothing but mock, until an old man took pity on them and covered them both with his shirt.

This incident certainly provides a picture of a very free, in fact a truly promiscuous society. Olearius was a visitor from a more orderly world, where sex had already learned to clothe itself in the garments of modesty—while the Russians bathed naked, drank to excess (even then!), and with their drinking bouts often just the prelude to other, less edifying diversions.

Still, we should not accept Olearius's moral pronouncements and

* Olearius, *Journey to Muscovy*, Paris, 1659, pp. 152–153. [See also L.E. Berry and R.O. Crummey, *Rude and Barbarous Kingdom*, Madison, Wisc., 1968, for the Elizabethan Englishman's view of Muscovite culture.]

premature conclusions uncritically. Just because a society is extremely permissive does not imply total freedom from restrictions, even if these are enthusiastically transgressed on every possible occasion. In contrast to these scenes of unrestrained debauchery, we might invoke the image of the Orthodox patriarch, the virtuous embodiment of these restrictions in a country that was still essentially ruled by the clergy. In any case, the mores of the peasantry in Western Europe were scarcely more refined, at least before they had felt the restraining hand of the Church.

Nonetheless, the early descriptions of Russia do suggest a society that was at only one remove from barbarism. Should we conclude from this that these primitive traits are inherent in the Russian character, or should we see them as the legacy of the Mongol conquest, which reduced the Russian people to a state of virtual slavery from the thirteenth to the fifteenth century? These are merely conjectures, of course, and they are tainted with the prejudices of the nineteenth-century slavophile intellectuals, who were always somewhat uneasy about serfdom itself and the moral character of the "honest Russian *muzhik.*" At any rate it does seem clear that the civilizing and repressive influences of the Church had far less impact on Russia during this period than on other rural societies in Europe.

Olearius has also supplied us with an interesting account of the *skomorokhi,* strolling mountebanks who doubled as acrobats, buffoons, sorcerers, and jugglers on occasion, enlivening the tedium of rural existence and the festivities of the princely courts:

> These charlatans and mountebanks enact fanciful tales before the public. They do not scruple to uncover their backsides and sometimes their entire persons for all to see. The bear leaders, who are accompanied by cup throwers and puppeteers, can rig up a stage in an instant, by means of a linen covering that they bind to the middle of their bodies, and drawing this up over their heads, they produce their marionettes and make as if to perform acts against nature, and other kinds of bestiality. It is by means of such spectacles as these that their children learn in earliest infancy to renounce modesty and chastity forever.

These "mountebanks" always took part in the traditional pagan festivals—Shrove Tuesday, the first day of spring, summer, and winter—which, like the Carnival in Western Europe, were marked by the complete relaxation of ordinary taboos, and it is hardly surprising that the songs of the *skomorokhi* do not always adhere to the highest standards of propriety. Although the Soviets have produced new editions of the Russian heroic tales, which date back to the earliest time, they have so far been reluctant to publish the texts of these comical, obscene folk ballads, which do seem to revel in everything that is forbidden in contemporary life.

Marriage is always held up to ridicule in these ballads: an unfaithful wife prevails on her lover to strangle her husband, which only makes the good man snore the louder. The balladeer seems here to have been a feminist long before his time. Religion is another target of the balladeer's wit: if a ballad shows Satan being buggered by a lesser demon, then for all his contortions he no longer cuts a very terrifying figure; and if Satan has lost all his terrors, then a sin is no longer a sin. Nor is the clergy spared by the balladeer, who claims to have "fucked" a priest and his wife and daughter as well—who show their gratitude by cooking him an omelette.

The ballads I refer to were collected by Kirsha Danilov at the end of the eighteenth century. So apparently the pace of life described by Olearius had not slackened in a hundred years, at least in the countryside. The *skomorokhi* were still drawing crowds in every village they appeared in, particularly during festivals and holidays—much to the distress of the Church, which, well into the nineteenth century, was still inveighing against the blasphemous and indecent character of these festivities.

Under Ivan the Terrible, for example, the Stoglav Council of 1551 denounced "the wearing of women's clothing . . . by men and young boys," games which "arouse many men and women to mirth and fornication," and finally "diabolical songs and dances and even more degraded acts" which only result in "the corruption of youth and the defilement of young virgins."

Pamphilius, a priest of the seventeenth century, complains that:

> [In June] virtually the entire town is in an uproar, together with a great clamor of flutes, fiddles, and tambourines. Wives and daughters dance and soil their lips with impious cries and songs, contorting their bodies and stamping and galloping with their feet. The men and young boys are sorely tempted to sin. . . . Matrons commit adultery and young girls are despoiled of their maidenhood.

Young Pagans and Wantons

If the Church's attempts at repression were real enough, in practice its influence was fairly limited. The pagan festivals were rechristened—the winter festival as Christmas, the June festival as St. John's Day—and some effort was made to restrain the populace "from running riot." But the sort of popular commotion that was decried by Pamphilius and his indignant brethren was still very much in evidence throughout the nineteenth century, as the enormous body of ethnographic literature from that period attests.

During the Christmas celebrations *(Sviatki)* boys and girls still dressed in one another's clothes and, as one author explained, "we are compelled to point out in all candor that these holiday pranks cannot by any stretch of the imagination be called innocent; even the young children are brought out of the cabins to give them a taste of this freedom." * Maximov also feels compelled "not to give any particulars of the more irreverent aspects of certain of these games," of which "easily half consist of pagan survivals which strike the observer as being frankly indecent."

Moreover, in certain parts of Russia these holiday celebrations also witnessed the resurgence of a phallic cult that was undeniably pagan in origin. In springtime villagers reenacted the burial of Yarilo (presumably an ancient Slavic deity) who took the form of an effigy with an enormous phallus. While the women ogled unashamedly the men would laugh and crack obscene jokes—though in a peasant community these probably would not have been regarded as such. During the mock burial the celebrants would kiss one another and, as Maximov tartly observes, "contact between the sexes was extremely free."

Here sexuality takes on a metaphysical dimension. This erotic ritual symbolizes the coming of spring and is intended to stimulate the fertility of the soil (the burial of the Yarilo effigy represents the sowing of the seed).

In one of the games described by Maximov, the Blacksmith Game,

* A. Maximov, *Powers of Evil,* 1903.

teenage boys disguised themselves as old men and the "blacksmith" made a few magical passes over their heads to restore them to youth, whereupon they threw themselves upon the village girls with renewed ardor. It is noteworthy that unmarried adolescents participated in these games, and that a certain amount of sexual freedom was tolerated before marriage—if not in the form of actual intercourse, at least of erotic games which were sanctioned by tradition and were hardly felt to be shameful.

Often these games retained a ritual, even magical character, whose significance transcended that of simple mass catharsis. During the Christmas celebration it was customary to try to foretell the future, particularly for young girls who were eager to find out what sort of husbands they would have. One method of divination required the girl to walk into the sheepfold at nightfall, quite naturally shivering with fear, bend over, and turn her bare buttocks toward the open door, intoning, "My dear, my promised one, caress me!" If the hand that reached out to caress her was hairy, this meant a rich husband; a smooth hand, a poor one. Here again, this erotic game was a prelude to marriage, of which it appears to be a sort of symbolic representation.

Certain ethnographers were occasionally able to overcome their scruples in order to record such songs as:

> The balls of the rye went sailing down the river
> Till they caught up with a cunt on a bridge between two legs.

This couplet is sung to accompany a wedding dance—the "balls" refer to the design traced on the loaf of rye bread which forms the centerpiece of the marriage feast. Such expressions, extremely indelicate by modern standards, were regarded as perfectly natural and lent themselves quite well to fanciful and poetic imagery of this kind. But what is most striking here is the complete integration of sexuality into ordinary life in the minds of the most "respectable" countryfolk. Marriage is openly proclaimed to be a physical union, and no attempt is made to conceal this truth.

The famous collector of Russian folktales, Alexander Afanasyev, never succeeded in publishing his *Secret Russian Tales* inside Russia itself; they were first printed in Geneva over a hundred years ago and have remained a rare collector's item, though a new French edition appeared recently. These folk tales are full of exuberant obscenity;

husbands are deceived and maidens seduced by the most unlikely subterfuges. The callow or merely stupid young man who doesn't know "how it's done" is made the butt of many tales, and the amorous intrigues suggest a comparison with the French *fabliaux* or Boccaccio's *Decameron.* (One of Afanasyev's tales is given in its entirety in the Appendix.)

In fact, it appears that sexual license can be tolerated in a well-ordered hierarchical world, since some conventions can occasionally be flouted as long as the essential structure remains intact. The center of this world, and of all peasant life, was the family. From the seventeenth century on, communal land holdings were parceled out to extended family groups, not individuals, in order of their importance. These allotments were cultivated by the family group as well; private property was unknown. The extended family might number several dozen people, all ruled by a father, grandfather, or elder brother whose patriarchal authority was unchallenged—he could even sleep with his daughters-in-law, as sometimes happened, without causing any particular scandal.

The *Domostroi,* a sixteenth-century handbook of domestic economy, advised husbands to be careful to avoid blows to the head or other sensitive areas when they beat their wives. This handbook was addressed primarily to the merchant class, but this was considered to be sound advice for any householder. The battered wife was not just part of contemporary reality, she was an archetype who was celebrated in Russian folklore. Here is one of Afanasyev's "secret" tales which says a great deal about the attitudes behind all this:

> Once there was a woman whose husband gave her a terrible hiding whenever she brought his dinner to him. What's more, he shouted at her, "Bottom's filthy! Bottom's filthy!" with every blow. So she went out to wash her bottom, scoured it with sand and sackcloth until she drew blood—but the next time she served her husband's dinner, he started to beat her again, still shouting, "Bottom's filthy! Bottom's filthy!" Then she went to her aunt's house to find out what the trouble could be. "Can't you tell me, Auntie, why my husband always beats me when I bring him his dinner, and why he shouts, 'Bottom's filthy! Bottom's filthy!' After all, I washed my bottom until I drew blood!" "How can you be so stupid, I wonder. It's not *your* bottom he wants you to wash, it's the bottom of the bowl." The woman went straight home and washed the bottom of the bowl, and her husband never beat her again.

This rigid domestic hierarchy, with its strict division of labor between the sexes in the household as well as in the fields, created a stable and enduring image that has given rise to all sorts of nostalgic reveries and lamentations for a vanished past. The way of life of the landed gentry closely resembled that of the peasantry; their lives followed the same seasonal rhythms, and they also were devout adherents of the cult of the family. How many idyllic evocations there are of domestic happiness in Russian literature, beginning with Aksakov's *Family Chronicle* and Tolstoy's *War and Peace!* Such happiness was usually described only in the past tense, however, since it was the young nobleman's unpleasant duty to leave his family and confront the rigors of military life or the cold, gray routine of the *gymnasium* in a city that might just as well have been in some other country as far as he was concerned, since he had been torn from his games, his old nurse, and his village playmates. . . .

This then is the face of rural Russia, which remained unchanged until the twentieth century.

The Tsars at Play

It is probably no secret to the reader that the Western concept of erotic love was almost unknown in Russia, and it would be fruitless to try to discover even a hint of courtliness or chivalry in the private lives of the Russian princes. At the princely court of Muscovy, until the eighteenth century in fact, manners were still extremely coarse, and the violence and cruelty of the age were hardly affected by an idealized image of love and womanhood—as they were to some extent in the West. The Muscovite tsars themselves, after all, did not set the highest standards of conduct for their subjects.

The career of Ivan the Terrible (1547 to 1584) is probably familiar enough in its broad outlines. Seven times married, he came to prefer rape as the ideal means of gratifying his sadistic impulses, and sometimes his political designs as well. On one occasion he raped the wife of a boyar, who had apparently done something to provoke his anger, then turned her over to his bodyguards, the notorious *Oprichniki.* His anger appeased, he sent the woman back to her husband with a note to the effect that the tsar and forty-nine of his faithful servants had "all taken great pleasure with her." In fact, Ivan preferred to take his pleasure with persons of both sexes—his chief favorite, Basmanov, enjoyed a long career at court—in elaborate orgies with the murderous thugs of his bodyguard.

But the peculiar tastes of an individual—even if he is the Tsar of All the Russians—are not necessarily shared by his countrymen, and we might recall that there were a number of French and English kings who set similar if less spectacular examples. What is still striking, to say the least, is the unrestraint and abandon with which Ivan indulged in these acts of sadistic cruelty and sexual degradation, for he was no stranger to the consolations of religion. In fact, he is almost equally well remembered for his periodic bouts of morbid depression, during which he generally retired to a monastery to do penance for his latest outrages. When we recall that this was also the age of the High Renaissance in Europe, a time when the spiritual ecstasies of love were being celebrated by painters and poets, we begin to think of Russia as suspended in a sort of time warp, or, to resort to the more usual cliché, "stranded in the backwaters of European civilization."

In the hundred years that elapsed between the accession of Peter the Great (1696) and the death of Catherine II (1796) the upper classes turned toward the West, and the enlightening influence of Western European civilization began to be reflected in Russian mores—although the ideal of the French libertine was just as eagerly emulated as the pastoral poet or the sentimental novelist. Russians of the nineteenth century regarded the moral decadence of Catherine's reign with horror, and this German princess who became Empress of Russia quickly showed herself to be a willing disciple of Casanova. A whole procession of lovers succeeded one another in the imperial boudoir, from Saltykov to Poniatowski, then from Orlov to Potëmkin, and finally an entire squadron of vigorous young men, hand-picked by the officers of the guard for their virility and stamina.

After Catherine, virtue gradually reestablished itself in the imperial household; Nicholas I, Alexander II, Alexander III, and Nicholas II were all sovereigns of regular habits—the life of Nicholas I was austere to the point of asceticism—and none of them would furnish much material for the historical novelist. There is of course the counterexample of Rasputin to provide a little variety, and his meteoric career was admittedly due as much to his sexual prowess as to his spiritual attainments. However, the details of Rasputin's ministry have certainly received sufficient attention in the West, and are most interesting in any case as a regrettable indication of the decadence of the monarchy itself in the period just before the precipitous collapse of 1917.

The Renaissance

In the nineteenth century the aristocracy and the intelligentsia had become completely devoted to Western ways, and the idea of love itself had acquired a certain touch of humor, of playfulness, of poetry, and of Eros.

It was during this period, which has aptly been called the Russian Renaissance, that an erotic literature appeared for the first time. The poem "Luka Mudishchëv," an extract from which appears in the appendix, has been attributed to Pushkin but in fact was written by Ivan Barkov at the end of the eighteenth century. The poem itself is a rather elegant pastiche of humor and popular obscenity. The climactic scene in which Luka impales the procuress on his monstrous phallus is borrowed directly from the folk tradition and the carnival ballads of the *skomorokhi*—the hero of one of Afanasyev's "secret tales" is endowed with an even larger engine of destruction, formidable enough to sink a ship in his case.

In the Soviet Union today "Luka Mudishchëv" is only available in a privately circulated *samizdat* edition, and I recall that at the end of a propaganda lecture I once attended in Kiev, on the subject of Soviet marriage, the speaker received a note from the audience requesting his comments on "Luka Mudishchëv." He replied more or less as follows, his voice rising in an angry crescendo:

> I have never read this poem, but I know that it is marred by certain grave defects, which can, of course, be explained in terms of the class origins of its author. The poem makes no mention of the popular liberation struggles of the period, nor of the sufferings of the peasantry, who were compelled to give up their sons and daughters to the matchmaker and the horrors of arranged marriage. Luka Mudishchëv is shown to be totally cut off from the masses. His struggle is waged only against the merchant class, and consequently he meets with a tragic end.

The audience was silent, dumbfounded—probably almost none of them had even read the poem. No one laughed, and this Marxist analysis of "Luka Mudishchëv" was, as they say in the USSR, adopted by acclamation.

But to return to the Russian Renaissance, the best examples of the joyous erotic freedom of this period are found in the poetry of Pushkin, the first and the greatest genius of Russian literature. Unfortunately, his complete works are only published in an expurgated edition, so full of ellipses that many of his humorous poems and epigrams are completely indecipherable. How, after all, could the Soviet censors permit a poem like this to be published in its entirety?

> When Orlov first his warlike garments shed,
> And fell on fair Laissa in her bed,
> The ardent warrior was quickly disarrayed,
> And ill-accustomed to a bareback jade.
> By now Laissa had abandoned hope,
> And from somewhere produced a microscope:
> "*Mon général*, you've stormed the Mount of Venus.
> Return the favor, please—present your penis!"

And what are they to make of his *Gavriliad*, a genuine treasure of erotic literature and a highly original account of the Immaculate Conception, which only occurs after Mary has submitted to the embraces of Lucifer and the Archangel Gabriel?

The Dying Eros

We have arrived at a time in which Russian culture was at its height, an age of great writers and composers whose works are cherished by the entire world. Without suggesting that this culture reflected all of Russian society at that time, I will pause to examine it as an expression of the attitudes of the aristocracy and intelligentsia during the long period of gestation before Russia finally emerged as a "civilized" country.

But after the brief display of skyrockets and Roman candles which marked the age of Pushkin, Eros begins to be presented in an increasingly dim light. Even in Pushkin himself there are hints that he was intuitively aware of a kind of malaise, or of a certain uneasiness in the presence of erotic love.

In his verse drama *Evgeny Onegin* it is the heroine, Tatiana, who declares her love to Onegin. This is not the classic Western European drama in which the woman is seduced by the man; here it is the woman who plays the active role of the seducer. But the most interesting aspect of this typically Russian drama is that Onegin responds coldly to Tatiana's overtures, and with an affected cynicism which only conceals his inability to love.

In fact, Onegin's virility is called into question by the structure of the drama itself. Tatiana, the demystified image of woman, does not correspond at all to the heroines of chivalric romances in which the hero's courtship of his beloved is depicted as a conquest. In *Evgeny Onegin* the hero is treated as a comic, almost contemptible figure, unworthy of Tatiana's love and quite impotent, for all that he plays the Don Juan.

Apparently this does not reflect the real situation of Russian women in the nineteenth century. But it does seem that the archetypal pattern found in *Evgeny Onegin* reflects certain pervasive titudes which reappear in many other works of the period. For example, the title character of Goncharov's *Oblomov* is so debilitated that he is quite incapable of winning his beloved, even though she is initially well disposed toward him. In the end she marries a German—and Oblomov wins nothing but a certain immortality as the national symbol of lassitude, impotence, and passivity.

Could this be interpreted as the resurgence of a slave mentality—the aftermath of the Mongol invasion perhaps, or of serfdom, which was much more comparable to the enslavement of black Africans than to medieval serfdom in the West? In any case, no sooner had romantic love appeared on the scene, thanks to the joyous eroticism of Pushkin and his contemporaries, than it was rebuffed with suspicion and abhorrence—a reaction that seems typical of Russian culture in general. After all, this is a culture in which love and sex are rarely dealt with directly, in which representations of the female nude are almost unknown, a culture which is exemplified by Tolstoy's *Kreutzer Sonata,* that hymn of hate directed against love and sexual passion, both of which are dragged through the mire along with woman herself; as always, assumed to be the cause of it all. (Not that this prevented Tolstoy from fathering a whole brood of children, to say nothing of his escapades with gypsies and serving girls.

But this conflict between guilt-ridden asceticism and a vigorous sexual drive is all the more revealing of a profound psychological split.)

It is in the work of Dostoyevsky, though, that we see the Russian Eros laid bare in an extraordinary spectacle of rape, brutal sadism, and masochism transformed into impotence. The hero of *Notes from the Underground* spends an entire day tormenting a prostitute with moral harangues while he decides whether to sleep with her; the main character of *The Possessed* is obsessed by the memory of having raped a little girl, the only expression of his sexuality of which we are given any evidence.

Such then is the ambiguity of the nineteenth century—a diffident attempt to embrace the Western concept of Eros, which gradually turns tragic and embittered, as if the entire culture had fallen under a curse.

At the turn of the century we see the appearance of a new imperative in the Russian attitude toward sex—the renunciation of all sexual activity in the name of the revolution. The small extremist sects which flourished at the end of the nineteenth century taught their adherents to disdain not only all of present society but life itself—which, they maintained, should be completely subordinated to an ideological ideal. As early as 1863 Chernyshevsky has the hero of his novel, *What Is To Be Done?*, devoting his entire life—even down to the smallest detail—to the task of preparing for the society of the future. Nothing is supposed to distract him from this purpose—certainly not love, which is imagined to be impossible in reality except as a kind of sympathetic attraction based on a common political program and a shared sense of militant activism. A bad novel, a ridiculous philosophy, you might say, and quite correctly. But this philosophy of renunciation became the credo of whole generations of revolutionaries. Many forced themselves to model their lives on the ascetic ideal portrayed in *What Is To Be Done?*—notably a certain Ulyanov, who later took the name of Lenin.

Chapter 2
From the "Socialization of Women" to the "Communist Family"

Make Way for Eros!

Moscow, 1922. A crowd of naked men and women surge through the streets. Some of the women are carrying hastily scrawled placards, some of the men are carrying flowers. Women walk hand in hand, singing, their faces shining with joy.

Love! Love! Down with shame! Down with guilt!

The onlookers are rooted to the spot with indignation, or with vicarious ecstasy. Occasionally a woman strips off her clothes and joins the marchers, and a grim-faced Chekist (secret-police agent) wonders whether he should fire into the crowd. . . .

It is hard to believe today that such a thing could have happened in the Soviet Union. Yet it is too improbable to have been invented, and in fact old people who lived through the "mad years" remember it very well. I myself knew a man who took part in this nude march through the streets of Moscow, and who spoke wistfully of this brief interlude of incredible freedom between 1917 and the days of the free-love leagues when everyone thought they would always be allowed to do just as they liked.

The Moscow demonstration of 1922 was only one of many that took place in various Russian cities, primarily in Moscow and Petrograd, but also in Odessa, Saratov, and elsewhere in this era. But the nude marches proved to be a nine-day wonder, quickly suppressed by the police, who were assisted by squads of "indignant workers" specially recruited for this purpose. The naked marchers were obliged to make their way home as best they could; the women were sometimes set upon and raped (another phase of the operation that was delegated to the "indignant workers").

The social history of this period is best understood as a sequel to the revolution of 1917 and the wholesale dissolution of traditional values and institutions which it brought in its wake. The newly installed Soviet regime had already embarked on its unprecedented campaign of terror and repression, but people all over Russia were still drunk with freedom and the memory of 1917. This is why the early twenties seemed to many contemporary observers a period of unrestrained anarchy, a time when the most radical ideas and the wildest social experiments captured the imagination of a whole generation of zealous young enthusiasts.

There is probably some truth to this picture. Because of the social chaos of the civil-war period, the sexual crisis erupted with the violence of an explosion—elementary physical drives had been denied an outlet for too long. There had never been a time when sexual questions occupied such a prominent place in the public mind, and sexuality could at last be discussed openly. Sexual conflicts and relations between the sexes in general became an inexhaustible source of inspiration for artists of all kinds, and writers in particular.

Lev Gumilevsky's *Dog Alley* (1927) is a typical novel of the period. It deals with a group of young Communists, members of the Komsomol. The main character is an adherent of the theory of "biological free love," which holds that love is no more than a biological need which should be satisfied as simply and directly as hunger and thirst. In this spirit he approaches a female comrade—a fellow student and member of his Komsomol group—with the following proposition:

> It's quite natural. I need a woman, and so I turn to you, simply and frankly, as one comrade to another. Anna's not here—so why

> can't you just do me this favor out of friendship? If I told you I was hungry and I had to go off to work, and you had a piece of bread, you'd share it with me like a comrade, wouldn't you?

This sort of frank and uninhibited language was a hallmark of the period. Free love became the fashionable idol of the marketplace, and the celebrated ménage à trois of the poet Mayakovsky and the Briks, far from giving rise to scandal, was held up as the model of the openminded and progressive way of life.

Alexandra Kollontai, whose feminist pamphlets have won her some celebrity in the West, was the self-proclaimed champion of free love unmarred by jealousy and possessiveness:

> Jealousy belongs to the past, and we are in the process of banishing the concept of property from our emotional lives. Anyone who seeks liberty for himself must also seek it for his partner. He must no longer try to poison his lover's mind with calumnies against his rivals, but must instead treat them with deference and respect, an attitude born of collective "comradeship" which up to now has been unknown.

At this time Kollontai still held an important post in the government, so that, far from being the ravings of the lunatic fringe, her views enjoyed more or less the full respectability of a government white paper.

Love itself was said to be "strictly physiological," as the current Soviet catchphrase had it, or to cite another cliché, "Love has nothing to do with cherry blossoms" (an allusion to a popular novel by Pantaleimon Romanov, *Without Cherry Blossoms,* in which the heroine gives herself to her lover in highly unromantic circumstances). Sexual gratification was said to be "as easy and as natural as drinking a glass of water." In her essay "Make Way for the Winged Eros" Alexandra Kollontai observed that sexual intercourse should be and in fact already was "completely casual, like any other activity that is intended to gratify certain biological needs which the partners are anxious to have done with lest this distract them from their essential purpose: revolutionary activism." *

* *Young Guard,* number 10, 1923.

This new ethos found its most enthusiastic adherents among the Komsomols. A Soviet bureaucrat, Sonya Smidovich,* has left us this ironic though scarcely exaggerated commentary on their "rules of conduct":

> Every Komsomol, every male student in a training academy or worker's institute, every young man who has not even started shaving, can and should be able to satisfy his sexual desires. I have no idea why this is regarded as an indisputable truth. Sexual abstinence is dismissed as a fetish of the petty bourgeoisie. Every female Komsomol or student to whom a young man has made his wishes known (I can't imagine how these jungle passions ever came to develop among a northern people like ourselves) is expected to submit to him straightaway; otherwise she is no more than a petty bourgeois element, unworthy of the name of Komsomol, of proletarian student. . . .

It becomes clear that "free love" often had nothing whatever to do with feminism; in practice it was strictly a "male prerogative." The content of the following document is admittedly rather bizarre, but it does say a great deal about the attitudes which were current in certain political circles closely allied to the Communists. It is in fact a "decree" of the workers' soviet of the city of Vladimir (a similar decree from Saratov has also survived): †

> From the age of eighteen onward all young women are hereby declared to be the property of the state.
>
> It shall be the obligation of every unmarried woman of eighteen or older to register, on pain of the strictest prosecution, with the bureau of free love.
>
> After registration women will have the right to choose a husband between the ages of nineteen and fifty.
>
> Men shall also have the right to choose a wife who has reached the age of eighteen, provided that they can produce sufficient proof of proletarian origin.
>
> Those who wish to do so may choose a new husband or wife once every month.

* Kollontai's successor as head of the Women's Department, a government agency which was abolished by Stalin in 1929. [Translators' note] Quoted in *Journal of Sociology,* number 4, Moscow.

† Quoted in A. G. Kharchev, *Marriage and the Family in the USSR,* Moscow, 1964.

> In the interests of the state men between nineteen and fifty shall have the right to choose any woman who has registered with the bureau even without her consent. All children born of these unions shall become the property of the state.

Needless to say, this sort of thing was quite exceptional, and most such experiments in "sexual communism" proved to be short-lived indeed. But the period abounded in radical ideas. Free-love leagues, group sex, nude marches, and even proposals that booths be set up next to the public toilets in the streets and parks for the convenience of couples in search of immediate sexual gratification were seriously discussed in public meetings and widely advocated in contemporary literature and the press.

In contrast to the male-chauvinist "decree" of the Vladimir soviet, Alexandra Kollontai has supplied us with a feminist variation on the theme of free love. (The feminist movement, by the way, was already active in the reign of Nicholas II: the Union for the Equality of Women had five thousand members in 1905, the All-Russian Congress of Women was convened in St. Petersburg in 1908, and a suffrage petition signed by seven thousand women was presented to the Duma.)

The heroine of Kollontai's *Love of Three Generations* says:

> As far as I'm concerned, sexual intercourse is just a simple human need. I change my lovers to suit my moods. At the moment I happen to be pregnant, but I neither know nor care who the father of my child is.

Always receptive to "advanced ideas" of any kind, the 1920s also witnessed a craze for psychoanalysis, which had already found its way into certain intellectual and medical circles before the war. A psychoanalytic association was founded in Moscow in 1921. Vera Shmidt ran a school for young children in which all instruction was based on Freudian principles, and psychoanalytic associations later sprang up in Kiev, Odessa, and Rostov.

An Age of Sexual Liberation?

So far we have confined our inquiry to the realm of words alone. But were these words really accompanied by a significant change in the mores of the Russian people? There are some indications that this was in fact the case.

Young people seemed to have begun experimenting with sex at an earlier age. A survey of students in Moscow, conducted in 1922, revealed that 41.5 percent had their first sexual experience before age sixteen and a half, and 7.5 percent before age thirteen and a half. The platform of the free-love leagues seems to have been already put into practice.

The ironic comments of Sonya Smidovich quoted above provoked an enthusiastic response from *Pravda*'s readers; this letter from a young woman appeared in the issue of May 7, 1925:

> Male students despise the Komsomol girls who refuse to sleep with them. They consider them to be politically backward petty bourgeois who haven't been able to free themselves from the prejudices of the old society. Some are even of the opinion that motherhood, like sexual abstinence, is also tainted by bourgeois ideology.

This corresponds quite closely to the basic impression created by the literature of the period. In the second half of the decade, after the predictable Party crackdown was well underway, the newspapers were full of adolescent sex scandals. Here are several examples from the pages of the *High School Instructors' Journal*:

> —In Yeysk, a port city on the Sea of Azov, a sixteen-year-old student committed suicide. His diary revealed that he had taken part in precocious sexual experiments with the young girls in his class. (Issue of June 19, 1926)
>
> —In Odessa School Number 49 the school play was followed by a program of dances which drew blushes from the adults in the audience. . . . There was also a [student] group called Tiso, which was devoted to the perusal of pornographic literature. (June 29, 1928)
>
> —In Novosibirsk another "secret society" composed of sixteen students put out a pornographic magazine entitled *Down with Virginity!* (June 22, 1928)

At the same time the new legal code favored the "sexual revolution." The Soviet regime had immediately proclaimed the emancipation of women, who henceforth were to enjoy the same rights as men. Divorce proceedings were drastically simplified; after the decree of December 1917, which legalized the "dissolution of marriage," a divorce could be obtained practically free on the simple demand of *one* of the parties. Illegitimate children were given the same rights as children born in wedlock, and so-called free, or trial, marriages were officially recognized by the code of 1923. In a country with such a strong traditional attachment to the institution of the family, these measures seriously disturbed the equilibrium of a society that was already profoundly shaken.

Finally, and especially, the liberalization of the abortion laws had a serious impact on Russian mores. It almost immediately became the most common method of contraception—and a well-worn theme of the "Komsomol" school of fiction in the 1920s, in which the abortion becomes the pretext for a great deal of sentimental histrionics, a rigorous unraveling of the characters' mismanaged love affairs, and the inevitable discussions of Communist morality. The number of abortions performed each year in the Soviet Union quadrupled between 1922 and 1926.* In 1928 in Leningrad there were 31.5 abortions, as against 22.6 live births, for every 1000 inhabitants. The abortion rate continued to climb until 1934, at which point there were 3 abortions recorded for every live birth in Moscow or for every 2 live births in rural areas.

Let us pause and take stock for a moment. Divorce and abortion may have had a completely unprecedented effect on Soviet sexual behavior, but this does not necessarily mean that the structure of the family was about to disintegrate or that this social metamorphosis had actually produced who-knows-what revolutionary or futuristic forms of sexuality.

First, the liberalization of sexual attitudes seems to have been confined to a minority of the population. And in spite of the new codes and decrees, the family remained the unshakable and indispensable foundation of rural life. With the civil war and the redistribution of land ownership, Russians began to rely increasingly on the resources of the countryside and the family. When the government organized discussions in the villages to explain the provisions of the new family code (adopted in 1926) †, the peasants protested vigorously: they regarded the liberalization of the divorce

* Rudolph Schlesinger, *The Family in the USSR*, London, 1949.

† In which the provisions of earlier government decrees—divorce granted at the request of one partner only, unregistered (i.e. common-law) marriage legally binding—were finally codified into law. [Translators' note]

laws as an overt incitement to immorality. In particular it represented a threat to the economic stability of the extended family group, which after all remained essentially patriarchal—or patrilocal, to use the precise anthropological term. This meant that a newly married couple would set up housekeeping in the husband's family farmhouse and thus become part of a social group dominated by the august figure of the family patriarch. If the wife were allowed to divorce her husband, to leave the farm, there would be one person less to work in the fields—and worse than that, she would be entitled to receive alimony payments, another recent innovation in the divorce laws. By what right, the peasant spokesmen demanded, should the father and brothers of a "bad husband" (since in their minds divorce could only be explained as the fault of the husband—perhaps he didn't beat his wife enough?), the entire family in fact, be made to pay? And worst of all, the divorced wife, as an equal partner under the law, would also be entitled to claim her share of the family's plot of land—whereas according to traditional law land was held, communally and inalienably, by the extended family.

Thus there was a considerable discrepancy between revolutionary precepts and rural traditions which had remained unchanged for centuries. It is easy enough—and the new regime certainly found it so—to issue paper proclamations of sexual equality or to hand down laws which must have seemed about as meaningful to the peasants as a transmission from outer space. And it is easy enough afterward to boast about "building socialism"—without giving any thought to the consequences that such colossal irresponsibility might bring.

To cite only one example, the newspapers of the day expressed a great deal of concern about the problem of "seasonal wives," as they were commonly called—homeless and unemployed women from the countryside who had drifted back into the cities. It seems that certain peasants had discovered an extremely practical application of the new divorce laws (nothing to do with sexual liberation, however) which they were quick to take advantage of. Thus they would get married in early spring—it was always useful to have an extra pair of hands around during the growing season—and get divorced as soon as the harvest was in; after all, there was no point in having an extra mouth to feed during the winter.*

The effects of the social revolution were not always apparent

* Kent Geiger, *The Family in Soviet Russia,* Cambridge, Mass., 1968.

among the urban population either. A survey of Moscow students in 1923 shows that 72 percent of the young men and 81 percent of the young women expressed a definite preference for a lasting sexual relationship, as opposed to the "glass of water" approach currently in fashion.*

It is especially striking how these "advanced ideas" were often grafted onto traditional attitudes, to produce some fairly surprising hybrids. Here, for example, is a question asked of a lecturer who had just put forward the proposition that love did not exist and that only sexual desire was real. "Comrade lecturer! If someone gets married, does his wife belong to just him or does she belong to everybody?"

It has not even occurred to this budding young patriarch that a wife could not belong to her husband like any other piece of property; the only question that remained for anyone who aspired to the correct collectivist line was whether such property should be considered to belong to the individual or to the collective.

But do any of these trials and experiments add up to a sexual revolution? Certainly not. A relaxation of moral values then? Very probably. And those who gained the most from it all were those who were in the best position to do so—the new Soviet ruling class. I am certainly not speaking here of austere old Bolsheviks like Lenin, who was too devoted to his lofty mission to concern himself with such trivialities; I mean the lesser Party officials, local commissars, and newly minted Checkists, latecomers and opportunists of all sorts who were simply out for what they could get.

The liberality of the divorce laws and the precepts of "sexual communism" made things very convenient for them. To divest themselves of their original wives was child's play, and then they could begin to enjoy some of the perquisites of their new positions of power. Here is an extract from a letter written by a young woman, a student and Komsomol member, which appeared in *Pravda* (May 7, 1925):

> It is not only the Komsomols but the senior Party members as well who are touched by this sickness. They embark on casual affairs which they break off almost immediately. They think that fidelity is very tiresome and that words like ***husband*** and ***wife*** are simply bourgeois fictions. They are shocked when you ask them what

* *Journal of Sociology*, number 4, Moscow, 1970, p. 104.

> their wives will think, or they just snicker or ask "Which one?" I knew one man, a high government official, who had a different wife in every city that he visited in the course of his administrative duties. . . . Another Communist, the husband of a friend, asked me to spend the night with him, on the pretext that his wife was ill and wouldn't be able to satisfy him that particular night. When I turned him down, he said I was a stupid bourgeois, that I could never even begin to grasp the true spirit of Communism. He never spoke to me again. This was a very painful experience for me, as I had always respected his integrity as a Party member and his knowledge of Party doctrine.

Certain local commissars were also stigmatized by the press as "backwoods Casanovas" * because they had forced the women teachers assigned to their villages to become their mistresses and threatened them with administrative reprisals if they refused to cooperate.

But over and beyond all this, it is essential not to lose sight of the incredible human tragedy which formed the background of the entire decade—the state of anarchy and social upheaval into which Russia was thrown by war and revolution. The civil war desolated entire regions and left millions of corpses in its wake. Towns and villages were utterly destroyed; rape, massacre, and violence of every imaginable kind were the common currency of the age. In the Volga region there were those who only survived the great famine of 1921 to 1922 by eating the flesh of children. The roving population of young vagabonds, abandoned children, orphans, runaways, and delinquents reached seven, perhaps nine million in 1922. And it is here that we have the real breakdown of the traditional family, the real "revolution," far more than in any of the fashionable slogans of the cities.

Rape was endemic, and the climate of sexual violence even after the civil war gave rise to numerous public scandals and prosecutions (followed by ideological self-criticism sessions on the part of the perpetrators.) *The High School Instructors' Journal* (June 26, 1926) reported that a group of schoolboys in Chelyabinsk had gang-raped a classmate. In Leningrad seven men (including several Communists) were tried for the rape of two women on Chubarov Street (*Leningradskaya Pravda,* December 17, 1926). The newspaper accounts of the crime emphasized that incidents of this kind—which came to be

* *High School Instructors' Journal,* December 4, 1926.

known ironically as "Chubarov Street morality"—had become very much a feature of the times. After all it was Mayakovsky himself who wrote:

> Any girl
> Who's young and pretty—
> I'll rape her,
> And spit
> On her heart
> With contempt.

This, of course, is only one of the poet's more lurid sexual fantasies, but the tone of cynical bravado only serves to illustrate the total collapse of moral values which characterized the 1920s.

I will conclude with a story that was told to me by one of my patients. This is surely an exceptional, not to say pathological case, but nonetheless symptomatic of the incredible savagery of the famine years, and also perhaps of the secret affinities that may exist between power and sexual sadism. This patient's mother was a peasant woman from a starving village in Bashkiria who had made her way to the city of Ufa. On the station platform she was accosted by an armed Checkist who took her home with him. Inexperienced in the ways of the world, she had hoped at least to sell herself for a piece of bread. When they arrived, he ordered her to strip off her clothes—and gave her to his dog. She made no attempt at resistance and allowed the dog to mount her. When the dog had had his fill of her, the Checkist threw her out of the house, with no money and nothing to eat.

During this period, then, traditional life clung desperately to the extended family structure which sustained it while all other moral standards were collapsing. The Communists had put morality behind them. Their motto was: All is permitted; "in the name of the revolution" was understood. Here, behind the bland mask of Communist morality, we have glimpsed the real face of Communism—the desire to live without any moral standards whatsoever. The "sexual freedom" of the twenties is strongly reminiscent of social experiments that have been attempted all over the world during the past two decades, but in the Soviet Union, in contrast to the experience of the West, these few years of experiments and exploration scarcely brought about any kind of mental or cultural liberation or any fundamental changes in sexual mores.

Sex: Enemy of the Revolution

So ran a Party slogan of the twenties. Naturally things were not as simple as this incisive formula made them out to be. At first it seemed that the Party was doing everything in its power to uproot the family and the old way of life and to promote "sexual freedom." Then, in the period that followed, the Party seemed to have gotten a grip on itself and to have accordingly tightened all the screws of its administrative and juridical machinery, inaugurating a sort of reign of virtue. In order to make sense of this contradiction, we will have to return to the ideological foundations of Communism.

The regime had encountered a serious obstacle in the path of the new society and the progress of "Communist man": the family, which continued to offer a place of refuge after every aspect of public life had passed under the control of the state. Children were still raised by their families, and thereby deprived of the states' tutelage. The family, particularly the peasant family, represented the permanence of tradition—the object of particular loathing on the part of the new pioneers of progress. Clearly such a reactionary institution could not remain intact, could not continue to cast its malevolent shadow on the soil of the workers' state. It must be cast down—it must be destroyed!

Here are Lenin's views on the traditional family. Setting himself up as the champion of women's liberation, in 1919 he wrote:

> Woman remains in a state of domestic servitude . . . , since the single-family household oppresses, suffocates, and brutalizes her . . . dissipating her energy in incredibly unproductive labor that is at once petty, enervating, dehumanizing, and oppressive.

He went on to call for a complete transformation of this "aberrant system" into a "great socialist economy."

These ideas leave no doubt of what Lenin's intentions were. The liberation of women was meant to furnish the labor force necessary for the construction of socialism—an ideal which was later to be realized. He was not disturbed by its sexual inequities as such, but he wished to expedite the "withering away" of the family by depriving it of its very reason for existence. His hope, as Anatol Lunacharsky, head of the People's Commissariat (Ministry) of Education and Culture, expressed it in 1918, was that "this little educational establishment that is the family, this little factory . . . this whole accursed business . . . will be over and done with."

"The state," added the worthy minister, well respected for his liberalism and moderation, "should take hold of the child the very moment that his mother lets him go." * There were also those who pointed out that the millions of children who had been abandoned already represented a bold step toward the dissolution of the "bourgeois" family.

So we understand why it was that Lenin signed the decree legalizing civil divorce in December 1917. The chronology is truly remarkable—only a month after the overthrow of the Provisional Government in October, during an extremely critical period for the infant Soviet Republic, Lenin still found time to concern himself with the revisions of the divorce laws.

But this hardly means that Lenin was a partisan of communal sex. He was actually disgusted by the "glass of water" theory, which he considered to be anti-Marxist, and by the excesses of his young disciples in the Komsomol. According to Klara Zetkin, the German Communist leader, he once remarked in 1923 that:

> The so-called new sexuality of our young people and adults alike often seems to be merely petty bourgeois, like a version of the fine old bourgeois institution of the brothel.

Lenin was not an opponent of marriage or the family in principle; he himself advocated "proletarian civil marriage based on love and ideology." In other words, the proletarian should not rush into marriage with the daughter of any bourgeois.

His pronouncements on sexuality, of a rather puritanical tendency, preach a doctrine of ascetic renunciation:

> The absence of self-control in one's sexual life is a bourgeois phenomenon. The revolution requires the concentration of all one's

* A. Lunacharsky, *Education and Instruction*, Moscow, 1976.

> forces, and wild sexual excesses are symptomatic of a reactionary outlook. We need minds that are healthy. . . .

Lenin's own private life seems to have been remarkably free of such excesses. All his attentions and energies were harnessed to the task of creating the Party. Like the hero of Chernyshevsky's novel whom he so much admired, Lenin left no place in his program for sensual or emotional detours. Eating, drinking, dressing, and the other necessary tasks of daily life were only the means which enabled him to continue the struggle. The pleasures of the flesh were denied to him; his entire life was devoted to the service of the revolution.

We only know of two women in Lenin's life: his wife Krupskaya and his friend Inessa Armand, who died in 1920. Nowadays the Soviets are at some pains to conceal the existence of his relationship with Inessa Armand, even though it was purely platonic, and perhaps the only human and truly moral episode of his entire life. He had no children. The only fruit of his militant marriage with Krupskaya was their shared mystical vision of a Communist paradise.

I do not know what the historians' verdict on Lenin will be, but a medical analysis of his behavior, particularly of his gestures and physical expressions, makes me inclined to believe that the Communist titan was in fact a sexual pygmy. In the USSR he is commonly supposed to have been impotent, and this may not be totally unfounded. The vigorous gesticulations with which Lenin punctuated his speeches (not to mention his notorious indifference toward women) certainly suggest a comparison with the characteristic gestures of countless impotent men whom I have seen as patients, gestures which appear as a kind of compensatory sublimation.

We have perhaps begun to stray into the realm of historical gossip, but the subject of Lenin's character is an important one nevertheless. It is far from my intention to suggest that his asexual temperament had an exemplary influence on the population at large (with the possible exception of the ceremonial visit paid by newlyweds to the Lenin Mausoleum, which must have a remarkably aphrodisiac effect). But Lenin's ascetic vision—the great revolutionary progress toward the society of the future, flattening everything in its path like a steamroller—was not peculiar to him alone, and it subsequently became an essential component of the Communist ideology.

This Soviet puritanism is a strange sort of puritanism indeed. To all appearances the new Soviet morality had eliminated all the oppressive taboos of the old society and still avoided a flight to the opposite extreme. In fact, the question of sex seems to have been approached very sensibly. In 1922 the Party leader Bukharin, in an address to "our revolutionary nihilist youth," spoke of "anarchy in all the rules of human conduct." But in reality the ideas which were embraced by all the "liberal" legislation and the programs of "liberation" tended in a single direction—toward communism. At the same time, love itself was done away with in the name of a "glorious future." It was no longer an adventure shared by two people but rather a pretext for the transformation of the old society and a springboard to the society to come.

The psychologist Zalkind became famous for his attempts to make Freudian recipes more palatable by dressing them up with Marxist-Leninist garnish. A collection of his articles, *Youth and Revolution*, which appeared in 1925 under the auspices of the Communist University, includes the following declaration:

> Our viewpoint can only be revolutionary and proletarian, strictly practical. If a particular sexual practice has the result of *isolating* an individual in relation to his own class, makes him less efficient in his work or less active in the struggle, it will become necessary to put an end to it. The only kind of sexual activity which can be tolerated is that which will contribute to the full flowering of the collectivist spirit.

He goes on to propound a set of rules which make such delightful reading that I can't restrain myself from quoting a few of them:

5. A couple should not engage in sexual intercourse frequently.
6. Nor should one change sexual partners too frequently.
7. Love should be monogamous.
8. When a couple does engage in intercourse, they should always take care to prevent the possibility of conception.
9. One's choice of sexual partners should be made on the basis of class origins, in conformity with the goals of the revolutionary proletariat.
12. The working class [that is, the Communist Party] has the right to intervene in the sexual life of any of its members.

Such intervention may entail, for example, forbidding a member of the proletariat from loving a class enemy:

> To be sexually attracted to a being who belongs to a different class which is hostile and morally alien to one's own is just as much a *perversion* as it would be to feel sexual attraction for a crocodile or an orangutang.

Even better still, the Party should be the guardian of the purity of the race. Zalkind proclaimed "the total and unconditional right of society to intervene in the sexual life of the population toward the goal of achieving the betterment of the race through the practice of an artificial form of sexual selection."

It is difficult to read these lines today without being overcome by a feeling of profound despair. The tune has become so painfully familiar by now that we cannot help but harbor certain uncharitable sentiments toward the performer; however, Zalkind was not alone in this. Preobrazhensky, the Party theoretician, for example, regarded sex as "a social problem, if only from the simple point of view of the physical well-being of the race . . ."; it was his hope that sexuality would be regulated with regard to "a better combination of physical qualities on the part of those who are engaging in sexual relations."

I will not dwell any further on the official attitude toward sex during this period, and I only hope the reader will agree with me that what is essential here is the utopian vision of complete control over every aspect of human life, including sexual desire—a vision which has left its mark on the entire history of the regime. In 1929 we encounter it again in the writing of one A. Sabsovich, who advocates that "children be taken from their mothers after a few days" and placed under the supervision of the state, and again in the plans for the cities of the future, in which every detail of everyday life will be collectivized, as we find in the latest city-planning projects of the present day.

However, I must reassure the reader at the outset that the government has never succeeded in abolishing the family, nor have "artificial selection" centers ever been set up—except possibly in the Gulag. A French survivor of the camps, Armand Malumian, reported that in 1948 male and female inmates were allowed to mingle more or less freely, although the sexes had been rigorously separated before that time. The orgy which ensued was indescribable, and a number of women became pregnant. They were given to understand that they would be set free, but after a year they were returned to the camp. Their children had been taken from them to be raised by the state and were later sent to special schools for the training of policemen.*

As always, the Communist utopia has only become a reality in the concentration camp. In order to fill the terrible gaps created by the purges and all the other calamities which have befallen the Soviet people, the regime could find no better remedy than to use its prisoners as breeding stock. As far as the children themselves were concerned, the old plan of taking them from their families was finally carried out, anticipating the program of the Pol Pot regime in Cambodia, where "family life" (for the mother and child only) was finally reduced to a period of a few months.

Stalinist Virtue

If the legislative policy of the Leninist period was aimed in part at the destruction of the family, under Stalin the family was totally rehabilitated—not the traditional "bourgeois" family, to be sure, but rather the "Soviet family." This marked the beginning of the reign of virtue.

Abortion was effectively forbidden in 1936; homosexuality was made a crime in 1934. It became extremely difficult to obtain a divorce after 1944. Illegitimate children were deprived of all the rights they had previously enjoyed, and from a legal point of view they were now worse off than they had been under the tsar.

Of course, there were pragmatic reasons for this policy change. The catastrophic sequence of World War I, the civil war and the famine of 1921, collectivization and the ensuing famine (1928 to 1931), a decade of purges, notably those of 1937, World War II, another wave of purges followed by another famine—all of these had brought the Soviet Union to the brink of the abyss. The mounting death toll, which has only been partially acknowledged by the Soviets, has been estimated by Western demographers at approximately 60 million for the entire period. The birthrate, very high in the early years of the regime and comparable to those of underdeveloped countries today, soon began to fall off dramatically:

Births per 1000 Inhabitants

1913 = 45.5
1920 = 31.2

* A. Malumian, *The Sons of the Gulag*, Paris, 1976.

1925 = 44.7
1926 = 44.0
1930 = 39.2
1940 = 31.2
1950 = 26.7

The objection is sure to be raised that a similar drop in the birthrate was characteristic of all European countries which have experienced fairly rapid industrialization. However, I must point out that in no other country has industrialization been achieved at the cost of millions of deaths. In examining these figures more closely, we can see that during the only period in which social conditions (particularly in the rural districts) were relatively peaceful—that is, between 1922 and 1928—the birthrate almost returned to its prewar level, whereas at the same time in Western Europe there was a spontaneous decline in the birthrate. In the USSR, however, the decline appears to have been a direct consequence of the successive calamities of the postrevolutionary era.

As a means of confronting this demographic catastrophe, the regime was at great pains to restore the stability of the family and to check the alarming rise in the divorce and abortion statistics, which threatened the very survival of the population. But this is not, in my opinion, the most fundamental explanation. The motive force seems rather to have been those puritanical attitudes which had already taken root in the 1920s, probably even in the nineteenth century, and which reached their fullest bloom in the 1930s.

These attitudes expressed themselves in a number of measures which had nothing whatever to do with stimulating the birthrate. Coeducation, for example, introduced in 1918, was abolished in 1943. Psychoanalysis fell under the ban in the late twenties along with all clinical and educational programs based upon it.

It was primarily the imposition of a new moral standard by the regime which brought the "mad years" to an end. This was a standard so narrow and inflexible that it might have surpassed the fondest hopes of the most hidebound peasant traditionalist, though it was traced a million times over in the arts and literature, in the press and the schools, and in meetings and public speeches.

In this scheme the family was more than a structure which gave life shape and form, a wellspring of happiness, and an economic unit; it became a public duty as well. A party ideologue called Makarenko prepared the *Handbook for Parents,* which outlined this novel Stalinist theory of the Social Contract in reverse—the family structure itself is created through the delegation of part of the state's authority to the parents. In turn, they were expected to "perform their civic duty toward Soviet society," which Makarenko likened to an orchard in which Stalin would be "the great head gardener." Parents who have failed to grasp where their duty clearly lies are "of doubtful utility to society."

Hence it was not just any family which could be "rehabilitated" but only the family pledged to the service of the regime.

The same held true for women, whom the Soviet system boasted of having liberated: "Never has woman been the object of so much care and attention on the part of a state or of a people as she presently is in socialist society." And this woman was preeminently a model citizen. Countless conferences, congresses, and public meetings of all sorts were arranged at which carefully selected women proclaimed their fidelity to the regime. Activists every one, they devoted all their energies to increasing production or, failing that, giving every possible support to their engineer (or technician or worker) husbands—or so we were informed, for example, by the conference of the wives of engineers engaged in heavy industry described in *Pravda* (May 10, 1936). The ideal Soviet woman was also the perfect mother judged not only by the criterion of her political consciousness but also by the many children she had brought into the world, an example of that "human utility" endorsed by Makarenko. Beginning in 1944 medals were awarded to especially prolific mothers—"Heroine Mother," "Maternal Glory," "Medal of Maternity"—and it is clear that the regime far preferred stamping out medals to patiently and unceremoniously carrying out the measures which would have been appropriate to the demographic crisis.

It may be imagined, then, that as the composite personification of all these imperatives, the model woman was something like Joan of Arc and the Virgin Mary rolled into one—such as Dunyasha, the heroine of *The Zhurbins*, a novel by Vsevolod Kochetov, the worst of the hack novelists inflicted on the reading public during the Stalinist period. The book first appeared in 1952, and millions of copies have been published since then. Dunyasha herself is both sweet and charming—the author speaks of the angelic perfection of her features; her other physical attributes are left to the imagination. She is a shock worker, a perfect mother, and a bit of a prig who somehow finds the time—between work, children, and dispensing words of socialist good cheer to everyone around her—to rush off to Komsomol meetings, trade-union meetings, and every other sort of meeting that she happens to get wind of.

Such was the new star of Soviet womanhood, and children too were provided with their own ideal of perfection. Organized into paramilitary brigades as "Young Pioneers," they "took an oath" and swore in the words of their seventh and last commandment, to remain "pure in thought, word, and deed"; the oath was adopted in 1922, when the organization was founded.

Purity was of course the essence of the Soviet hero. As Makarenko put it, the Soviet family had attained "a level of morality which is only possible in the classless society."

But all of this catechism is nothing in comparison to the supreme hero of the regime: the very model of the modern male militant. Literary examples of this type abound in the works of Leonov, Fadayev, and Ostrovsky, to mention only the classics of the genre. He is the worthy descendant of the protagonists of Chernyshevsky's *What Is To Be Done?* and he even surpasses his fictional predecessor by a fair distance, since he has the advantage of living in a socialist society, which gives free reign to the exercise of his hyper-proletarian virtues. He does not smoke, he does not drink, he hardly ever makes love—even platonic affection is often postponed until happier, future days. He gives everything he has to the political "struggle" and to his work. If he happens to be the father of a family, we may wonder by what supernatural agency this came to be, since this automaton has parcelled out his entire day and left not a moment for his private life: morning calisthenics, the joys of labor, political or trade-union meetings (where he nudges his errant comrades back into the fold), and study of the works of Marx and Engels in the ten minutes that remain. Where would he find the time for sex?

The hero of Nikolai Ostrovsky's *How the Steel Was Tempered* is the most egregious of these Stalinist supermen. He spurns the love of a girl of bourgeois origins who asks nothing more than that he love her in return. With her unreliable social background she obviously does not have the makings of a good militant. Then he meets a true militant, an attractive one at that, and falls in love with her. After a moment's hesitation he gives her up as well, since conjugal life might not allow him to live up to his full militant potential. From the impotent hero of Romantic literature to the perfect Communist, by way of the nineteenth century revolutionary, the cycle is complete.

The ailing Eros is finally dead in Russian culture, once and for all.

And what was the reality of Soviet sexual life during the Stalinist era? I could easily devote the rest of this book to this single question, since the Soviet Union of today is still living on the "accomplishments" of this period. For the moment however I will limit myself to the problem of the "Communist" family.

Nothing could be more hypocritical or more artificial than the Stalinist morality which was disseminated through every available propaganda channel. The ideal "Soviet family" has never been anything other than a myth, with no more reality than a sea serpent or a unicorn. In practice the regime had systematically dismantled the structure and the foundations of the traditional family, which was certainly not necessary to secure the civil rights of its citizens. Moreover, it is not even clear that it was Stalin's intention to deal a mortal blow to the traditional family system. But the machinery of terror—the very fact of its existence—and the permanent interference of the state in every sphere of human activity were certainly sufficient to the task.

I have already discussed the magnitude of the demographic crisis. The reader will acknowledge that it is not very meaningful to speak of sexuality or family life in a village that has been devastated by famine or despoiled by a punitive expedition intended to bring about "collectivization."

These catastrophes left their imprint on people's minds even when their bodies were unaffected. And so it was with the denunciations. Everyone was involved; everyone mistrusted his fellow worker, his neighbor, his relatives. Husbands and wives denounced each other. Pavlik Morozov, the Young Pioneer who denounced his own father during collectivization, was held up as a special example; an entire article was devoted to him in the *Great Soviet Encyclopedia,* and statues were even erected to his memory.* When a man was arrested, it required true heroism on the part of his wife not to divorce him immediately, as the law allowed her to do, since the husbands and wives of "enemies of the people" were also threatened with the most terrible consequences, including arrest and deportation to the camps. Try to imagine, then, what sort of love could exist in a household in which everyone was afraid to make the most inconsequential politi-

* Pavlik Morozov was murdered by fellow villagers in 1932, after he reported his father for hoarding grain. This incident was also the subject of an unfinished film by Eisenstein, *Bezhin Meadow.* [Translators' note]

cal remark in front of the others, in which the parents were forced to carry on a permanent charade in order to maintain the image of perfect "Soviet happiness."

A paradoxical situation: during the twenties the state was bent on destroying the family, and during the thirties it made every effort to strengthen it. The actual result was quite the reverse; as the terror mounted and the regime took on an increasingly totalitarian character, the disintegration of the family continued to accelerate. The number of households headed by women are a significant indication of the decline of the traditional family. The war, and the purges as well, decimated the male population: men represented only 45 percent of the total population according to the 1959 census, and only 37 percent of the total population of those 32 or older (in other words 170 women for every 100 men). This is exactly the age group which was affected by those terrible years. This tremendous imbalance was tilted even further in rural areas by migration to the cities (most often it was the man who left the village in search of a better life), and it had a genuinely traumatic effect on the Soviet family. The disturbing effects of a father's absence are well known in Russia and were magnificently portrayed in Tartovsky's film *The Mirror.* There are other statistics which allow us to perceive how widespread the problem actually was: again according to the 1959 census, 29 percent of Soviet households were headed by women, widows, divorcees, or unmarried mothers. For the Russian Soviet Federated Socialist Republic (RSFSR) alone the figure was 31 percent, 34 percent in rural areas. A study carried out in the Kalinin region showed that this figure may be as high as 41 percent.*

The discrepancy between the official image—the mendacious propaganda extolling the superiority and radiant happiness of the Soviet family—and the tragic reality itself recalls the idea of the split personality to which I alluded earlier. The goals pursued by the regime—the transformation of Eros into a purely procreative instinct, the subordination of one's sexual impulses to the economic and political interests of the Soviet state, and total control over the individual's freedom even in his private life—have finally been brought to fruition. This is not to say that the ordinary Soviet citizen carries out the orders of the totalitarian state with the precision of a well-oiled machine: the terrors imagined by Orwell are still largely confined to

* L. Anokhina and M. Shmeleva, *The Culture and Everyday Life of Collective Farmers in the Kalinin Region,* Moscow, 1964.

the pages of his *1984*. However, the ultimate effect of all this has been that sexuality itself has been forced to take refuge in the deepest recesses of the oppressed Soviet psyche. In other words, the private lives of ordinary Soviet people can only be compared to the lives of convicts in a prison or soldiers in a barracks, since normal sexual drives are either repressed completely or can only be expressed in ways that would ordinarily be considered deviant. I would say then, and I am choosing my words very carefully, that just as it has become a commonplace of our age to compare the Soviet Union itself to a vast prison camp, the sexual behavior of the Soviet people exhibits striking similarities to the sexual behavior of convicts and the inmates of other "total institutions."

But I still would like to end this chapter on an optimistic note. The family, even in its battered state, and love, even with its wings clipped, can still provide a refuge for the Soviet people from the rigors of daily life. How can we fail to admire, for example, the constancy and fidelity displayed by the woman whose story I am about to tell? During the famine of 1947, when the people of the Ukraine were dying by the tens of thousands, her husband was the president of a collective farm in the Khmelnik region. He organized a gang which looted the stores in a neighboring district and distributed the booty among the members of their collective. He was picked up, quite by chance (the village had kept the whole affair strictly to themselves), and sentenced to twenty-five years in a camp at Kharkov. At the time of his arrest he and his wife had one child. His wife waited patiently while he served out his sentence and came to visit him every six months, as the regulations permitted her to do. As a result of these brief reunions they had five more children by the time he was released. There can be no doubt that it was her love for him that saved him from perishing in the camp. By defying the barbed wire and the watchtowers, their love was able to endure and their family at last to be reunited.

II
HUSBANDS, WIVES, and LOVERS

CHAPTER 3

The Modern Soviet Family

I WOULD LIKE to begin this study with an analysis of the family, since the family group is still the privileged domain of sexuality in the Soviet Union. People still get married in the Soviet Union, and their children are still raised, at least in part, within the family. I mention this lest anyone think that Soviet society has devised some entirely new form of sexual relationship—neither Communism nor "the Slavic soul" has so far given birth to such a mutation.

In the previous chapters I have tried to sketch the broad outlines of the evolution (or perhaps revolution) of the Russian family, from the stable, traditional patriarchy to the family on the verge of dissolution under the Stalinist terror. How far have we come since then?

Suffice it to say that the apparatus which was assembled gradually and brought to sinister perfection under Stalin is still effectively in place. The perfect Communist family, based on the twin principles of labor and duty to the motherland, its children educated "in the Communist spirit" (as Lenin put it), renouncing all self-interest and individual emotion for the sake of "the collective good"—the entire litany still resounds through the media, the classroom, and even the marriage ceremony. However, what interests us at present is the real Soviet family.

At first glance the contemporary Soviet family seems scarcely different from its counterpart in the West. Since the extinction of the traditional clan with its bearded patriarch, surrounded by swarms of young descendants, the typical family has become the couple with one or two children, perhaps a mother-in-law as well, living in a single room or a small one-bedroom apartment in a complex that dates from the Khrushchev era or later. What could be more ordinary or, if I may say so, less exotic?

As we have already seen, one characteristic which the Soviet Union shares with other industrialized countries is a rapidly declining birthrate. Let us bring these statistics up to date:

Live births per 1000 inhabitants

1950 = 26.7
1955 = 25.7
1960 = 24.9
1965 = 18.4
1968 = 17.2
1969 = 17.0
1970 = 17.4
1974 = 18.0

The figures would seem to speak for themselves—except that the slight increase between 1970 and 1974 is illusory; Soviet demographers themselves have offered the explanation that the children who packed the classrooms of the fifties had simply reached childbearing age. Another explanation can be found in the runaway population growth of the Muslim republics, which has already begun to taper off.

The latest available figures on the average size of the Soviet family (1970 census) are 3.7 for the USSR as a whole, 3.5 for the urban Russian Soviet Federated Socialist Republic (which includes most of European Russia and Siberia), 3.4 for the urban RSFSR, 3.4 for the Ukraine, 3.1 to 3.4 for the Baltic republics, and 3.1 for the city of Leningrad. The tendency toward smaller families is reflected in another series of statistics: in the RSFSR (again according to the 1970 census) 21 percent of families were childless, 38 percent had only one child, and 26 percent had two children. In the cities this tendency was even more pronounced: 20 percent of families were childless, 43 percent had only one child, and 28 percent had two children.* I have given only the figures for the RSFSR since the situation in the Central Asian republics is very different. In the Ukraine, Byelorussia, and the Baltic republics, however, the population statistics confirm the same overall decline in the size of the family.

Is the average Russian couple approaching the goal of the one-child family? Today, in the streets of the big cities a family with three children is likely to attract attention; however, in a study conducted in Moscow in the late sixties 47 percent of the women questioned said that they felt that the ideal number of children was two.† A revealing figure—these women dream of having two children, but in reality they seem to be satisfied with only one.

One could offer any number of explanations for this trend (I am speaking now of the recent past, not of the demographic catastrophes of the Stalinist era), and demographers have not been reticent in doing so. Since I am not a specialist in this field, I will not add any weighty pronouncements on the subject, but I do wish to make two brief observations of my own. First, the decline in the birthrate in Russia is indicative of a profound change in attitude: the conscious attempt to limit fertility presupposes the belief that nature can be made subject to human control. This would have been unthinkable in prerevolutionary Russian society, as it is in most of the Third World today. In this respect, at least, we are justified in concluding that Russia has finally caught up to the West.

My second observation is somewhat more complex. Why, it must be asked, are people choosing to have fewer children? There can be no doubt that the motives are essentially "selfish"—parents are hoping to get something more out of life, wives are scarcely inclined to devote their entire lives to raising six or seven children in a two-room apartment, and so forth. I should also mention that at the beginning of this century it was to the peasant family's advantage to have more children; children meant not only additional hands to work in the fields but actually more land as well, since the size of the family's allotment was determined by the number of family members. But the current scarcity of accommodations—in the country as well as in the cities—has converted the advantages of a large family into lia-

* Results of the census of 1970, volume 7, tables 4 and 25.

† V. Belova and L. Darski, *Public Opinion Statistics in Population Growth Research*, Moscow, 1972.

bilities. As we shall see later, the lot of the Russian woman is harsh indeed, and even women in the United States or Germany, who enjoy an infinitely higher standard of living, still hesitate to have more than two or three children. All the more reason then for their Russian sisters—who, under the influence of Western ideas, have begun to aspire to a better way of life—to regard the prospect of raising several children under present conditions as an intolerable form of slavery.

Who is actually responsible for the day-to-day management of the new Soviet household? Does the traditional division of responsibility still exist—the wife looking after the household and the children, while the important domestic decisions are left to the husband? Here we are embarking on troubled waters. Formally, one suspects, the husband is still the head of the family, and the patriarchy still reigns supreme. But, it appears that many men have abdicated their traditional responsibilities and left the entire burden of running the household to their wives. A study conducted in Leningrad revealed that in 56 percent of the families interviewed it was the wife alone who was concerned with raising the children, in 23 percent of the families these responsibilities were shared by both parents, and in the remaining families it was not the husband but the children's grandmother who shared the task with their mothers.* And even if the law still recognizes the husband as the head of the family and still charges him with certain obligations as such, another survey of public opinion revealed that 29 percent of the women questioned considered themselves the real heads of their families, irrespective of what their husbands might think.† In 1977 *Literaturnaya Gazeta*—that pallid substitute for a journal of public opinion which often promotes "discussions" of domestic and social problems—opened its columns to women readers who were dissatisfied with their husbands. Here is one such letter from a woman named Yeletskaya:

> What is going on? It seems like the idea of "the man of the house" has lost any real meaning. The man of the house is either a capricious, petulant child or a roaring lion who abuses his wife on the flimsiest of pretexts. All the women I know have the same complaint, with a few rare exceptions. . . . Every one of them says that

* *Journal of Sociology,* number 4, 1970, p. 65.

† A. Pimenova, "The New Life and the Implementation of Equality," *Journal of Sociology,* number 7, 1971.

> it's easier to take care of two children than it is to look after a husband. . . . Only one of my friends is lucky enough to have a husband who can fix things around the house. All the rest of us, myself included, have to get out the hammer and the drill ourselves. One of my friends tells me that when the elevator is broken, her husband gets annoyed—"What are we waiting for? Why don't you go ahead and call the electrician?" If the sink's broken, it's the same story—"Why didn't you call the management two days ago?" It never even enters his head to make the phone call himself. . . . What shall we call this then? Childishness? Laziness? Meanness? Frivolity? I don't know, but it seems to me that husbands have just about given up the right to be called the master of the house . . .

A harsh verdict, but one which the editors acknowledged to be shared by a great many:

> We had thought that the writer of this letter showed too great a tendency to generalize from her own unhappy experience. But as the mail kept coming in, we were compelled to admit that her opinion was typical of the views of most of our women readers.

In spite of the naiveté of many of these letters, the situation itself is too serious to be dismissed lightly. The husband who acts childishly, irresponsibly, who allows all the burdens of parenthood to fall on his wife's shoulders, has become a bona fide social archetype. This phenomenon has a very specific origin—the "fatherless" families which were so common in the Stalinist era and which are not unknown today. It may also have a more profound origin, as though the emasculated hero of nineteenth century Russian literature had been reincarnated in the Soviet Union of today. And in fact the Soviet male appears to have undergone a kind of moral castration, which appears to be inevitable in the context of Soviet society. For in reality it is neither the husband nor the wife who bears the responsibility for the family, but the state itself. It is the state that is the parent, guardian, and teacher of children and adults alike. As a recent sociological work* expressed it:

> . . .these intimate family interactions cannot be left to develop on their own. . . . Only reinforcement by means of an educational

* *Sociology in the USSR*, 1966.

> work program for each family makes it possible to supervise these interactions and to reorient them in the desired direction. It will therefore be necessary to organize an educational work program aimed especially at the heads of families.

The ascendancy of the state is so complete that, socially, the individual no longer exists. This means that children are confronted with a weakened moral authority. Their upbringing and education are monopolized by the school, in which children are indoctrinated and regimented by the Young Pioneer organization. It is scarcely my intention to defend the patriarchal system in which the husband beats his wife to prove his affection for her. But the contemporary Soviet family is neither patriarchal nor matriarchal nor egalitarian—it can only be likened to a band of castaways who have been set adrift in a rudderless boat. The fundamental bases of its authority have been undermined, and it has not been able either to reestablish itself on its traditional foundations or to reconstruct itself according to a new blueprint that would allow it to adapt to new circumstances.

And so we find ourselves at a far remove from the comforting, banal image of the "happy little family." The modern family is rootless and divided against itself.

The population of Russian cities is made up of recent migrants from the countryside who have not found a stable, structured social context that would enable them to adapt to urban life. In 1913, 82 percent of the Russian people lived on the land; in 1939, 68 percent; in 1959, 52 percent; and in 1970, 44 percent. In other words, this rural exodus is a quite recent phenomenon. Although the peasant family structure was destroyed in the villages as an adjunct of the process of collectivization, this explains why the contemporary family retains certain archaic traits. According to the 1970 census about 22 percent of urban families still include two generations of adults—the grandmother, often widowed, remains a pillar (if not *the* pillar) of the family. A patient of mine from the city of Chita used to call his grandmother "Mama" and his mother "Auntie."

I am certainly not making the claim that it is impossible to live a normal family life in the USSR, and in fact, as we have already seen, the family may offer a kind of refuge from the exactions of society. But conflict between the generations (as well as between the sexes) is probably more acute than in other societies. Parents and children seem to experience a great deal of difficulty in communicating with one another. According to a study carried out at the University of Tartu, 75 percent of the students who were interviewed were not satisfied with the way they got along with their fathers, 60 percent were dissatisfied with the way they got along with their mothers; only 10 percent reported that they had any kind of "emotional contact" with their parents.

I do not know what form the family will take ultimately, but I can state that family ties are very fragile and that the moral values which they depend on are crumbling. I knew a thirty-six year old Muscovite woman who had been married three times, had lived with ten different men, had had more than ten abortions, and still maintained that she was leading a perfectly normal life. I mention this not in order to make any kind of moral judgment but because her experience seems to be typical of the profound changes that the microcosm of the family has undergone in the USSR.

Chapter 4
Marriage and Divorce

Marriage à la Mode

Russians marry later today than they did before the Revolution. According to the 1970 census, the average age is nearly twenty-five—and there is rarely a significant age difference between husband and wife. A survey conducted in Leningrad reported that most people marry coworkers, fellow students, or neighbors.

The search for a husband or wife sometimes presents problems. In fact it is so difficult to make contact with members of the opposite sex that many Russians would gladly resort to the personal columns of the newspapers if such things existed in the Soviet Union. In 1977 a prominent Leningrad doctor called Shlyapentokh suggested in *Literaturnaya Gazeta* that an "introduction service" (matrimonial bureau) be established. This proposal, an extremely audacious one by Soviet standards, attracted more than 10,000 letters from unmarried readers who were eager to set up housekeeping with someone, more than 80 percent of them from single women. A plan to match compatible couples by computer was seriously discussed in the press and by the sociologist Chechyot in his book *Youth and Marriage* (1976).

All of this has remained in the realm of speculation, however—at once a sobering and amusing confirmation (if confirmation is needed) that the Soviet authorities are eager to interfere in the private lives of their citizens but simply cannot conceive how they could use the resources of the state to benefit the individual even in the most innocent ways.

On his wedding day the Soviet citizen is still very much aware of the presence of the state, beginning with the ceremony itself. Church weddings, quite understandably, are almost unknown today. Until recently, civil ceremonies were performed in the rather dismal surroundings of a state registry office and were over in few minutes—as long as it took to get to the head of the line and dispose of a few formalities. Accordingly, in the late 1950s it was suggested that "palaces of happiness" might provide all the pomp and pageantry that anyone could ask for on such an important occasion; it was even proposed that the newlyweds don special costumes embellished with Party slogans and the hammer-and-sickle emblem. And so it was that "Wedding Palaces" were erected in all the major cities though many couples still preferred the brisk efficiency of the registry office. The ceremony itself is a fairly faithful imitation of a civil ceremony in the West, but is heavily impregnated with Communist ideology and has an artificial quality—almost as if the entire proceedings had been parachuted in from some other country.

The Wedding Palace can accommodate up to fifty couples a day—hence the interminable waiting. The wedding party arrives on the appointed day, and from then on everything proceeds according to an unvarying formula. The couples are immediately separated in the waiting room—the brides with their women friends and relatives on one side, the grooms and the rest of the men on the other. The walls are decorated with portraits of beloved Party leaders and slogans, such as, "Workers of the World, Unite!" "Long Live the Communist Party of the Soviet Union!" and "The Soviet Family Is the Best in the World." When their turn comes, the couple, accompanied by their friends and relatives, proceeds to the great hall, where an official wearing a red sash awaits them. He mumbles a few selections from "The Moral Code of the Young Builder of Communism" and treats them to a few heartfelt ideological exhortations; the bride and groom exchange rings, are given their passports, duly stamped, and pose for their wedding picture. But that is not all—and it is at this point that the ceremony becomes a blatant caricature. The couple is ushered to a taxi and whisked off to lay a wreath at the foot of the Lenin statue which is found in every Soviet city worthy of the name. In Leningrad the first stop is Mars Field; in Moscow, as I've already mentioned, it is the Lenin Mausoleum itself, where the newlyweds will be lucky enough to get in without having to stand in line.

All of this sounds rather comical, and I can assure you that most Russians have the same reaction. But I do not present this scenario of "marriage Soviet style" simply for the sake of amusing my readers. The nature of the ceremony says more about the uneasy relationship between private life and public authority in the USSR than a whole volume of learned commentary. If young couples choose to have their marriage solemnized in a Wedding Palace, it is not because they are passionately eager to behave like model young builders of Communism or to throw themselves at the feet of the great Lenin, presumably to invoke his blessing on the fertility of their union. It is because they want to celebrate the occasion and to escape the gray routine of the registry office. In exchange, they are made to pay for the festivities by taking part in an ideological charade stage-managed by the regime to which they are, after a fashion, swearing allegiance.

By exacting this homage the state manages to falsify the meaning of the ceremony. Even if the participants are totally indifferent to politics and ideology—as is the vast majority of the population—they are still brought into unfamiliar surroundings, required to go through certain motions, and assailed with ritualistic language which is completely foreign to them.

The state clearly does not exercise this sort of supervision over the individual's choice of a marriage partner—contrary to the utopian goals, of the early years of the Revolution. Just as marriage and the family continue to exist, the choice of a spouse remains "free"; the state only intervenes directly when Soviet officialdom wishes to put obstacles in the path of certain individuals. Here, for example, is the *samizdat* account of a Soviet dissident, Vladimir Gusarov. (The crucial fact to bear in mind here is that all Soviet citizens are legally obliged to register as residents of such-and-such a place. A notation of this appears on their passports, and failure to register is a criminal offense. It is forbidden to remain in a particular place for more than three days without the permission of the authorities.) Gusarov writes:

> At eleven o'clock the doorbell rang. Inspector Ivan Chernyavsky was at the door.

> "Open up, you've got someone living here who isn't registered."
>
> After a fruitless attempt to parley with him, I opened the door and let him in, along with several affable policemen. My fiancée and two of our friends were sitting at the table; my ninety-year old grandmother was sleeping in the next room. They asked for all our papers except for my grandmother's and my own.
>
> "You have someone here who isn't registered."
>
> "This is my future wife. Here's the notice from the registry office—we're getting married in three days. Now I think you should offer us your apologies and your best wishes, and leave."
>
> "No, you're coming down to the station with us—she's not registered in Moscow."
>
> "In other words, you expect her to cool her heels in the train station until we can get married."
>
> "We expect her to stay in Kiev, where she's registered. . . ."

Gusarov's encounter with the inspector was only the first round, however; he was later carted off to a mental hospital, since in the Soviet Union anyone who insists on exercising his rights as a citizen is regarded as a dangerous sociopath until proven otherwise.

Another class of Soviet citizens whose motives are automatically suspect are those who take it into their heads to marry a foreigner. After 1947, when Stalin imposed a rigid ban on these "mixed marriages," there were a number of notorious cases which stirred up a great deal of indignation in the West. The ban was officially relaxed in 1953, but the fact remains that a Soviet citizen who marries a foreigner is still completely at the mercy of the authorities, who may choose to prevent the marriage from taking place or at least do everything in their power to prevent the couple from living together—or to magnanimously grant their approval regardless of the normal legal and administrative requirements. I will give only one example of the kind of pressure and intimidation which Soviet citizens may be subjected to if they take it into their heads to marry a foreign national. An official of the Ministry of Trade was dismissed in 1970 after having dinner with a foreigner who was none other than her future husband. She was immediately summoned to the police station, where the following conversation took place.

> "Why is Mr. T. staying with you?"
>
> "Where is he supposed to be staying?"
>
> "At the hotel—he's a foreigner."
>
> "But we're going to get married."

"No, he's a foreigner.
"Very well then, he *is* a foreigner, but he's also my husband."
"He has no right to be staying with you."
"I don't understand—a husband has no right to stay with his wife?"
"A foreigner should be sleeping at the hotel."
"So perhaps I should move to the hotel too?"
"Watch out, Comrade T., we could very easily arrange for you to move to Siberia and live with the bears."

For Comrade T. things worked out much better than this conversation might lead one to expect. She is currently living in Paris, like many other Soviet citizens who have made the same choice. For all that it may be easier to marry a foreigner today than it was ten or fifteen years ago, it is still just as uncommon. Although they are not really representative of the ordinary Soviet marriage, such marriages clearly demonstrate the fragility of individual privacy under the Soviet system.

Tradition and Degradation

Do Soviet husbands and wives live happily together? As happiness is highly subjective, this question can hardly be addressed profitably. I would prefer to examine the forces which favor the survival of the institution of marriage, as well as those which threaten its existence.

A wedding is still a joyous occasion, celebrated by a banquet which brings together the couple's families and friends, and marked, naturally enough, by a great deal of drinking. The dowry, an even more surprising survival of the old traditions, is still extremely common in rural districts—not as the inevitable object of negotiations between the two families which exclude the couple themselves, but in the form of paraphernalia accumulated by the bride-to-be, which may be anything from bedclothes and table linen to a bicycle.

In fact, young women, particularly in the countryside, are still eager to marry, even if they are legally and financially independent. And to this end many a young woman still resorts to the time-tested custom of getting pregnant deliberately, with the object of compelling the young man responsible to accompany her to the registry office. If the prospective husband proves recalcitrant, the young woman may fall back on a much less traditional strategy: she may threaten to take her case to the local Party committee, the managers at his place of work, the Komsomol, or finally the trade-union council. And these guardians of Soviet morality are often successful in guiding the young scoundrel back onto the straight and narrow path.

Husband-hunting is all the more actively practiced since, as I have mentioned earlier, men are still a scarce commodity in the USSR. In the countryside this pursuit may give rise to morbid excesses, as the following story illustrates.

Engineer Boris Reidisov is a man of highly passionate temperament, a veritable force of nature. During his military service he was troubled by frequent and prolonged erections. As furloughs are rarely granted in the Red Army, millions of Soviet soldiers are deprived of a normal sexual outlet for two or even four years (depending on the branch of the service). Reidisov was inspired to bribe his superior officer to grant him regular leave in the nearest town, where he embarked on an affair with a young woman. She interpreted his sexual ardor as a proof of love and decided to make him her husband. Boris refused, explaining frankly that as far as he was concerned their relationship was purely physical. Shortly before he was to be discharged, she invited him to spend a final evening with her. Not suspecting any malicious intent, Boris readily agreed. That Sunday, when he arrived, the young woman's parents and her brother were not at home. They began to make love, but just as he was about to enter her, her brother burst into the room, armed with an enormous cudgel, which he brought down on the back of the unfortunate Boris. Boris only managed to escape, relatively unscathed, by making an inglorious exit through the window.

Notwithstanding the tragicomic character of this episode, it does illustrate the paramount importance of marriage, at least for a certain kind of mentality. In fact, for this young woman, sexual license serves only as a preparation for marriage, which in turn is the culmination and crowning achievement of her sexuality. Here again it is the woman who appears the force for stability in marriage. In his *Involuntary Journey to Siberia,* Andrei Amalrik recalls a lecture delivered by a jurist in a remote village in Siberia. His subject was the dangers women faced when they lodged complaints against their husbands for beating them. Soviet justice, blind and expeditious, would send such a man straight to the camps, and the horrified woman, who had never wished for this, would seek out the authorities and ask to have her husband back.

Soviet married life is often disrupted by quarreling. One published study * reveals that 74 percent of the families in the sampling reported an habitual pattern of conflict. In 44 percent of the cases the husband provoked the dispute, in 22 percent, the wife. The sociologist who conducted this study comments:

> Many women age prematurely, have almost no time to devote to their personal appearance, lose their attractiveness and their femininity, become ill-tempered and surly. . . .

To put it bluntly, the woman turns into a shrew, while her husband flees the house and consoles himself with a bottle.

The marriage may be shaky, torn by conflict, but husband and wife still manage to carry on all the same: this is the picture that emerges from these brief glimpses of Soviet domestic life, and only time will reveal whether such a volatile combination can endure. What seems to me to be the most serious threat is the degradation of the idea of marriage itself as a binding human compact. Marriage sanctioned by the Church has endured. Official morality and the grotesque rites promulgated by the regime seem like alien grafts that have not really taken root in the Russian soil. Quite the contrary, they have helped turn the institution of marriage into a laughingstock. The best proof of this is the recent proliferation of unconsummated "marriages of convenience." The typical case—which has become a significant sociological phenomenon in Russian cities—involves a young woman from the provinces who is attracted by the affluence and excitement of life in Moscow, Leningrad, or any other major city. However, the city is "closed," in the sense that registration as a resident can only be accomplished with great difficulty. She locates a needy "fiancé" who will accept her "dowry" of up to five thousand rubles. After the ceremony, she is registered at the address of her new husband without having to take the trouble of moving in. The couple petition for divorce almost immediately, the young woman finds herself another apartment, and the job is done.

The marriage of convenience may be equally useful for the Soviet citizen who is not actually of Jewish origin but who wishes to acquire Jewish "nationality" as a pretext for emigrating. Here he will arrange a fictitious marriage with a Jewish woman who is agreeable to playing the role of his wife, out of either friendly or financial motives. In certain Soviet circles today foreigners are much in demand as hus-

* *Journal of Sociology,* No. 4, 1970.

bands or wives, despite all the risks involved. A man who has married a foreigner—the procedure is easier for a woman—will generally succeed in rejoining his wife in her country after some time has passed and a great deal of red tape has been unraveled. The marriage of convenience has become so much a part of contemporary Soviet life that an entire black-market service industry has grown up around it, and a "marriage expediter" can find you a wife to fit your specifications in return for a cash payment.

Divorce

I will simply mention some data which have attracted a great deal of attention on the part of Soviet sociologists. Here, for example, are the results of a study conducted in Perm, a city in the Urals, from 1966 to 1967. The question was asked, "Do you consider your marriage to be happy or unhappy?" Thirty-eight point nine percent of factory workers (46.8 of women workers), 47.6 percent of office workers (48.8), and 28.8 percent of managers (37.5) replied that they considered their marriages to be unhappy. These results seem all the more striking when we consider how difficult it is for people to admit that they are "unhappy" in their personal lives, and indeed, how frequently they may not even be aware of it themselves. A subjective appreciation of the human emotions these statistics represent will be more informative than any description I might give of the prevailing sense of dissatisfaction with the institution of marriage.

Despite this, divorce is still not as simple as putting on a clean shirt, although the reader will recall that during the early months of the new regime it became possible for a couple to get a divorce in a matter of minutes. In fact, since only one of the parties was required to appear, the cast-off husband or wife could remain perfectly oblivious to the fact that he or she was divorced until much later. Beginning in 1936 the presence of both parties was required, and, as we have seen, the revised civil code of 1944 abolished this freedom of divorce altogether. A divorce decree could only be granted after a public hearing before a tribunal, and the appearance of a public notice in a newspaper, and only by mutual consent except in certain unusual cases. In 1956 the requirements were relaxed again, but a couple who have children can still only be divorced by decree of a tribunal. And divorce is more expensive than marriage—fifty to two hundred rubles, as againt 1.5 rubles. The decree of the tribunal settles questions of child custody and property division and legally allows the woman to resume the use of her maiden name.

One further obstacle to the freedom of divorce is the intervention of the authorities. When a Soviet citizen submits a petition for divorce, he opens himself up to all sorts of inquiries at his place of work, which transforms the entire procedure into nothing less than an irksome display of dirty linen in public. The husband and wife are summoned to meetings, jointly or separately; all sorts of attempts are made to talk them out of it (their friends and acquaintances are urged to take part), and no effort is spared to fix the blame on one party or the other. Thus it is not just the tribunal that sits in judgment, it is "society." And this is why the real grounds for the divorce are often concealed, particularly if they might prove damaging to the couple's reputation. The less scrupulous, of course, can fabricate charges which redound very much to their credit—a wife who accuses her husband of "political instability," for example, will immediately find that she has "society" on her side. This is an infallible ploy—even more reliable than an accusation of impotence—which is sure to get the matter settled very quickly.

In 1968 the husband of a well-known Moscow television announcer, Anna Shilova, filed for divorce after he discovered that she had been unfaithful to him. His petition was bitterly contested, and at one point in her testimony Shilova recalled that during the war the theatrical company her husband worked with had been evacuated to the east. "You didn't even go to the front!" she intoned solemnly. "You didn't defend the motherland!"

Bad citizen, unpatriotic—the classically simple accusations which enabled Shilova to keep her complicated private life from being exposed to public scrutiny. Recently another such tactic has been devised: to disgrace one's spouse completely in the eyes of "public opinion" all one has to do is inform the tribunal or the appropriate authorities that he or she is planning to emigrate. There is no need for any proof; it is enough that he or she might have been considering it. And once again, the divorce goes through, and one's hapless ex-husband or -wife is permanently stigmatized as a traitor to the Soviet motherland.

Taking one's case to the authorities does not really change the nature of the dispute between the parties; it merely provides it with an ideological coloration. While there is probably no miraculous solution to such delicate and complex personal conflicts, the moral and ideological standards inherent in the regime, the lack of separation of political and judicial authority, and the fact that the couple is compelled to air their dispute in public—these factors only tend to exacerbate a conflict which calls for nothing more than a judge's decision as to whether there is sufficient evidence of adultery and who should be awarded custody of the children.

Even worse, the intervention of "society" (the Party, Komsomol, or trade union) can actually change the result of the proceedings. For example, a thirty-seven year old office worker in Moscow filed for divorce, accusing her husband, a prominent research scientist, of carrying on an affair with a young actress. The case was brought before the Party organization to which her husband belonged. The Party committee began to pressure him, and, mindful of the consequences of expulsion from the Party, he agreed to mend his ways. This is essentially the same situation as described by the singer and songwriter Alexander Galich in his well-known song "Red Triangle," in which Comrade Paramonova, an important Party official, learns that her husband has been unfaithful while she was out of the country. She summons him to a meeting, at which he is thoroughly brainwashed and forced to confess that he has not been behaving properly. Finally he is forgiven for his misconduct, and the reconciled couple go off together to drink to the health of the "model Soviet family."

What are the reasons for divorce? Soviet social scientists have devoted a great deal of attention to this question, probably in an attempt to check the spread of what they regard as a virulent social plague. As we have seen, the reasons offered by the couple themselves are often not the true ones, but simply pretexts that will make it easier for the divorce to go through—hence the catchall formula, "temperamental incompatibility." Still, their investigations into the problem have resulted in some rather interesting findings.

For example, 40 percent of divorces are said to be the result of some sort of dispute with the parents of one spouse or the other. Remember that many couples continue to live with their families—the traditional values are still strong enough to keep the generations together under one roof but not strong enough to ensure that they will be able to live together in harmony.

This brings us to the problem of the housing shortage. In 1965, according to the Soviet sociologist Kharchev, 31.7 percent of divorced couples did not have accommodations of their own but lived with their parents, with another family, etc. Another 63.2 percent lived in a communal apartment. In other words, virtually 95 percent of divorced couples did not have adequate living space. In 1977, 79 percent of divorced couples did not have an apartment of their own when they got married. This situation does not require any further comment. The housing crisis, although less severe than it once was, still remains critical, and it may introduce unexpected complications into the problem of divorce. Often the divorced couple continues to live in the same room, separated by a folding partition. Impelled by necessity, they may one day conclude a nonagression pact and resume their sexual relationship. The Leningrad artist Semënov and his wife went through several such cycles of divorce and reconciliation. Their marriage broke up periodically because Semënov could not control his passions for his various models. However, the couple never succeeded in locating another apartment and invariably wound up getting married again. They finally decided that their regular expenditures for the successive divorce proceedings (and upkeep and maintenance on the folding partitions) could not be sustained indefinitely, and they are currently living quite happily together.

Other reasons given for divorce include sexual incompatibility (which will be the subject of a later chapter), "loss of affection," adultery, of course, imprisonment (usually of the husband), alcoholism, and physical maltreatment. The battered wife, much less submissive today than she once was, often ends up by divorcing her husband. In Leningrad in 1975, 375 out of 500 divorced women had cited their husbands' alcoholism and brutality. A comparison of the statistics for 1964 and 1977 shows that infidelity has been a rising cause of divorce—from 15 percent to 24.4 percent of all divorces.

The following statistics only take legal divorces into account and not unofficial permanent separations, or "dead marriages," as they are commonly called in the USSR. Here are the figures:

1950	67,000 divorces
1960	270,000
1973	679,000
1975	783,000
1976	861,000

The statistics for 1977 and 1978 show that a third of all marriages end in divorce; in cities such as Moscow and Kiev the proportion may reach one half. In addition, couples are very often divorced before they have been married for even a year; only 48.4 percent of divorced couples had lived together for more than a year, according to a study carried out in 1965, and more than 36 percent had lived together for less than six months. In Kiev in 1978, 55 percent of all married couples between the ages of twenty-five and thirty were divorced in the first few years of their marriage.

In conclusion, marriage has become fragile, dispensable, even meaningless. Most often, it seems no more than a stab in the dark, a futile, inconclusive gesture. It might be supposed that the institution of marriage itself is giving way to less formal living arrangements, but that is not the current trend. Russians continue to get married, but for many divorce is the inevitable outcome.

Chapter 5
Liberated Women?

I am not introducing the subject of women's liberation simply to pay homage to the prevailing intellectual fashions of the West. In fact, this is a very real problem in the USSR, a problem posed by the regime, which claims to have brought about the liberation of women and the equality of the sexes. It has also been posed, as we shall see, by those who are most closely concerned with it: women themselves.

If the equality of men and women has been realized at all, it is in the area of employment. At present 44 percent of the women in the Soviet Union are employed, and they represent 53.5 percent of the work force (this because women still make up far more than half the population). This is the result of a real revolution (at the beginning of the century women worked almost exclusively in their homes or in the fields) which was accomplished in two separate stages: first, industrialization, for which women furnished the bulk of the necessary labor (82 percent of those who entered the work force between 1932 and 1937 were women), and then the war. I use the term *revolution* because women were not brought into the work force gradually, as in Western countries, but were recruited en masse, out of necessity, to replace the casualties of a succession of historical calamities. Like all revolutions, this one had a traumatic impact on women, which I will discuss further on.

Today the working woman is an accepted figure in Soviet society. The majority of women can no longer imagine themselves not working; and too, the average couple, still not far removed from a life of economic hardship, aspires to a higher standard of living which would not be possible on a single income.

But has the equality of sexes truly been achieved? If women are indeed offered equal pay for equal work, in practice this equality is illusory, for as a general rule women are employed in less highly skilled jobs than men. *Literaturnaya Gazeta* (February 15, 1967) noted that in the construction of the dam at Saratov there were 119 women and 17 men employed as heavy laborers, and 142 men and 10 women employed as crane operators. In the USSR it is common to see a male foreman directing a crew of women laborers, particularly in the construction trades.

But the worst aspect of this inequality is the "double work" women have to do, a phenomenon recognized throughout the world wherever women work outside the household. In the USSR this has become a very serious burden, given the government's estimate that women devote between three and a half and five hours a day to household tasks (in my opinion this estimate falls somewhat short of the mark). Interminable lines in the food stores, the scarcity of material comforts (there are few washing machines, the public laundromats are extremely inefficient, and hot water, and even indoor taps, are still considered something of a luxury), child-rearing methods that have not changed since the Stone Age—all this, in addition to seven hours of work and the routine annoyances of public transportation, conspires to reduce the Soviet woman to a state of virtual slavery.

And yet the most profound and probably the most crucial form of inequality is cultural and spiritual. It was Sholokhov himself, the prose laureate of this self-styled egalitarian regime, who announced in 1965 that "only men are capable of creating true literature. . . . Furthermore, women should be very strictly taken in hand, wives in particular."

It seems perfectly natural to Soviet men that women should take care of the children, do the housework, and the shopping. I will never forget the occasion on which one of my patients aired his grievances to me about his wife:

"When I get home and I'm ready to have a little fun, she always turns out to be too tired after making dinner and doing the washing and getting the kids to bed. She doesn't even want to hear about it. All she's good for is sitting in front of the TV for awhile and watching that stupid drivel that even the kids can't stand. Then she gets up and goes to bed. It can't go on like this! I'm going to smash that damned TV and throw it out the window."

"You aren't the only one who has that problem," I told him. "But believe me, it has nothing to do with the television set. The real problem is that your wife has so many responsibilities that take up so much of her time and drain away so much of her psychic energy that she really can't be expected to take a very active interest in lovemaking. I'd advise you to try to share some of the burden."

"Me?" he cried. "Not a chance! I already bring home the money. I don't even drink. And now I'm supposed to put myself on permanent KP and waste my time standing in line all day? Don't make me laugh!"

I doubt that this story is likely to make anyone laugh—certainly not the sex therapist, who must grapple with problems that have very little to do with sex, nor the woman, who has been turned into a beast of burden, nor the frustrated husband, who may already be thinking about a divorce. Yet unfortunately this sort of attitude is typical of the majority of Soviet men.

And how do women react to all this? Traditionally Russian women have been docile and resigned, but increasingly, and particularly in the larger cities, they have begun to embrace certain feminist attitudes. This is a timid sort of feminism to be sure (the women's liberation movement does not exist in the USSR), an intellectual feminism, and even, I would say, a moral feminism, but it is feminism all the same. Thus, at the end of the sixties a survey of women in Moscow, Leningrad, and Penza showed that 25 percent believed that their situation could only be improved by a more equal apportionment of household tasks. Such a proposal might be quite unrealistic, but it is significant of a profound change in attitude: these women were not only unwilling to work as domestic servants, they understood that the remedy must come, not from the State, but from a reorganization within the family itself. And this points to the awakening of a new consciousness and a new sense of responsibility at the individual level.

In 1968 the magazine *Novy Mir* serialized Natalya Baranskaya's novella *A Week Like Any Other,* an hour-by-hour account of the life of a young Moscow woman. Though her married life is happy enough (her husband does not drink and is even willing to help out around the house), she seems constantly on the run, straining every nerve to keep ahead of the thousand routine difficulties of daily existence which finally impose their own hellish rhythm on her life. The publication of this simple, rather maudlin story prompted an enormous amount of discussion (within permitted limits, of course) and filled *Novy Mir*'s correspondence columns for many weeks afterward; it has since become something of a classic of Soviet "feminism." But what seems more important to me is the portrait the novel draws of a woman who has lost touch with herself. It is true that the peasant woman of years ago worked from dawn till dusk with scarcely a pause for breath, but her labor was an integral part of an entire way of life, a stable pattern of tradition which did not permit her to imagine that things might be otherwise. But, the modern Soviet woman is a "hybrid" entity. On the one hand, she is constantly being assured that she has more freedom than any other woman in the world; on the other, she has to put up with a set of cultural prejudices and a grinding daily routine, both of which are demoralizing. Torn between tradition and modernity, she always feels out of place, both at work and in her own home.

As is the case with marriage and the family, there are almost no cultural, ideological, or ethical standards which the Soviet woman can look to—certainly not the model of the militant wife, mother, and worker, which no one has been able to believe in for decades, though literature, films, and the press are still haunted by her ghostly presence. The standard of female beauty in less sophisticated circles still conforms to the peasant ideal of the buxom, apple-cheeked *baba* who is any man's equal at hard physical work—"tits and ass, half a pood [roughly twenty pounds] each," as the Ukrainians rather crudely put it. But it is tragic how quickly this beauty fades. Peasant women and laborers of thirty or thirty-five already look old and worn-out; so much so that I often felt obliged to check my patients' passports to make sure they had given me their correct ages. Graceless and haggard, prematurely aged by a wearisome existence and embittered by a profound sense of dissatisfaction, these women end up losing their femininity altogether.

As the editors of *Literaturnaya Gazeta* wrote, in 1977: "Women who look like cowboys do very well for themselves. They are the ones who raise large families, whose husbands never leave them, while their frail and helpless younger sisters can expect to end up old maids." And rather than asserting their womanhood in the face of male expectations such as these, some women react by becoming more masculine, by emulating the sort of male example that they see all around them. These are the women who become alcoholics (and their numbers are steadily increasing), or even the brutal Amazons who become policewomen and are notorious for the ferocious enthusiasm with which they carry out their duties.

Women in the most comfortable and more privileged strata of urban society take great pains to keep up with the tastes and fashions of the West, even to the extent of embracing "advanced" ideas like feminism. But the sexual inequality and oppressiveness of their own culture is such that these borrowed fashions, in ideas as well as in dress, always have a skimpy, makeshift air about them, as if women were clinging to these rags and patches of Western culture as a signal of protest against the sort of deprivation for which no remedy is permissible in their own country.

The following story illustrates this apparent evolution of consciousness. During a 1970 medical conference in Moscow a colleague invited me to his dacha on the outskirts of the city. When I arrived, he introduced me to his three other guests—all women in their late thirties—and announced that the numerical equality of the sexes, at least, would be restored when our Swedish guest arrived. The women lept to their feet. "A Swede?" "Yes, I have asked a Swedish colleague to come over, to even out our party and help us stave off boredom for a while."

The conversation languished as we waited for our Swedish guest to materialize, even though we had drunk several toasts to the progress of medicine in the meantime. Finally he arrived, making his excuses as best he could with the handful of Russian words at his disposal. The women were overcome at the sight of this exotic apparition. One of them, a plumpish assistant professor, decided to break the ice by showing him how to drink vodka neat, the Russian way. She sat down beside him and tried to start a flirtation, but the Swede appeared to be unmoved by her Slavic charms and sank stolidly back in his armchair.

The conversation that followed was concerned with the biological differences between men and women. After an anatomical excursus in which the assistant professor explained the physical superiority of women (the clitoris only serves as an organ of sexual pleasure, whereas the penis has another, very different function), the Swede inquired:

"What are you discussing, exactly?"

"The liberation of women," answered another of our female colleagues, who was dressed in black. "Men do what they like, sleep with whomever they like, and no one thinks any the worse of them for it. I only wish that I had a chance to do the same. If my husband knew that I was spending the evening here with three men, all hell would break loose . . . even though my husband is completely impotent. Do you understand what I mean?" She tugged at the Swede's arm to keep him from nodding off. "This is the first time I've ever spoken openly with a foreigner in private. How does it work in your country then, in Sweden? Can a woman go to bed with any man she wants?"

"I . . . I am not a woman. . . . I suppose so. You know, I'm not really very interested in that sort of thing."

"You see how it is then—in Sweden the women have liberated themselves. Their men aren't interested anymore, they let them alone so that they can do what they want. Isn't that right?"

"Yes, yes," replied the Swede, beginning to get a little alarmed.

"But here in our country women have no sexual freedom at all. You have to play up to your husband to get him to do what it is he does for you once a year, and that's our whole existence in a nutshell. If I were running things, I'd shut them all up in camps and give them numbers instead of names and let the women choose the numbers they liked and keep them for as long as they wanted, until any time of the day or night, and then send them back to the camp. That's real sexual freedom, don't you agree?"

But the Swede has disappeared. He had gone off to get his briefcase and returned a moment later with a pornographic magazine.

"Here . . . a present for you . . . from me . . . to bring sexual freedom . . . very pleased . . . if you would take it," he said in his halting Russian.

Our colleague's reaction was truly extraordinary. Her eyes opened wide, her eyebrows flew up, her mouth dropped open.

"It's just not possible . . . it's incredible," she muttered as she riffled frantically through the Swedish magazine.

"Today anything is possible," our host remarked philosophically, but she was no longer listening; she seemed to be in a state of shock, but she was also obviously sexually aroused. By the time she reached the middle of the magazine, her neck and cheeks were scarlet, and she fell back onto the couch in a near faint.

The astonished Swede got up from his armchair and asked, quite matter-of-factly and this time in English, if this was the Soviet version of women's liberation.

His question was not as frivolous as it sounds. In the USSR the sexual repression of women is so extreme that a woman might well faint at the sight of a nude body. Sexual frustration, feminist ideas picked up piecemeal from the West, and profound sexual inhibitions—such is the curious amalgam that is the pseudo-liberation of Soviet women.

All this has led us to a very important observation, one which will be invaluable in understanding everything that follows. Women can be the equals of men and still not be truly free, and this, I submit, is the Soviet brand of women's liberation. Women have not been raised up to the level of free men; rather men have been brought down to the level of oppressed women. This creates the illusion that women have been liberated, whereas it is only a matter of the alienation and emasculation of Soviet men.

Chapter 6
The Deserted Garden

I come now to the heart of my subject—the sex life of the Soviet people. And here I am treading on dangerous ground, for if there is one aspect of a people's existence that cannot be approached with scientific rigor, it is precisely this one. Here one cannot generalize from the particular, since the expression of sexuality is always highly individual and no two sexual relationships are alike. Besides, as I have pointed out, circumstances in the Soviet Union make it impossible to undertake an objective and comprehensive study such as the *Hite Report*.

It must be remembered too that my observations are those of a doctor whose business it was to treat people who were by definition ill, in some sense of the word. Even so my patients' attitudes and behavior, and their problems, were so similar that I believe I am justified in viewing them as representive of the Russian people as a whole. And too, very often my patients' complaints were not of a sexual nature at all, so that it was only incidentally that I could gain some insights into the sexual aspects of their lives.

How Do Russians Make Love?

By far the most popular sexual position is what the Russians call the "crayfish"—the woman kneels or bends over, and the man enters her from behind. Russian folklore and a myriad of erotic anecdotes, as well as my own observations, confirm that this is the favored position among all classes of society. It is apparently also the usual position among so-called primitive peoples and the higher mammals. I will leave it to the reader to judge whether this might suggest that the Russian people have remained closer to their origins than most.

The general level of sexual sophistication in Russia is very low. The woman is usually inexperienced and passive, and the man, hurried, tactless, and even brutal. The man often behaves as though it were enough to penetrate the woman's vagina to cause her uncontrollable ecstasy—and should this prove not to be the case, he is likely to become violently angry, or withdrawn and depressed. He seems to be unaware that there are female erogenous zones other than the vagina, for he rarely engages in foreplay, and after ejaculation, he is quick to dismount, turn his back, and go to sleep.

In fact, the majority of men in the Soviet Union are quite simply unaware that clitoral orgasm exists. And as anything that relates to sex or sexual technique is strictly taboo, the woman dares not mention the possibility of such a thing to her husband. Consequently a man might have the greatest affection for his wife and still not have the slightest clue as to what really gives her pleasure. As one may well imagine, sex here is, to say the least, somewhat lacking in originality and refinement. Russians almost never make love in the daylight hours; they prefer darkness, so that one need not look at the partner's body and can rest assured that one's own is equally invisible. To make doubly sure, they often pull the bedclothes over their heads when they make love, and to clinch the matter, close their eyes. Recently, however, they have begun to react against this traditional prudishness, sometimes with disastrous results. Prompted by their scanty knowledge of Western pornography and determined to prove their mastery of imaginative sexual technique, some couples attempt to execute maneuvers that are, at the very least, ludicrous. In Vinnitsa, for example, a young wife was advised by a friend that her husband would be very pleased if she were to pull him around the room by the testicles. I was present when her husband was rushed to the hospital unconscious. Again, in Moscow a dentist took it into his head to sodomize his wife on their wedding night. His efforts were so vigorous that his wife went into shock. (Luckily for her, her husband was able to administer artificial respiration.)

Erotic play and fantasy—in fact erotic pleasure itself—are not considered appropriate to the marriage bed. To the extent that they are ever contemplated at all, they are confined to extramarital affairs or encounters with prostitutes; that is, to relations with women who play "outside the rules." I once saw a woman who had come to complain about her husband, an engineer named Nenaydov. The couple and their two children had lived in a small basement room for many years. Finally, in 1970, they were allotted a small two-room apartment with a rather primitive bathtub near the stove. Apparently this unaccustomed luxury had gone straight to the engineer's head.

"We have been married twenty-two years," his wife told me, "and we still love each other. But my husband has gone quite mad. He wants me to do it with him in the bathtub!"

I tried to explain to her that there is nothing intrinsically abnormal or horrifying in this suggestion, that so far as sex was concerned, there were no strict rules about what one could or could not do, and that there would certainly be nothing wrong in her complying with her husband's request. At this she exploded: "What? How can you say such things? Here I come to you for advice, and you tell me to commit perversions!"

With this she stalked out of my office, slamming the door behind her.

Soviet women cannot imagine that marital sex be anything but straightforward and unadorned. Their attitude toward oral sex is typical in this respect. If a husband even suggested such a thing, his wife would immediately begin to suspect that he had been leading a life of secret debauchery. A respectable woman is not supposed to know about fellatio, even though it is practiced by some couples before marriage, among other reasons, to avoid pregnancy. One of my female patients was subject to periodic attacks of nausea during intercourse; it turned out that she had engaged actively (though, it seems, reluctantly) in fellatio before she was married. This left her with a profound disgust for all forms of sexual activity.

With such a limited repertory of sexual techniques, orgasm remains almost exclusively a male privilege. As we know, a couple can only experience maximum pleasure when both reach orgasm simultaneously—which means that since the man is more quickly aroused, a great deal of patience, consideration, and sensitivity is required for him. What distinguishes erotic love from simple procreation is the ability to "make the pleasure last," to prolong foreplay and find new techniques of precoital stimulation. The practice of the art of love demands a certain amount of control over the sexual act, in order to enhance the pleasure of both partners, but in the Soviet Union "holding back" is almost regarded as a perversion. Thus, it often happens that the man's ejaculation becomes the sole raison d'etre of the sexual act. The word *orgasm* itself, a foreign loan-word, is used primarily by doctors, and there is really no way of expressing the concept in colloquial Russian. The closest equivalent is the verb *konchat'* (literally, "to finish up," "to put an end to something"), which is truly a sad commentary on the Russian Eros.

This does not necessarily mean that the average Russian is completely unaware of the female orgasm. The popular image is of a volcano in full eruption, a high-voltage electrical current—with the result that some women who take this literally attempt to conceal their frigidity with a fixed, ecstatic smile (a painful grimace, of course, would be more realistic but less "convincing").

This erotic charade seems to typify the relations between men and women in the Soviet Union. By the dead hand of puritanism and prudery, by the slavish mimicry of some incomprehensible "ideal" not only in public but even in the most intimate aspect of human existence, the act of love is transformed into a mindless caricature of itself, a tasteless farce.

One of my patients had slept with her husband for fifteen years and never once had an orgasm (her husband was unaware of this, for she could give a passable imitation of "mad, volcanic love," as the Russians would say), or more accurately, she could only reach orgasm by masturbating. One day her husband came home from work early and caught her—she had not even heard him at the door. He started screaming obscenities, gave her a good beating, and immediately filed for divorce. By the time this woman came to see me, she had become genuinely frigid as a result of the emotional shock of being caught in a shameful act, the traumatic effect of a physical beating, and guilt. This poor woman, perfectly normal before this incident occurred, was a permanent sexual invalid, if you will, and this story can be read as a classic tale of woman's oppression, or more to the point, a short course in the ways that relations between Russian men and women have been poisoned by lies, brutality, and ignorance.

Finally, I would like to present a much more unusual case, which nevertheless says a great deal about the kind of grotesque mythology that surrounds the "mysteries of the orgasm" in the Soviet Union. A student by the name of Lomonosov, who had recently gotten married, had nothing but praise for his new wife: "She's more of a dream than a woman. I've never known anyone like her!"

What he prized so highly in her, apart from her other excellent qualities, was her "passionate temperament." Lomonosov was astonished by his wife's extraordinary responsiveness when they made love—sometimes, according to his account, she would writhe convulsively, cry out with pleasure, and faint dead away as soon as she reached climax. When she regained consciousness, she still felt weak and shaken; she could not even remember the final moments of their mutual ecstasy.

The next time I saw Lomonosov, which was sometime later, he was still totally content with married life, though he was somewhat puzzled by the fact that his wife seemed to drool so much when they made love. This, of course, aroused my suspicions immediately; I asked him to tell me more about his wife. Lomonosov seemed disturbed by this: "She's gotten to be very irritable, even what you'd call aggressive, but at the same time, very sluggish. She still takes care of the house and all, but she seems sort of eccentric, obsessed with *things*, if you know what I mean. She's getting to be really hard, and bitter. . . ."

Though I said nothing about it at the time, Lomonosov had just given me a textbook description of a personality type that is frequently associated with epilepsy. Neurophysiological tests confirmed my suspicions, and before long his wife began to have seizures when they were not in bed together. She also had assumed all along that these extraordinary convulsions were simply proof of her unusually passionate temperament. However, after she received treatment to control her seizures, she discovered that she was totally frigid.

If female sexuality is more often totally passive than passionate and volcanic, its complement can be found in the male ideal of sex as a show of strength, a performance that has become its own reward. Such men are not trying to make love, to give or to seek pleasure;

they are content with a simple demonstration of their manly prowess. This sort of behavior is not uniquely Russian, of course, but there is an additional element of deceit and self-deception which is peculiar to *Homo sovieticus*, and which seems to color all of his social attitudes as well. Since he is no more than a cipher in his public life, he must find some other arena in which to prove himself. (In fact, his wife's reactions are not as important as proving he is "somebody" to himself.) This machismo is often just another pose, a way of concealing genuine feelings of inferiority and self-doubt.

I have had hundreds of men trooping through my office, complaining that their penises were "underdeveloped." This was such a common affliction, the patient's accounts of their symptoms were so repetitious, that I became as familiar with the "atrophied-penis complex" as is the general practitioner with the common cold.

In many cases this male "show of strength" takes the form of aggresssion. Even if the woman is really attracted to the man, she must put up a corresponding show of resistance. I encountered an extreme example of this syndrome in the camp at Kharkov—an inmate who told me that he could only make love to a woman if she pretended to struggle the entire time. If she had not figured this out for herself, he would set the scene in such a way that she would have to struggle in earnest. After the last of these playful sessions, he found himself in the dock, and shortly afterward in a camp.

The fetish for "a woman who fights back" is actually quite common: there is a popular Russian anecdote about a rich Georgian on a visit to Moscow who brings a prostitute back to his room in the Hotel Rossiya. She immediately sheds her clothes, hops into bed, and invites him to join her. His first attempt is a fiasco; he tries again, still without success. Finally he jumps out of bed and shouts "Get dressed!" The prostitute hurries into her clothes (assuming that he's about to throw her out), but he stops her before she reaches the door: "All right—just try and get away!"

All this notwithstanding, male aggressiveness is not particularly funny (nor is it restricted to the inhabitants of the Caucasus). Some men beat their wives as a form of foreplay, an indispensable prelude to the sexual act, which is reminiscent of the traditional belief that a husband who never beats his wife cannot really love her. There is even a current slang expression for sexual intercourse, *trakhnut'*; the primary meaning of the word is "to hit," "to strike a blow."

In fact, there is really no absolute standard of "normality" where sex is concerned. As soon as they begin to transcend their purely physical instincts, human beings have already arrived in the realm of fantasy, and every sexual relationship is to some extent unique. And for this reason I am not about to set myself up as an arbiter. But I would like to make two observations that apply to the sexual practices I have just described—that the woman is purely passive, the object of the sexual act, and thus is prevented from experiencing pleasure, and that the introduction of a sado-masochistic element into the relationship seems necessary to fulfill the needs of both partners. In 1953 a retired lieutenant-colonel came to consult me about his declining sexual drive. After I took down his personal history, I asked him to undress for the physical examination. His back was covered with welts, as though someone had slashed him with a sharp knife. He replied evasively to my questions, but I later found out the true explanation: after the war he had returned to Vinnitsa, met a woman there, and married her. He began to beat her on their wedding night when he discovered that she was not a virgin. He only made love to his wife when he was drunk (this sexual sadist was still tormented by the memories of his experiences in the war), and his wife could hardly stand the pain of the inevitable beatings. She began to offer some resistance, digging her nails into his naked back. Gradually their sexual relations assumed a stylized pattern—he could only become aroused when he felt his wife's nails digging into his flesh—and so the roles of sadist and masochist were reversed. After some time he found that he could only get an erection when the pain was too great for him to bear; anything less could no longer excite him. This relationship was neither "normal" nor "abnormal," but simply self-destructive, since it finally became impossible for them to have any sort of sex life at all.

I know of no better (or more absurd) illustration of the ways in which power can displace sexuality in a relationship than this one: I treated a woman, a twenty-six year old economist from Byelorussia, who expressed her coldness toward her husband, an army officer, not by refusing to sleep with him, but by deliberately preventing herself from reaching orgasm. Here at least everything comes together—female passivity and masochism, the idea of sex as a power relationship and of the orgasm as a kind of "tribute" the wife bestows on (or withholds from) her husband. It may seem as if her rebellion was entirely directed against herself, but in fact, as far as she was concerned, the orgasm was only hers to give away, not to experience for herself; for her it was a symbol of male prowess, and thus she could avenge herself on her husband by denying him the token of his virility—a curious kind of vengeance, though, which one inflicts on oneself.

This brief description of Soviet "sexual technique" leaves me with the impression of imbalance and disharmony—the man is selfishly concerned with his own pleasure, and the woman, totally submissive, consoles herself with outrageous overacting in what is, after all, a purely secondary role. For the man, the conjugal bed is simply a proving-ground for his virility, and for the couple the act of love itself becomes no more than a furious, painful paroxysm which momentarily draws them together, though they are perhaps even more unaware of each other than at any other time.

Puritanism at Work

At this point I should explain to the reader that when I use such phrases as "fallen under a curse" and "banished from Soviet territory" to describe the vicissitudes of the Russian Eros, I am not simply indulging in metaphor. These abstractions are actually embodied in powerful social forces which affect the everyday lives of the Soviet people and which are largely responsible for the fact that ordinary human relationships are systematically deformed and degraded in contemporary Soviet society.

Here I would like to add another entry in the catalogue of the psycho-sexual consequences of the Stalinist repression—the phenomenon of *penis captivus*, which is caused by severe involuntary contractions of the vaginal muscles (vaginismus). The result is that the couple is "welded together" during intercourse; the man finds that he is physically unable to withdraw. Such cases (usually very rare indeed) were relatively frequent during the Stalin years. I recall one incident that took place in the students' dormitory of the Odessa Pedagogical Institute, in 1937. When the couple's plight was discovered, the doctors were sent for immediately. Someone threw a sheet over them, and they were trundled unceremoniously out to the waiting ambulance, still locked in an involuntary embrace, while a large crowd gathered and hooted with derision. The whole affair was handled as conspicuously and insensitively as possible by the school authorities; they obviously intended to dramatize the incident for all it was worth, to make the sexual act seem shameful and ridiculous, even though the couple themselves as it turned out were respectable married students and not "illicit" lovers.*

In more recent years, with the gradual relaxation of moral standards, official repression has become less stringent. However, the old system of moral censorship is still intact and always ready to clamp down on casual offenses against public decency. "Immoral" young men and women may find their photographs (along with their addresses and the particulars of the offense) posted on a public noticeboard in the center of town. This is not only inhumane but self-defeating, since the only people who stand to benefit from this "object lesson" (as the practice is called in Soviet parlance) are prostitutes and their prospective clients. On the other hand, ordinary young women who have been subjected to this kind of public humiliation often end up quitting (or losing) their jobs and moving to another city.

Here is an incident which took place in Ulyanovsk (Lenin's native city): a man went out to fill a bucket with water, but right by his doorway he caught sight of a young couple and began to take them to task for their "immodest" conduct. The young man lost his temper, grabbed the bucket, and brought it down over the older man's head; he started to rouse the neighborhood, and the young couple took to their heels. Only the young woman was caught; she refused to give her boyfriend's name to the police. The next day's "object lesson" attracted a large crowd of loafers and curiosity-seekers; the young woman's photograph was accompanied by a doggerel poem which accused her of supplementing her regular income (she was a schoolteacher, in fact) by entertaining a steady stream of male clients. Before long she was trying to find a teaching job in another city.

Soviet law prescribes that "economic parasites" (that is, persons who cannot provide evidence of regular employment) may be expelled from their city of residence, and thus the police are accus-

* The doctors at the scene could have resolved the problem immediately (a slight pressure on the rectum causes the levator ani muscle to relax, and the man's penis can be withdrawn), but Soviet doctors were (and still are) ignorant of such things, for reasons all too easy to imagine. [Author's note]

tomed to receiving anonymous letters denouncing young women for receiving male visitors in their apartments. The Soviet national press (which usually remains sublimely indifferent to ordinary crime reporting and "human interest" items) still publishes accounts of such cases for the edification of its younger readers. *Isvestia* reported that a twenty-year old woman was expelled from Kiev for "immorality" after she was denounced by several of her neighbors. Such denunciations can be a very efficient way of settling an old score or annexing an extra room in a crowded communal apartment. In a similar case, in which the farcical aspects of this legally recognized vendetta were more apparent, a young woman was denounced for entertaining a male visitor in her room. She had already received her expulsion order before she was given a chance to explain that the mysterious stranger was her husband.

Sometimes merely "suspicious behavior" is enough to get a young woman into serious trouble, without benefit of a denunciation, as in the case of Inga Markelov, a student at the University of Moscow. A friend of hers had heard that she was ill, and he telephoned the dean of students to ask if there was anything she needed—a doctor, medicine, money. . . . As soon as Inga recovered from her illness, she was summoned to the dean's office.

"What is the nature of your relationship with this man?"

"We're friends."

"It's all too clear what sort of friends you are. When a man offers to give you money like that, he's not just acting out of pure friendship."

Professors and students alike became involved in this affair, spreading idiotic rumors and engaging in lofty moral discussions. The Komsomol committee convened a special meeting and voted a resolution censuring her for "immorality." Shortly afterward she was expelled.

This form of moral censorship requires two further comments: first, that once more its victims are primarily women, as always, condemned to a life of virtue. In this respect Russian women are no more liberated than they were a century ago. Second, there are some areas in which official and popular morality intersect. Lovers are not only stigmatized by the regime, they are also constantly being badgered by self-appointed moral vigilantes. If a young couple is embracing in a doorway, kissing on a bench in a park or a public square, there is certain to be someone who will call them back to order—a concierge, one of the old pensioners who sit in the park all day, most often a middle-aged matron. Kissing in the streets, according to the vigilantes, is immoral, and particularly not a fit sight for the eyes of children. In a country where lovers are harrassed and pursued like criminals, where the individual has lost control over his private life, you begin to feel that society is telling you, in its loudest, harshest voice: "None of this belongs to you. You don't really live here, we do—and it all belongs to us."

There is no room for lovers in the collectivist state. Love has not been "collectivized," as the free spirits of the twenties had hoped; instead it has been expelled from the city, and the triumph of the bogus "collective spirit" has brought about the death of individuality. As a Ukrainian newspaper recently reminded us, "The honest Soviet citizen has nothing to hide; he has nothing to fear from an examination of his private life." The threat of blackmail is open and unrestrained. Though every social group exerts a certain amount of pressure on its members, at least their privacy is secure, and there is still one corner of their lives they can call their own. But the Soviet regime has taken great pains to rout everyone out of his private corner (since everyone is happy and honest, there is no need for concealment), just as the moral fervor of the mob, already ingrained as an instinct, still hunts down "immorality" in the most secluded doorway.

Humor is the eternal antidote for all the ills of Soviet society, and there is a popular joke about a police patrol that comes upon two lovers kissing in a Moscow street. One of the officers confronts the couple:

> "Who taught you to carry on like that?"
> "Maupassant."
> "Sergeant! Run a check on this Maupassant fellow and bring him down to the station!"

The Loss of Sexual Appetite

After the Soviet sociologist Kolbanovsky had given a lecture in Moscow, a man in the audience asked him: "How many times in his life can a man fall in love?" The professor replied, "Everyone is capable of loving many, many people. An unlimited number. . . ." A pause. "Of course, I'm not talking about physical love. I mean that everyone is free to love whomever he wants—so long as he or she is not an enemy of the people." This statement sums up admirably the regime's unrelenting assault on love—which has ended by distorting the very meaning of the word itself. "Real" love is no longer the love of a man for a woman or a woman for a man, but the love of all good Soviet persons (in the neuter gender). In other words, it is no longer love at all.

One doesn't have to have read *Romeo and Juliet* or Petrarch's *Sonnets* to know what love is. But in the USSR Romeo and Juliet have been replaced by Lenin and Krupskaya—the Soviet version of the "ideal couple" held up as an exemplar to all schoolchildren. There is something worse than the absence of cultural ideals, and that is the attempt to palm off bogus ideals on a people who are all too aware that they are not being offered the real thing. For in fact, the Russian Eros has not been reborn from the ruins of the Stalin era. In what one can only facetiously call modern Russian culture, there are no love songs (except for the traditional ones); there are no romantic stories that move the reader to tears (again, except for the literature of Russia's glorious past). In fact, despite their distance in time, Pushkin's characters seem far more real to the Soviet people of today than do the "perfect" heroes of Soviet literature—which perhaps explains the enormous formative influence nineteenth-century literature still has on the population, a phenomenon that has no real equivalent in the West.

Perhaps more than anything else, it is language that transforms sex from a stark physical encounter into an act of love. But in Russia today lovers no longer talk to one another. What would they talk about? One can hardly discuss the last Party congress while one is making love—and Soviet "culture" offers them few other topics of conversation. There is no "language of love" in Russia today; there is no longer even a vocabulary of love. And as a result men and women can no longer communicate with one another.

This lack of communication between lovers, between husbands and wives, even between the members of the same family is the source of another peculiarly Soviet phenomenon: the enormous value that is placed on friendships between persons of the same sex. For not only does friendship offer a refuge from the hypocrisy and deceit of society at large, it transcends the difficulties that plague sexual relationships; in fact, it often supplants those relationships, along with all other family relationships. When a Russian first comes to the West, he is baffled and disappointed by the coldness and reserve, the "dryness" of the relationships between "friends." Here friendships are not the intense, intimate pair bondings they are in the Soviet Union, where friends often visit each other daily and share intimacies that they would not share with members of their own families. This is perhaps because the Westerner has a large circle of acquaintances, a public and social world within which he can circulate freely. In the "prison world" of the USSR social life is oppressively restricted, for the party member and the peasant alike—so that the few genuine friendships one does have take on a vital importance that they do not have in freer societies. Friendship is one of the few human relationships that remain beyond the reach of governmental manipulation or control, and a friend is the only person in whom one can confide one's most intimate feelings and most private thoughts—feelings and thoughts that one hides even from one's husband or wife or lover. Friendship is the only compensation for the breakdown in communication between the sexes.

And if communication between men and women is all but nonexistent, this alienation is most apparent in the sexual domain. Even in their search for a partner, men and women alike are hampered by a kind of awkwardness, an inability to relate to members of the opposite sex. As an emigré, I was struck by the ease and spontaneity, and even the elegance, with which a Frenchman, for example, would approach a young woman—an ease and spontaneity which would be viewed with suspicion and mistrust, and even outrage, in the Soviet Union. Discontent and frustration breed aggression, with the result that the common courtesies which govern social intercourse in the West are rarely observed in the Soviet Union. (It is not for nothing that Intourist guides must be coached in the rudiments of ordinary politeness before they are judged fit to deal with foreigners.) One of the most popular films to come out in the USSR in the sixties, *July Rain*, is a love story about a man and woman from two different cities who meet by chance while taking shelter from a rainstorm, and then fall in love in the course of a series of long telephone conversations. The tenderness, openness, and humor of their growing affection for each other had an enormous appeal for the Russians—precisely because love, for them, is all too often a crude, awkward, heavy-handed affair. For example, here is the story of a young woman who sold mirrors in a large Kiev department store:

> One day a young man came into the store wearing large fur mittens. To the young woman's astonishment, he walked up to one of the mirrors on the floor and put his fist through it, leaving only the frame intact.
>
> "What are you doing?" she cried. "Are you crazy? Don't you know you could be arrested for that? Do you have any idea what that mirror was worth?"
>
> "Yes, I know what it was worth," the man said calmly, and he took a fat roll of bills from his pocket and tossed it on the counter. "And that one over there—what's that worth?" He pointed at the largest mirror in the store.
>
> A shiver of fear ran up the young woman's spine. "Why do you ask? Do you want to break that one too? That mirror's worth more money than you'll ever see in a year—a thousand rubles, as a matter of fact."
>
> "And what makes you think a thousand rubles is all that much? Have you ever seen a thousand rubles?"
>
> "Well, no."
>
> "Which is more—a thousand rubles or ten thousand rubles?"
>
> "Ten thousand rubles, of course."
>
> "But if you've never seen either one, how can you be so sure?"
>
> She began to laugh. "I don't need to see them to know!"
>
> "Ah, that's the difference between you and me. *I* have to see something first, to get acquainted like. . . . So what do you say—may I see you when you get off work?"

In this way the barrier between the sexes was breached—but only at the price of a shattered mirror. That evening the young woman discovered the reasons for her suitor's strange behavior. For three days he had been wandering about the store trying to attract her attention, but she had not even noticed him. He had decided that a more dramatic approach was in order, since his vacation was almost over and he would soon have to return to Surgut, the oil town in Siberia where he worked. It seemed that although the town had 80,000 inhabitants, it consisted of nothing but suburbs and its nightlife began and ended with a couple of movie theaters and a single café. (The only other forms of recreation were hunting and drinking.) When the workers were finally given a vacation, they would head for one of the larger cities with a few years' wages burning a hole in their pockets; the salaries in Surgut were four times higher than in Kiev, but as there was nothing to spend it on in Surgut, it all had to be frittered away in a few short weeks.

Of course not all Soviet men work in the oil fields—or initiate courtships by smashing mirrors—but as the story of a man who is so inhibited about chatting up a pretty woman that he is forced to resort to slapstick violence and absurdity—this is thoroughly typical of the plight of the Soviet people in general.

The barriers between men and women are often so great that they can only be surmounted after a great deal of alcohol has been consumed. More than one of my patients has said to me, "No man who doesn't smell of alcohol is a real man." And it is surely true that even the virtuous pair portrayed in Mukhin's statue *The Worker and the Collective Farmer*—so pure and martial in their militant poses, brandishing the hammer and sickle with such pride and dignity—would thaw out a bit if one provided them with the third necessity of Soviet life, a bottle of vodka. It is paradoxical that alcohol—which diminishes virility—should be so widely used as an aphrodisiac. Although it is true that alcohol dissolves the inhibitions that imprison the libido, the woman who must submit to a drunken and often violent husband—who cannot make love to her except when he is drunk—surely does not derive a great deal of pleasure from the effects of this "aphrodisiac." Women also drink, usually at parties, and although their behavior may provoke a good deal of fondling and groping, these affairs usually end in something far short of an all-out orgy.

I will conclude this chapter by attempting to answer the question which every sex therapist is inevitably asked: How often do people in the Soviet Union make love? I should say that these figures are by no means definitive, for, once again, they are based on information supplied by my patients:

from 20 to 25 years	every day
from 25 to 30 years	twice a week
from 30 to 35 years	once a week
from 35 to 40 years	once a month

Thus it would appear that Soviet men and women lose their sexual appetite rather early in life. It is not uncommon for men to become completely impotent at the age of forty—a predictable consequence of the official banishment of Eros from Soviet society. Love, forbidden at the outset, and all too often degraded by brutality and drunkenness or transformed into hatred—finally grows weaker, and with the loss of desire, dies. The very sources of life, long before they can be exhausted naturally, are smothered beneath the rubble of the deserted garden of love.

CHAPTER 7
Frigidity and Impotence: A National Sickness

ONE DAY a middle-aged couple came to my office to consult with me. The woman, in her mid-thirties, shoved her husband toward me—for he seemed reluctant to approach—and with the delicacy of a drill sergeant announced: "Cure this impotent idiot for me, will you? I've lived with him for ten years and he's managed to saddle me with three children, but he's never once given me any pleasure."

As it turned out, the man was not impotent in the strict sense of the word, but he did have sexual problems, particularly with premature ejaculation. His wife had never had an orgasm—until she began an affair with someone she had met at a health resort. It was only after she had discovered real sexual pleasure with her new lover that she began to view her marriage in a different light.

I could cite hundreds of such cases: of men who suffered from incomplete erections, who could not sustain erections, or who did not have erections at all; of women who had never had an orgasm. Problems of this sort, which are responsible for the disintegration of so many marriages, are very rarely organic in nature. Typically, my female patients showed no clinical signs of frigidity, and my male patients were able to have erections and to ejaculate. But again and again, these couples had no sex lives to speak of, and their marriages, deprived of a physical basis, had become empty shells, emprisoning them both—insofar as they were mutual victims of a plight for which they were both responsible. This, then, is the outcome of the loss of sexual appetite which I described in the preceding chapter: sexual difficulties which affect both potency and the ability to experience orgasm.

Male Sexual Disorders

If sexual disorders among men are as common as I believe they are (I estimate that they affect almost nine tenths of the male population), then their causes clearly go beyond the purely sexual realm. To repeat what I have already said: impotence is such a common affliction in the USSR that it amounts to a social epidemic, a psychological aberration of national proportions, as well as a strictly medical problem.

This national catastrophe affects all classes of Soviet society. In 1969 the problem received public recognition in the Soviet press, when the *Literaturnaya Gazeta* claimed that "thousands afflicted [with impotence] awaited help." The official response to this claim—which was not made public until 1974, a time when candor was no longer very fashionable—was that fully a hundred percent of Soviet men had experienced orgasm. This is no more credible than most government statistics in this area: admitting the truth would be tantamount to confessing that all was not well in the workers' paradise. Nor did the statisticians mention the frequency, or quality, of the orgasms experienced by Soviet men—in other words, precisely those factors most commonly affected by male sexual disorders.

This reticence is shared by the victims themselves. The sexually inadequate man is reluctant to confide in his doctor—a universal reaction, no doubt, but exaggerated in the Soviet Union, because of the Russian "virility complex" to which I have referred, the general sense of inhibition with regard to sexual matters, and also because of the inadequacy of Soviet medicine to deal with such problems.

Traditionally, when a doctor takes a patient's medical history, he touches on the patient's sex life only in passing, asking, with lowered eyes, "And your sex life?" The patient responds in kind, his eyes lowered as well, "Normal," and the matter ends there. Should the patient take his courage into his hands and pursue the matter, he would receive the time-honored assurance, "Don't worry. You don't have cancer or an infection. And what you have, you won't die of. Give it a little time and it'll cure itself." This easy optimism, however, is seldom justified by the facts; and ultimately, despite the doctor's predictions, the patient discovers that his problem has only been aggravated by the passage of time. Problems with sexual performance are traumatic in their effects: as the failures multiply, the man's impotence crystalizes in a fixed reality from which he cannot free himself.

Things would be very different if the victims of impotence, the doctors treating them, and the governmental authorities were able to examine the problem objectively, without cultural prejudice or inhibition. A colleague of mine from Moscow, Professor Povyansky, once treated a couple who had had virtually no sex life during three years of marriage. Only their love for each other had kept them from seeking a divorce. Four hours of psychotherapy in the form of hypnosis sufficed to solve their difficulties. But at the other extreme there are untold cases in which the physician's attempts to intervene come to nothing—and untold others in which the victims dare not even broach the subject with a doctor.

Sex therapy in the Soviet Union is still little more than a craft: the physician must play it by ear, improvising from case to case. I've referred earlier to the story of the engineer Boris Reidisov, who was attacked by his girlfriend's brother at an extremely unpropitious moment. Reidisov was so severely traumatized by this experience that he could no longer function sexually: just as he was about to enter his partner, he would lose his erection. He spent many years seeking the advice of neurologists, psychiatrists, and urologists, but to no avail. He married twice, but both marriages ended disastrously, for he could not consummate them.

When Boris came to see me he was thirty-five and about to marry for the third time. He wanted desperately to solve his sexual problems before his wedding night. He had been referred to me by a colleague of mine, a psychiatrist named Mozrukhin, who had tried unsuccessfully to treat him with hypnosis. I questioned Boris extensively about the history of his problem, his life, and his fiancée, and decided to try a different tack.

"I'm sure that I can help you," I told him. "But first I would like to speak with your fiancée."

"What?" he responded. "Never! If she were to find out about my problem . . ."

"Don't worry. I've no intention of telling her anything."

This was a calculated lie. Ordinarily, conjoint therapy is simply not an option in the Soviet Union; in fact it would all but constitute a crime against "Soviet morality." But since there is no doubt that were it not for this preposterous prohibition thousands of couples' sexual problems could be solved, I have always found a way to get around it when conjoint therapy seemed necessary.

When Boris's fiancée came to see me, she was confused and embarrassed. I spent an entire afternoon with her, for the task I had to accomplish was not an easy one. I was convinced that she alone could help Boris to have a normal sex life, and perhaps more important, prevent his disorder from crystalizing into a pathological reflex. The method I had decided upon was a very simple one; the difficulty was in presenting it to Boris's fiancée.

"You must overcome your sense of shame," I told her. "Your happiness with your future husband depends entirely on you. The only way that tragedy can be forestalled is this: when Boris gets an erection, don't wait for nature to take its course. Instead take his penis in your hand and guide it into your vagina."

My "therapy" worked wonders. On the day after the couple's wedding night, Boris came rushing into my office, radiant, quite oblivious to the patient I was seeing at the time, and full of his accomplishments—he had "done it" five times. Proof that the human factor, in an atmosphere of trust and honesty, can be far more effective than any kind of professional therapy.

Sexual performance is a delicate matter; the physical mechanism can be disrupted by the slightest thing. In 1967 to 1968 I treated a patient named M. R., a rural postman. There was nothing whatsoever wrong with the patient's libido; in fact he had never experienced sexual problems of any sort until he had come across a pornographic *samizdat* publication which informed him that it was possible for lovers to stimulate each other's genitals orally. He had heard of fellatio—though he had never asked his wife to try it, for fear of "humiliating her"—but cunnilingus seemed like the very thing. However, the result was disastrous. Peter the Great had once instructed Russian courtesans to wash themselves thoroughly before receiving foreign visitors in their boudoirs. As R. discovered, the problem had survived the seventeenth century. He was so disagreeably affected by the odor of his wife's vagina that he became impotent. What is striking about this case is that my patient's innovation was not something that occurred to him spontaneously while he was making love, but a formula he had decided to try out much as one might try out an exotic recipe—something completely out of the ordinary and designed to break the monotony of the usual routine. In other words, sex has come to be viewed as an alien commodity, and in the circumstances it is not surprising that the average Russian's mastery of his own sexual impulses may be somewhat precarious.

Poor hygiene is still widespread in rural areas. A peasant woman who came to see me was in the habit of bathing only twice a year; she and her husband lived in a hut on one side of a small partition, and their pigs lived on the other. But if body odors can be offensive, as in the case of the postman, they can also be stimulating. One of my patients forbade his wife to bathe, for the only thing which aroused him sexually was the odor of sweat and dirty linen. Sexual stimulants can be quite varied and sometimes unexpected: the odor of alcohol, gas, or urine; the dark, a woman's tears, even bodily deformities. . . .

This leads me to another aspect of male sexual insecurity: Without being impotent in the strict sense of the word, a man may be incapable of making love except under certain very specific conditions. For example, I treated a patient who felt no attraction at all for women when he was alone with them, but was quite stimulated by any woman who was with another man. It was the presence of the other man—a rival with whom he could compete—that aroused him. He was undoubtedly suffering from the "virility complex" I discussed earlier, along with an unconscious homosexual tendency.

A more extreme example is that of the police officer who came to consult me about his "impotence." Although he was indeed impotent with his wife, he was passionately attracted to women who were afflicted by some sort of physical deformity: a limp, paralysis caused by a bout with polio, the loss of an arm or a leg, and so on. Driven by this obsession, he had taken a job as Party secretary in a state enterprise which provided employment for handicapped women. However, he had been guided by convention in the choice of a wife and had married a pretty woman who was quite healthy. The fact that he was impotent with his wife appeared to be a manifestation of an inferiority complex: whereas "normal" women made him feel inferior, handicapped women gave him a sense of superiority.

It was not a matter of chance that this patient was a policeman. I don't mean that impotence is a sort of occupational hazard of police work, but I have observed that men suffering from sexual insecurity often choose a profession that offers them some sort of social compensation: the KGB, the police, the judiciary, the prosecutor's office, the army; such a man may even become a police informer. One of my patients, a KGB man, spoke to me with obvious envy of a Ukrainian nationalist whom he had executed shortly after the war: "You see, I made him dig his own grave and stand beside it, and just as I was about to shoot him, I saw that his cock was stiff, enormous. [The man was naked.] God, would I love to have a tool like that!"

The impotent executioner, jealous of the virility of his victim: the symbolism is obvious enough.

To the extent to which the police official is respected and feared in his professional capacity, he can allow himself to appear weak at home. A patient of mine, the wife of a police official, told me with obvious pleasure that she once spat in her husband's face as an expression of contempt for his sexual inadequacy.

It is quite common, then, for men to join the police in order to compensate for their personal inadequacies and, in fact, logical enough, for such a career offers a great deal of personal power in return for a small expenditure of effort and few risks. This is illustrated by the case of Vladimir P., a young man from a privileged family (his mother was a singer, and his father held an important post in the Ministry of Culture). Vladimir inherited his parents' apartment when they moved to Moscow, which left him free to spend the next few years in the relentless pursuit of debauchery. He presided over endless orgies in his new apartment, sometimes slept with several young women in a single day, but all this finally came to an end one day when he realized, after an attack of acute exhaustion, that he had become impotent. When he was called up in 1965, he volunteered for the military police (which in the Soviet Union is an arm of the KGB). He first distinguished himself during the suppression of an uprising in the Tashkent region, when he succeeded in rounding up several of the ringleaders and having them shot. A brilliant career had opened up before him—but he remained impotent. When he told me his story later, I was immediately struck by the fact that his decision to join the military police coincided closely with the onset of his impotence; the link between sexual inadequacy and overcompensation in some other sphere of life is often hidden or indirect, but in this case the connection was clear.

I have also already touched on the more direct causes of impotence—those for which the Soviet governmental apparatus itself is primarily responsible. I met many men suffering from impotence as a direct result of their experiences in the Gulag. I remember one in particular—an inmate of the Vinnitsa prison who had become impotent after ten years in the camps. He had earned his latest sentence—this time the death penalty—by murdering his wife's lover, cooking the man's body, and forcing his wife to eat it, bit by bit. "Labor camp" impotence was a mass phenomenon under Stalin, but it is still very common today.

The "arrest complex" which I mentioned earlier can also produce serious sexual disorders. I once treated a man who served fifteen years in a camp near Karaganda before his "rehabilitation" after Stalin's death. When he returned home, he discovered that he was unable to make love to his wife: as soon as he became aroused, he would ejaculate almost immediately, even before he could enter her. Treatment proved difficult, and progressed very slowly. Then one night something happened which destroyed all hope of cure. While the couple was making love, the doorbell rang. The man attempted to get up to answer it, but discovered that he could not: his penis was imprisoned in his wife's vagina. A violent spasmodic contraction of her vaginal muscles had literally locked the couple together, and it was several hours before they were able to separate. As it turned out, it had not been the police but merely a relative who had dropped by for a visit, but the damage was nonetheless irreparable. The experience was so traumatic for the man that his fear of a recurrence rendered him hopelessly impotent, and all my efforts to help him were futile. He died several years later of a heart attack, at an age when many men are still looking forward to getting married.

Often the ordinary stresses of life in the Soviet Union are responsible for sexual dysfunction. Socially vulnerable and legally defenseless, the individual is subject to mental harassment that may actually threaten his psychological stability. A teacher at the Institute of Highway and Bridge Construction in Petrozavodsk, a town not far from the Finnish border, received a summons from the police. He hadn't the faintest idea why he had been summoned, and it is not difficult to imagine how he dreaded the approach of the appointed day. As it turned out, the police wanted him to work for them—"without compensation"—as an informer. In return, the official promised, he would be given help in finding an apartment, advancing his career at the institute, and so on. He wanted nothing to do with such a proposition, but he disingenuously explained that he would not have time for the job as he had to continue working on his thesis. The police official replied that his thesis could wait—and sweetened the bait by hinting that collaboration with the police might involve travel abroad, where his knowledge of foreign languages would be useful. As the conversation dragged on, he continued to come up with fresh excuses; when the official realized that the "gentle" approach was getting him nowhere, he frowned and pushed a button on the intercom, whereupon a secretary bustled into the office and deposited a thick dossier on the desk.

"Could you tell me about Comrade Podlesnaya?" the official asked.

"Podlesnaya? The name doesn't ring a bell."

"You don't know the name?" The official riffled through the dossier. "Let me refresh your memory. It's a name that I'm certain would be of considerable interest to your wife and your cell members."

The official proceeded to relate the story of a brief affair this man had had three years earlier with a woman whose name he didn't know. He had all but forgotten about it himself, but in their mysterious fashion the police had found out about it and written it up in his dossier.

Although this patient assured me that he had not given in to the blackmail (something which I found difficult to believe), after his visit with the police he gradually became incapable of making love to either his wife or his mistresses, all of whom left him. My attempts to help him failed.

Of course, not all cases of impotence are the result of police interference, but this particular story is of interest on two scores. First, the teacher was the victim of a kind of manipulation that is extremely common in the Soviet Union. One must have tremendous moral and mental resources to withstand the terror the secret police inspire—and as a result the number of informers, as in all totalitarian states, is enormous. Some are volunteers, of course, but the majority are recruited by coercion. The story is also of interest as an illustration of how easily a socially and sexually well-adjusted man can be destroyed, isolated as he is and with no help to be had from any quarter. As all forms of duplicity are destructive of the personality, the double life of the informer is by far the most extreme form of duplicity.

The "indirect" causes of impotence, are those that can be traced to the very conditions of daily existence rather than to the regime itself. These causes are responsible for the large majority of cases of impotence, especially among ordinary working people. The chief indirect cause of impotence appear to be alcoholism and malnutrition; a third—the psychological effects of the housing shortage—I will discuss in a later chapter.

The effects of alcoholism on sexuality is another subject to which I will be returning later. Here I wish only to mention a phenomenon which I have come across many times. Men suffering from sexual disorders who attempt to "treat" themselves without the help of a doctor (whether for lack of a physician or out of shame) often use vodka as a panacea. And in fact, alcohol does often produce the hoped for results: drink allows the sufferer to forget his problems, frees him from his inhibitions, and thus restores his sexual prowess. What he is unaware of, however, is that the "treatment" creates a new illness—a crippling dependence on alcohol itself. He soon discovers that he cannot function sexually without the help of alcohol, and as time goes on, he finds that he must drink more and more to achieve the desired effect—much like the drug addict who must continually take larger and larger doses. Sooner or later he reaches the critical stage when alcohol ceases to have a beneficial effect and begins to aggravate his impotence. In the end he is not only impotent but an alcoholic as well. I have treated countless cases that would serve as an illustration of this pattern, but the one I am about to describe, unlike most, was more of a comedy than a tragedy and had a happy outcome.

A twenty-six year old woodworker came to my clinic the day after his wedding night with a severely bruised penis. He had been unable to break his wife's hymen and had come to me so that I could cure his "impotence" (an extremely temporary impotence, I should add). When I questioned him, I discovered that he was a chronic alcoholic. And, ironically enough, he had begun to drink in order to conquer his inhibitions, in fact, to prepare himself for his wedding night. As he was young, and strong-willed enough to give up drinking on my advice, his virility soon returned, and he and his wife began to enjoy a normal sex life.

Finally, malnutrition is still an important cause of sexual dysfunction in men. Certainly there has not been a true famine in the USSR since 1947. I remember that year very well, when thousands of Moldavians poured over the border into the western Ukraine, where the famine was less acute; many died before they could reach a hospital. Nowadays the problem is one of inadequate nutrition; except in Moscow, Leningrad, Kiev, and the other larger cities, the Soviet people consume less than half of the recommended minimum intake of protein. There are towns and villages where the population lives almost entirely on tea and potatoes; they may go for months without eating meat. If a man does not have enough protein and fats in his diet, his body will be unable to synthesize essential male hormones, resulting in sexual dysfunctions, and in aggravated cases, impotence, even where there are no contributing psychological factors.

I will conclude by discussing the consequences of impotence. I hope I have succeeded in showing that impotence is a particularly distressing affliction in the USSR—both because open discussion of the problem and usual medical intervention are the exception rather than the rule, and because tradition places such a high premium on virility as a source of male honor (I know of an inhabitant of the Caucasian town of Sukhumi, for example, who hung himself because he had failed to deflower a young woman). The most obvious and immediate consequence of impotence, and one of the most serious, is its effect on marriage. Impotence, when it does not lead to divorce, can create a living hell for both husband and wife.

The number of divorces due to sexual difficulties—and impotence in particular—has been on the increase since World War II. I was accustomed to seeing dozens of patients in a single day who had already separated or divorced because of the man's impotence—in other words, when it was simply too late to do anything about the problem.

Another and possibly even more serious consequence of impotence is the loss of the woman's ability to achieve orgasm—the subject to which the remainder of this chapter is devoted.

Frigidity

Under Stalin frigidity was extremely common in the USSR. In that era the merest hint of femininity was condemned as evidence of "bourgeois decadence." Any woman who dared to wear a touch of lipstick or dress in colorful clothes could expect to be heckled on the streets and summoned to a Komsomol or trade-union meeting, where she would be roundly censured. Given this ideological stance in conjunction with the traditional oppression of women, it is not difficult to understand how complete indifference to sex came to typify model feminine deportment, the virtue of the "honest woman." It is difficult to say with precision what percentage of Soviet women suffered from frigidity during the Stalin years. I would say that between 60 and 80 percent of my female patients at that time were never, or rarely, able to achieve orgasm.

And what is the situation today? Certainly it can still happen that a woman wearing a miniskirt will be subjected to a certain amount of constructive criticism; but destalinization and the liberalizing influence of Western mores have bettered the situation of women considerably. The percentage of frigid women—or women labeled as frigid—has diminished, particularly since 1970. Currently, and again judging by information supplied by my own patients, I would estimate it at 45 percent.

In almost half the cases, the woman is either indifferent to sex or disgusted by the idea of intercourse to the point where the act amounts to physical and mental torture for her. Some of these women sense that there is "something missing" when they make love, or experience nervousness or moral distress, but are unaware that these feelings are related to sexual frustration or other, unconscious factors. On the other hand, an almost equal proportion of women suffer no painful or disagreeable sensations whatsoever during intercourse, and some—though they have never achieved orgasm—experience a feeling of pleasure while making love which is easily mistaken for orgasm.

Among women who are labeled as frigid, it is important to distinguish those who suffer from secondary, or "acquired" frigidity—that is, those who at a given point in their lives ceased to have orgasms—

and those who suffer from primary, or absolute frigidity, who have never experienced either sexual desire or pleasure, and who have never had an orgasm.

I estimate that 30 percent of Soviet women fall into the first category. Many of them are the wives of alcoholics, who must submit to sex with a drunken and brutal partner despite their disgust.

The physician encounters primary frigidity less frequently, for the simple reason that women who have never experienced orgasm are often unaware of, or skeptical about the existence of such a thing, and so have no desire to experience it, and thus no motive for consulting a doctor. And those women who do seek out a doctor do so because they have heard others speak about orgasm—a rare circumstance in the USSR, given the general lack of candor about sex. One of my patients was a thirty-seven year old married woman who was pretty, healthy, and the mother of two children, but completely frigid.

"What is this thing people tell me about, doctor?" she asked me in a detached and rather ironic tone. "My friends all say it's very nice, but I really don't know what they're talking about. For me, sleeping with my husband is a job, and none too pleasant. I look at the ceiling and wait till he's finished. I've tried it with at least a dozen lovers, but it's always the same. A friend of mine told me that if I closed my eyes and began to moan, I would have an. . . . what do you call it?. . . an orgasm. Well I tried it. I closed my eyes and moaned like a half-wit—and nothing!" She burst out laughing.

This woman seemed quite unconcerned about her frigidity—in fact, I think she came to see me more out of simple curiosity than anything else. There was nothing I could do for her, not only because her ironic attitude toward the whole business created a barrier between us, but because there simply are no effective techniques for treating primary frigidity in the USSR. The problem is never discussed in medical journals, and the tentative methods which I developed by trial and error were rarely successful. By contrast, I had much better results treating cases of secondary or partial frigidity—for it is a great help when both the patient and the doctor know what it is they are talking about when they use the word *orgasm*.

Unlike impotence, which, as we've seen, is primarily a middle-age affliction, frigidity is often the direct result of a childhood trauma. One of my patients, a woman who worked for the police in Vinnitsa, told me of a childhood incident that was almost certainly responsible for her frigidity.

When she was seven years old, her mother remarried, and her step-father, who was an ardent Communist, changed the child's given name from Valya to Stalina. Happy as she was with this new name, she did not feel comfortable with her step-father, for reasons she did not understand. And one day when she was home alone with him, he came into the room flushed and trembling, dressed only in his bathrobe.

"I asked him what was the matter, but he didn't answer. Then he poked 'it' out from under his robe, squeezed it with his hand, and put it on my knee. I'd never seen 'it' before in my life. I was so horrified that I couldn't move. Then it spouted on my knee, and ever since I always get nauseous whenever I see 'it.' "

How can frigidity be treated under the conditions that prevail in the USSR? Frigid women do not consult doctors as readily as men with sexual difficulties. Women who suffer from periodic frigidity, which involves a temporary loss of sexual appetite, often seek their own "cures" in extramarital affairs with men who are able to arouse them. Many women turn inward and console themselves with sexual fantasies. These are often highly suggestible, somewhat hysterical women whose rigid emotional control blocks orgasm or even sexual excitation. One of my patients was thoroughly and uncontrollably repulsed by sex. But when I asked her if she was still able to experience sexual pleasure, she replied, "Oh, yes. In my daydreams." For her, erotic fantasy had become a substitute for physical sex and a refuge from it.

If the problem of impotence is sorely neglected in the Soviet Union, frigidity is, for the most part, simply ignored—beyond a bit of homespun "counseling" so far as the women themselves are concerned, and now and then a pseudoscientific debate among the doctors.

For the last ten years official Soviet medicine has obstinately insisted that the majority of women experience sexual arousal only after the birth of their first child. Although this may be true in some cases, in my experience it is valid for only about 3 percent of all women. The majority of nonfrigid women begin to experience clitoral orgasms well before their first pregnancy, in fact, when they first become sexually involved with men. The capacity to experience orgasm reaches its peak at about age thirty and may remain there till age sixty or seventy. So it is clear that the purpose of this preposterous official declaration is not to ameliorate the problem of frigidity at all, but to increase the birthrate, which, as we have seen, is quite low. It is also recognized in the USSR that sexual decline begins for men precisely when sexuality in women reaches its peak, at about age thirty—a situation aggravated by the fact that men rarely marry women who are older than they are. The official medical conclusion: the situation calls for a change in male expectations; as it is, men overestimate the sexual needs of young women and underestimate those of mature women. Sound advice, tainted with "Communist morality"!

In 1974, a Leningrad psychiatrist named Svyadoshch published a book entitled *The Sexual Problems of Women*—or rather the book was distributed in a limited edition, for it had been written strictly for physicians. But the book caused a sensation, and was sold on the black market for forty times its actual price. Notwithstanding, Svyadoshch's book was a tendentious fraud. He claims, for example, that only 18 percent of Soviet women are frigid, hastening to compare this figure with those of France (40 percent) and England (41 percent)—a perfect example of the typical Soviet use of statistics for propaganda. Even in a realm as seemingly remote from political preoccupations as frigidity in women, all that would appear to matter to the authorities, and those who serve them, is the affirmation of the superiority of the Soviet Union over Western nations. As a cure for frigidity, Svyadoshch recommends a vacation in the Crimea or the Caucasus, and douching with mineral water. All in all, this only serves to illustrate the pronounced tendency toward self-parody of the Soviet medical establishment, which is really no more than an appendage of the state propaganda machine.

The extent of women's sexual problems becomes fully apparent when we consider a curious, indeed a unique, contrivance, for which patent number 329698 was granted by the Committee on Inventions of the Council of Ministers of the USSR in 1972—"A Device Intended to Enhance Female Sexual Response." Given the puritanism of the Soviet regime, the fact that such an invention was patented indicates that the problem of frigidity has not—Svyadoshch's statistics notwithstanding—gone wholly unnoticed.

The patent is quoted in its entirety in the Appendix, but I will give a few of the particulars here. The exterior surface is covered with small protuberances which are intended to adhere to the woman's "erogenous zone," that is, the vaginal canal. First the man inserts his penis into the device. Then the woman takes over. She inserts the device, now fully loaded, into her "erogenous zone," pushes a button, and the device starts to vibrate. As I picture it, this stage of the operation must be as thoroughly perplexing to the woman as it is terrifying to the man, who must certainly be starting to worry about his virility remaining intact. Nevertheless, the instructions specify that the woman should not switch the device off until "erotic sensations have been aroused." Then sexual intercourse may proceed.

The logical question posed by all this is, "Then what does he need a penis for in the first place?" But of course there are times when asking logical questions can be prima facie evidence of anti-Soviet agitation.

So, from the shameless bluff of the man who must savage his wife to prove he is a man, to the burlesque of an invention that all but takes the place of a man, we still find, just beneath the surface, the same telling apathy, the same sense of futility.

Chapter 8
A Gap in the Hedge: The Breakdown of Official Morality

In 1975 the Soviet demographer Perevedentsev published an article in the magazine *Sovremennik* which was intended as a warning: the stability of the Soviet family was seriously threatened by the increasingly casual attitude toward marriage. He suggested that the principal danger was the decline in the birthrate, which was likely to jeopardize future economic growth. But this was far from being the only peril: "Not so very long ago premarital intercourse was condemned by society and thus was fairly rare," he went on to say. "But what is the present situation?" In reply he offered these statistics: there were 400,000 illegitimate children born every year in the USSR, one out of every ten; in the city of Perm in the Urals the figure was as high as one in three.

This article, then, represents a substantial admission—that the USSR is in the throes of a sexual revolution and that official morality has been severely shaken. I agree with this entirely. And I feel that Perevedentsev is right to discuss premarital sex among young people and extramarital sex (particularly insofar as it contributes to divorce) under a single heading, for they are, in fact, two different aspects of the same recent and widespread phenomenon which has significantly eroded the traditional basis of morality and posed serious questions about the future of Soviet society.

As far as I know, the same thing is taking place all over the world, or at least in all the industrialized nations. To be sure, the proportion of illegitimate births is higher in the USSR than in most of the rest of Europe, but this may be explained by the unavailability of contraception in the Soviet Union. A greater tolerance in sexual matters and a certain skepticism about marriage are certainly not attitudes unique to the Soviet Union. There are, however, two essential characteristics of Soviet society which ensure that this phenomenon will be more painful and brutal than in the West: that is, an omnipresent state and a very rigid official morality.

In a society where the role of the state is limited, where it does not attempt to monitor every aspect of its citizens' lives and thoughts, social change is accomplished progressively, to fill a definite need. Society itself carries out the transformation, unhampered by the state's attempts to oversee the reorganization of the society or else to maintain its status quo in the name of a social "ideal." The state plays a more modest role in the West; one might say that it serves to "domesticate" the evolutionary process, and in order to prevent it from becoming too anarchical and unruly, it hands down laws which institutionalize this process. It is true that Western countries have had some experience of various doctrines and ideologies which have imposed great restrictions on human freedom—Puritanism, for example. But even then, it was not a case of a rigid, unalterable, and alien ideal which was forcibly imposed on the population. This may seem like a highly idealized portrait of Western society, but that is the way it appears from the outside, from the East.

The Stalinist system, which managed to diffuse an atmosphere which was at once sterile and suffocating throughout the Soviet Union, is beginning to break down. The traditional attitude of obedience and resignation to authority is in retreat, and the Iron Curtain is not as solid or impenetrable as it once was; a certain amount of information about Western tastes and manners, about the Western standard of living, is allowed to filter through. The Soviet people are beginning to make demands of their own; often these demands are naively and awkwardly expressed, but they are nonetheless sincere. Thus, a climate of greater sexual freedom has only recently become the focus of the aspirations of younger people in the Soviet Union.

As we have seen, the "model" Soviet citizen of the Stalinist era—asexual, entirely devoted to the Communist cause to the total exclusion of any kind of private life—only exists today as a target for the satirist and an icon for the propagandist. The possibilities in the latter case, however, seem virtually limitless. To choose only one example among thousands, a recent addition to the Family Library Series, aimed at young mothers, praises the "tranquil gaze, suffused with inner strength, of Marya Alexandrovna Ulyanova . . . who brought humanity so much happiness when she brought Lenin into the world. . . ." * Today this entire mythology has been transformed by the Soviet people into a stock of more or less humorous anecdotes in which the great heroes of the past are held up to ridicule and the sexual foibles of a Lenin or a Chapayev (a hero of the civil war) are subject to a searching examination in what is surely the supreme form of sacrilege.

Thus, on the one hand we have the state, which hides its true face from its people and is unwilling or unable to adapt to social change—in sexual matters as in all others, the prospect of liberalization is greeted with much the same enthusiasm as a death sentence. On the other hand, we find a greater gap than ever before between the real life of the people, their ardent desire to see society transformed, and a value system that they no longer believe in. Imagine the effect that the phrases quoted below would have on a young man who has had several sexual experiences and who has nothing but contempt for the idea of marriage and for the adult world in general:

> The best way to learn emotional sensitivity . . . is through your attitude toward your mother, toward all women and girls. . . .
>
> Your attitude toward women is the best indication of your sense of honor, your conscience, your sincerity, and your sense of chivalry.†

And these are not selections from a third-rate manual of Communist morality for primary-school pupils; they are the reflections of the well-known liberal Sukhomlinsky, published in *Novy Mir*, the best of the Soviet literary magazines.

Now it should be clearer why I have chosen the title I have for this

* T. Ryabikina, *A Sacred Task on Earth*, Moscow, 1971.
† V. Sukhomlinsky, "Conversations on Ethics," *Novy Mir*.

chapter. The current transformation of Soviet society seems to lag behind the pace of social change in Western countries, but that does not mean that it is any the less violent, anarchical, or irreversible. It is just as if, beneath the shroud of official prudery that envelops the private lives of the Soviet people, a spirit of cynicism and amorality were developing, a clandestine sexual revolution that is all the more violent because it is denied a socially acceptable outlet.

Premarital Sex

The increase in premarital sex is a reality that no one has tried to deny. As a recent sociological work expressed it, "A significant proportion of young people have their first sexual experiences before marriage." * We even have more precise data which tell us how significant this proportion actually is: 53 percent of the eighteen year olds and 64 percent of the twenty-one year old girls who took part in a study in Leningrad, and 25 percent of the students between the ages of fourteen and seventeen surveyed in Odessa in 1973. In 1965 there were 1,774 single mothers or married women living alone with their children—2,041,000 children in all. In 1972 42 percent of married women reported that they had had sexual relations before marriage, 38 percent with more than one man. Finally, of the growing number of women who give birth to illegitimate children, more than half are under twenty.

To evaluate the real significance of these figures we would have to compare them with the corresponding data from the Stalinist years, and the collection of such data was evidently not encouraged during that puritanical era. But the most important development, as far as sexuality is concerned, has been the appearance of attitudes which are being expressed openly in a country where the public expression of any sort of opinion is so severely controlled. Premarital sexuality is increasingly considered a perfectly normal practice. One unpublished study suggests that it would be difficult to find a teenage girl in all of Moscow who has not had some sexual experience. Two thirds of the women who took part in this study approved of this sexual experimentation; the others expressed no opinion one way or the other. A more extensive study conducted among students revealed that 53

* *Journal of Sociology,* no. 4, p. 67.

percent of young men (38 percent of young women) approved of premarital sex, 16 percent (27 percent) disapproved, and the rest expressed no opinion.

All this confirms my own experience. Formerly, a young woman of twenty was expected to be a virgin, and usually was. During the postwar period girls began to have their first sexual experiences at progressively earlier ages, and today, in the schools, particularly the occupational-training schools, young girls are losing their virginity at fourteen, thirteen, or even twelve. Two parents brought their daughters to me, girls of nine and ten, who had both already had sexual relations. These young girls were sexually precocious, to be sure, but not pathologically so—as with a case reported by my colleague Khozhinov in Kharkov of a little girl who became pregnant at the age of six. This precocious sexual experimentation can certainly be explained, at least in part, by biological factors; young people today reach puberty very quickly, physically as well as psychologically. But the essential factor here is a profound change in attitude, which is readily apparent at the most ordinary, everyday level. Until the sixties, for example, there was an unwritten code that governed all social encounters between young men and women. On the day they met, if all went well, they would go to the movies. A friendly goodnight kiss was permissible at the end of their second date, and on the third the young man might put his arm around the girl. Only at this point could things become more serious. Today, however, young people pass blithely and almost instantaneously through these various stages of intimacy, and well beyond, in the course of their first evening together.

Naturally enough, the principal casualty of this new attitude toward premarital sex is the idea that a young girl's virginity is a precious capital asset, an idea promulgated both by the traditional culture and by official Soviet morality. Chastity (*purity* was the usual word for it) was one of the sacrosanct virtues on which the traditional marriage was founded, and of course these ancient virtues are still staunchly upheld in many areas. In the Caucasus, for instance, the father or brother of a "dishonored" maiden may still resort to his dagger to avenge the outrage against the family name. Tradition also dictates that a bridegroom may send his bride away on their wedding night if he discovers that she is not a virgin. Cast out by her husband, she will not be able to return to her family, for her father will refuse to take her back. But for the most part, and particularly among the

Slavic majority, this sort of attitude is undergoing a process of rapid revision, as the following anecdote will illustrate.

In Vinnitsa there was an ear, nose, and throat specialist called Dr. Rakhlin. Since his practice was only bringing in a meager income, he decided to respecialize in the more lucrative black-market business of restoring lost virginity by surgical means. For a long time he never lacked for patients, but when I ran into him on the street once in 1973, he appeared very gloomy and depressed. He was quick to explain the reason for his despondency—his patients had stopped coming, and he found himself once again on the brink of economic disaster. Young women had been "corrupted," he explained; today they were certainly not the way they used to be. And the young men? They had been corrupted too; their future wives' virginity didn't seem to interest them in the least.

Sometimes virginity is still considered an indispensable attribute, but with the recent liberalization of manners, this has given rise to a certain amount of confusion. One of my patients had allowed her parents to persuade her that she would forfeit any chance of ever getting married if she did not remain a virgin. As soon as my conversation with her touched on sexual matters, she began to blush and stammer.

"How old are you?"
"Twenty-eight."
"Occupation?"
"I've just gotten my degree in chemical engineering at the Polytechnic."
"You are married?"
"N–no."
"How would you describe your sex life?"
"N–n–none."
"What about masturbation then?"
"N–n–no never."
"But you still experience sexual desire?"
"Y–y–yes."
"And how do you go about satisfying these desires?"
Silence.

If this young woman had not stammered so eloquently and expressively, I would probably have had a great deal of difficulty in discovering that she had long since decided that oral sex was the only permissible form of sexual gratification which would allow her to keep her hymen intact and thus not irretrievably ruin her prospects for marriage.

Another example—the daughter of a physics professor, fifteen years old and still a virgin—nonetheless had sexual relations with several young men; anal intercourse was the preferred substitute in this case. One of her partners, however, who was more enterprising or simply more awkward than the rest, did manage to deflower her. This brought down her father's terrible wrath on the luckless young man, who was subsequently prosecuted for statutory rape and sent to prison.

I have spoken of "unrestrained" sexuality, and I am tempted to return to the formula used by Bukharin in 1922 to describe the sexual mores of Communist youth—"anarchy with regard to all the rules of conduct." I myself have come across hundreds of examples of this sort of anarchy, in the schools, for example. In the boarding students' dormitory of a school in Sutisky, not far from Vinnitsa, a group of fourteen year old boys set upon their housemistress and stripped her naked. One of the 176 rapes reported in the city of Sumgait (in Azerbaijan) in 1971 involved three students of the school for young workers who dragged a young woman teacher into a classroom and raped her while twenty-nine other students looked on in silence; none of them made any attempt to come to her defense. In the Vinnitsa schools twelve year old girls were already expecting their first baby. The principal of a school in the Ukraine, a man called Solevëv, told me that during a Russian class a boy and a girl of fourteen who were sharing a desk had been caught masturbating each other. Solovëv had the boy expelled, and his parents had a great deal of difficulty getting him accepted by another school, from which he was expelled in turn when a number of his subsequent sexual escapades came to light.

The sexual precocity of teenage girls is partially linked to the consumption of alcohol, that indispensable companion of Eros. Many of them have their first sexual experiences when they are drunk, and over the course of the last twenty years the consumption of alcohol and drugs has considerably increased in the secondary schools and universities. Formerly, young women tended to drink only when they were in the company of young men, but today it seems that women, and even girls, have acquired the habit of drinking with other women, as men drink with other men, apparently for the simple purpose of stupefying themselves. This represents a particularly sordid example of the new "equality" of the sexes.

From the doctor's point of view, the primary consequence of premarital sex is abortion. After a pregnant fourteen-year old girl came to me one day and explained, "I did it just to see what it was like," I began to realize that, preoccupied as I had been with the day-to-day practice of my profession, I had not really understood the profound changes that had taken place in young people's attitudes toward sexuality. What had until quite recently been considered totally unacceptable, strictly forbidden, and even unthinkable had become perfectly commonplace. It is not for the doctor to pass judgment on young girls who have become pregnant and seek abortions, even when they are barely past the age of puberty. However, he may well reflect on the attitude that adolescents seem to have toward these events. This particular patient did not feel the least bit guilty; nor did she feel that her "trouble" was the outcome of an irresistable passion or, on the other hand, that she had suffered a "fall"; in fact, she was motivated by nothing more than simple curiosity.

What is most striking here is the degree to which adults appear to be unaware of this phenomenon, or at least totally unprepared to deal with it in any way. The subject of the teenage mother has been raised in the press, however, and in recent years it has even appeared in the headlines of *Komsomolskaya Pravda* (February 16, 1975) and *Literaturnaya Gazeta* (June 15, 1977), among others. The author of one of these articles, a woman called Laptera, wrote:

> This subject is such a delicate one that I scarcely know how to approach it. It is something that is only spoken of rarely, and then in whispers. It is true that the whispers sometimes become cries of warning, but as a general rule, the warning arrives too late to be of any use. . . .

Laptera goes on to refer to cases of abortion in which the girls involved, teenagers or even younger, were afraid to see a doctor. Some of them ended up being treated by "ignorant old women, murderous quacks." One little girl began to feel nauseous every morning; her mother had to take her to see several doctors before they found one who realized that she was pregnant.

Another such article included a number of selections from letters written by adolescent girls, all of them between thirteen and fifteen. Here is one of them:

> All of us live on the same street, and we are all little girls who have already become women, but our mothers know nothing about it.

The response to this, as I have already indicated, has been either a simple refusal to recognize that the situation exists, the result of a general abdication of all responsibility, or an attempt to terrorize young people into chastity with various sorts of dishonest scare tactics. Good sense dictates that the first step should be to establish a minimal sex-education program and a counseling program for parents and teenagers, but the guardians of public morality have chosen a different tack. The press, for example, is filled with particularly telling extracts from letters written by young readers (in the Soviet press nothing ever gets printed by accident):

> I was sixteen. I was waiting for Prince Charming, the way every girl my age is. I met a boy in the South. I didn't love him, I didn't even like him, but the damage was done all the same.

The writer goes on to demand that the young man be brought to justice:

> I could never forgive a pig like that. . . . It was a real swindle, a betrayal of trust, a crime—a murder if you like.

Another letter sounds a distinct note of warning:

> I have made a stupid mistake, a terrible mistake. He used to be so nice to me, so affectionate and attentive, but as soon as he found out I was expecting a baby, he started to treat me like a stranger.

Or, to put it more clearly, it's all the fault of the boys, who don't know how to control themselves and don't have the faintest notion of chivalry. As for the girls, they should be more careful, leery of anybody who might lead them astray. It would not be surprising to hear such words from the mouth of a Russian peasant woman, but to find them in the columns of a newspaper which is supposedly devoted to educating young people is a different matter altogether.

It is hardly remarkable that young people have become cynical about sex. The survey of Odessa students I mentioned earlier showed that their attitude toward sex was rather "practical"—for them, love is only a physical need which should be satisfied without undue sentiment. Essentially, this is nothing more than the return of the "glass of water" theory but this time in the guise of a subversive ideology directed against the regime rather than harnessed to its service, as it was in the twenties. There is an added note of bravado here, of revolt against the cardboard moral stereotypes that have been sickeningly familiar to young people since their first days of kindergarten.

As we have seen, the nature of this revolt is often violent, elemental, and profoundly disturbing. Clearly it is not an ephemeral or superficial phenomenon, and the authorities are quite wrong to avoid their responsibilities by ignoring it. The fact that this youth revolt cannot find any context in which to express itself other than sex and the family only makes it more serious. But it does sometimes happen that these newly awakened aspirations can take on a more mature, more reflective form.

In the winter of 1973 some friends of mine brought their fourteen year old daughter to see me; they felt that she was spending too much time with her boyfriend. It was arranged that this private consultation would be conducted under cover of an ordinary convivial evening. The girl's parents had asked me to explain the dangers of spending so much time at such close quarters with a young man, but instead this fourteen year old schoolgirl treated me to a stern lecture that made me understand that the times had truly changed and that the children of today had begun to educate their parents in earnest. She cut me off abruptly in the middle of my prepared speech, saying: "If two lovers want to be alone together, that has nothing to do with false values. False values are what make parents or society spend their time peeking through the keyhole and imagining all the while that they have the perfect right to do it."

My young patient had expressed herself so clearly and so forcefully that I was left with a feeling of great respect for her. In the face of such strong convictions, I began to wonder whether the advice handed down by the adult world and the restrictions it imposed weren't somewhat naive. The Soviet press has criticized young people for kissing each other in the streets, for wanting "to find out about life," to "sample the pleasures of the flesh," accusing them of immorality. In other words, when young people behave frankly and openly, they are accused of immorality; but when they seek privacy, they are immediately berated about the dangers they are exposing themselves to—the dangers of pregnancy for the girl, the dangers of venereal disease for both of them. It is indeed true that there has been a new epidemic of venereal disease; the authorities are currently very disturbed by this, and such warnings are not mere demagogery. In 1971, the Ministry of Health opened an entire network of clinics, and a great many prostitutes were brought in for compulsory treatment. But it seems incredible that a newspaper for young people such as *Moskovsky Komsomol* could have published an article (as it did, in 1973) admonishing its readers not to risk impotence, venereal disease, and severe psychological damage by engaging in premature sexual experimentation. (This article especially stressed the point that girls should be careful to keep their honor intact.) Such exhortations are, in fact, a mixture of charlatanism, shameless lies (for example, the reference to "impotence"), brutal bullying (the threat of venereal disease), empty moral clichés, and a sublime ignorance of the real situation, for it is quite evident that their influence on young people is absolutely nil.

I will mention a few more examples of this new spirit among young people. In a girls' school in Leningrad the students went so far as to organize a protest demonstration against the compulsory wearing of the maroon school uniform, which prevented them from expressing their femininity. This may seem childish and trivial, but such things take on a great deal of importance in a country where uniformity reigns. For many years Russian clothing was ugly, drab, and completely standardized. Today young women and girls are eager to dress more attractively and more colorfully, and they need no longer worry about provoking "public opinion." It was widely reported in the West that the appearance of the miniskirt in the USSR in the late sixties was the harbinger of a genuine cultural revolution. The most significant repercussion of this was probably not the fact that puritan taboos had been trampled on, or the increase in the number of reported rapes; it was that the new style brought about a profound change in outlook. Until then the human body had never been displayed in public, and women's clothing had not been designed to please. The significance of this new fashion was not simply that it provided a subject for ribald improvisations on the part of a handful of voyeurs; in fact, the gray mediocrity of the

Stalinist years had finally been dispelled from one possibly trivial but nevertheless highly visible aspect of public life.

During this period there was also a considerable agitation by students against the regulations which restricted visiting hours in student housing and university dormitories. Male guests were not allowed in women's rooms after eleven at night, and the regulation was enforced by frequent inspections. The more intrepid male students dealt with this inconvenience by hanging from the windowsills while the monitors checked the rooms, and sometimes, as in Moscow, these acrobatics were performed on the twentieth floor. The names of women students who infringed the regulations were prominently posted. There were disturbances in 1964 and 1969 in the universities of Novosibirsk, Leningrad, and Moscow, where the students proclaimed, "Down with hypocrisy! A student dormitory isn't a public bathhouse, where the sexes have to be segregated!" The students at Novosibirsk went on a hunger strike for a day. The upshot was that *Komsomolskaya Pravda* finally stopped denouncing the aficionados of the twist as "bourgeois decadents," and even began to extol its many virtues. The faith and enthusiasm of youth can move mountains, even the sort of mountains that are notorious for bringing forth mice.

We can discern from the correspondence columns of certain newspapers that a more sophisticated attitude toward love and sex is beginning to emerge. Included under the heading of "teenage mothers," mentioned above, were several letters criticizing the impersonality and emotional sterility of the schools:

> I don't know why it is that in our school we never discuss love with our teachers. You can always talk about the love affairs of Tatiana Larina [the heroine of *Evgeny Onegin*] and Anna Karenina, but the minute you bring up your own personal experience, the answer is always the same: "You haven't even finished school yet, and you're already an authority on love!" You get the same thing from your parents too.

Another correspondent cited a literary precedent for these new ideas: "And Romeo and Juliet, how old were they?"

I will conclude with a brief account of a debate that was carried on in the correspondence columns of *Komsomolskaya Pravda,* in 1969.

This paper had already launched a campaign that was intended to combat the spread of immorality when it printed an article by Lev Kassil, author of numerous books for children and young adults. I quote from the article:

> You may be wearing a miniskirt, but that is certainly no reason to condemn yourself to a life of abbreviated mini-emotions, which very quickly give way to more primitive urges. . . .

Kassil goes on to explain:

> Girls reach sexual maturity before boys do. . . . But adolescent boys are the first to experience those almost uncontrollable impulses. . . . Nevertheless, this certainly cannot be said to justify the kind of cynical, even animalistic attitude which some boys have toward girls and women.

Kassil does not use doubtful words like *sex;* he prefers to speak of "uncontrollable impulses" and the like. Still, he does manage to discuss the subject on a relatively human level, which may be why this article elicited more than fifteen hundred letters from all parts of the USSR. Some of the printed responses took issue with Kassil's article. For example, a young woman from Tiflis by the name of Chakhazarova wrote:

> I don't really understand why it is that for such a long time honor has been equated with virginity in the literal, physical sense of the word. And what I find genuinely incomprehensible is how it was ever determined how much time should elapse before the first kiss! Who was it who researched this question and finally came up with such an arbitrary decision? Don't you feel that this sort of cliché is more appropriate for robots, who can be programmed to feel a particular emotion at a particular time?

Another letter, simply signed "Tatiana," constituted a kind of naive manifesto in support of love with no restraints:

> If you are in love, you should really be in love. You should loose your head, and more besides. Even if it's just a few days' happiness and you end up paying the price—still it's the kind of happiness that getting an interesting job or a scholarship to Moscow University could never take the place of. . . .

These letters, as frank as they are, seem to me to break out of the vicious cycle in which the youth of today are trapped. The moral and ideological pap which they have been spoon-fed since childhood, the saccharine sentimentality which permeates literature, the cinema, and even the cadences of "public" speech—this cloying mass of hypocrisy has filled the present generation with disgust for any sort of emotionalism or sentiment. Is it possible then that some young people have been able to transcend both the official morality and the cynicism which underlies it, and thus to free themselves from the weight of the past? It is really too soon to tell, but if there is any hope at all in the present situation, then it is surely this.

Extramarital Sex

Just as with premarital sex, it is impossible to make a quantitative evaluation of the situation in the absence of statistical data. However, here is one arresting finding: in 1977, there were 1,500,000 more married women than there were married men! This discrepancy certainly requires a word or two of explanation. Soviet sociologists maintain that these are unmarried mothers who simply told the census-taker that they were married. As a forty-six year old woman wrote to *Literaturnaya Gazeta:*

> I don't really consider myself to be a single woman. Single means alone, and I don't feel alone, because I have a son.

In other words, for this woman, and a great many others like her, the significance of motherhood far outweighs that of marriage. I believe, however, that the real explanation of this odd statistical discrepancy is this: these women claimed to be married in perfectly good faith; for even though they may not have been legally married, the Soviet Union does contain a large population of "migratory husbands," as they are called, incorrigible polygamists who have several different families in as many different localities.

In any case, these statistics point to an inequality between the sexes which is very much in the Russian tradition: the adulterous woman is considered a criminal, while the man's adventures go unpunished, or even unnoticed. In this respect, the past is still very much with us; in the rural districts of Russia and the Ukraine there are still peasant women who accept this fate with resignation, compliant and uncomplaining victims of their husbands' infidelity.

Crimes of passion are just as much a part of this tradition, and of course there is little to distinguish the Russian crime of passion from those committed in any other country in the world. More interesting are incidents involving violence which indicate that the traditional attitudes toward adultery itself may be changing. For example, in the suburbs of the city of Pskov a woman went to her husband and told him quite openly that she was having an affair but didn't know what to do, since she still loved her husband as well. He replied by breaking a bottle, picking up a sharp sliver of glass, and planting it in his wife's throat. His reaction—which earned him a long term in the camps—was entirely "traditional," while his wife—who felt that adultery was no longer a shameful act which had to be concealed—was clearly an adherent (or a victim) of a new standard of morality.

This is another contradiction, then, another discordant strain within the Soviet Union today. In Turkmenia in Central Asia, even after World War II, unfaithful wives were still being buried alive in the desert with the sand heaped up over their mouths to stifle their cries. (I witnessed such a scene in 1944.) By way of contrast, among the intelligentsia in the larger cities adultery has become tasteful and "civilized"; husbands and wives are completely free to do as they like, and make no attempt to conceal anything from each other. Today, even in less refined circles, wives may commit adultery out of mere curiosity or simply to gratify a momentary impulse. Here again we find the cynicism and the purely physiological conception of love so widespread among younger people.

There can be no doubt that extramarital sex has become more common in recent years. But even if this were not the case, the change in attitudes could not be any more apparent. One survey revealed that 50 percent of women who considered themselves happily married considered extramarital affairs to be perfectly normal. This is yet another indication that a genuine cultural revolution is taking place, the lasting consequences of which are only beginning to appear. Compare this attitude with the opinions expressed in the following letter, which the People's Commissariat of Public Health received from a peasant in 1923. Today this letter has the fragile and poignant air of an antique, and I am quoting it both for its curiosity value and as another demonstration of the sweeping changes in outlook which have overtaken the Russian people:

> I got married in 1918 and it was then that I made love for the first time. I lived with my wife for six months, then I was called up for the Red Army, and I served for a year before I got my first two week furlough so I could go home and sleep with my wife. Then I went back to the army and served for another year and then came home on furlough again, also for two weeks, but since April 1920 I haven't slept with my wife at all, since they didn't give me another furlough and she didn't come to see me, and nowadays I'm having a lot of trouble with my sex life, because I haven't had the opportunity. As far as prostitution goes, I swear I'm against it, because I can't stand them and I'm afraid I might get a venereal disease. This makes two years and four months that I haven't slept with my wife, but I'd rather wait another two years than have anything to do with prostitution, or if I did, it would only be because I had to. I hope they'll let us go home on furlough at the end of this tour and I'll be able to make up for lost time with my wife, and so from now on I'll just keep waiting for that furlough, because I'm really anxious to make love to my wife.

I have just described two diametrically opposed attitudes toward extramarital sex—one, rigid and traditionalist, the other, which is currently gaining the upper hand in the USSR, permissive. Naturally this is an oversimplification, for in reality these positions are often less sharply defined, but these antagonisms seldom make it easier for husband and wife to live together. Traditional morality may seem intolerable, but at least it had the advantage of offering a positive model of the family. Permissiveness, after all, may be no more than a fad. Although it does pose certain dangers—in the form of cynicism and the devaluation of monogamous love—it most definitely contributes to the expansion of human freedom, particularly for women. Nothing is more odious and degrading than the atmosphere of jealousy and backbiting that pervades many Soviet institutions. Even the most solid marriages cannot resist this sort of corrosion, because even if manners become increasingly freer, official standards of morality will still hearken back to the Stalinist dogma from which they were derived. A man or woman who is "guilty" of adultery is considered "morally unstable," and thus in need of rehabilitation. (He or she will be found unworthy of the privilege of traveling outside the country, for example.) The simplest way to do someone an injury in the USSR is to spread malicious gossip about him, and since accusations of political unreliability are not to most people's taste, sexual scandal is the obvious alternative—who's been sleeping with whom. Nothing is more effective than a choice anonymous letter, addressed to the local Party committee or the Komsomol, exposing the moral decadence of your chosen victim.

Let us consider, for example, the National Institute of Marine Geological Research in Riga. The institute regularly organized exploratory drilling operations in foreign waters—off the coast of Bulgaria, Cuba, or India. Before each voyage, while the participants in the next expedition were being selected, the institute was transformed into a field of mortal combat. The Party committee spent entire days reading through the voluminous file of anonymous letters they had accumulated with minutely detailed accounts of the most intimate activities, the debaucheries and perversions, of every member of the staff. The department head whom everyone thought was such a splendid fellow was actually a vicious and depraved homosexual; Galya, the meek little technician, had slept with more than half the men in the institute, and more than that, she always did it on the beach. Finally a peaceable family man was transformed into a sex maniac—it seemed that he even daubed green paint on his testicles. The poor man was compelled to produce a doctor's certificate before he would be allowed to join the expedition; as it turned out, he did not even *have* any testicles—or, that is, they had never descended properly.

Gossip and character assassination have always existed and probably always will, but in the Soviet Union they have become a virulent social sickness. In addition, they furnish evidence of the degradation of traditional moral values, of obvious sexual frustration, and of the error of assuming that there has been any real liberalization of values. Morality is no longer the affirmation of an ideal way of life with a corresponding set of rules; it has become a means of destroying one's supposed enemies, of perversely gratifying one's repressed sexual desires. If the sexual life of the Soviet people is to be restored to health, it must certainly rid itself of this contagion.

This brings us back to our discussion of extramarital sexuality, an area in which the boundary between traditional and modern attitudes is sometimes difficult to detect. It might be possible to find an explanation for this phenomenon in the Russian national character, which—and this has already become something of a cliché—is fundamentally anarchical, disorderly, indifferent or even hostile to all rules and conventions. It would be hard to imagine a Frenchman, an Englishman, or a Swede dropping by a friend's just to have a chat at three o'clock in the morning, though many Russians would think it the most natural thing in the world. This bohemian way of life, particularly common among the intelligentsia, can largely be accounted for in terms of the need for human contact—much as snowbound travelers must huddle together to keep warm in a blizzard. Unconventionality in general, and an unconventional sex life in particular, may be accompanied by alcoholism and an almost total contempt for creature comforts, clean clothes, and appearances in general—an attitude which is also characteristically Russian. To a certain extent, a Russian never really "settles down" after he gets married, and his sex life may continue to be no more restrained, or "domesticated," than that of an adolescent. This last point suggests a certain connection between extramarital and premarital sex.

For women, extramarital sex often represents a kind of compensation for the dreariness of their lives, for their sexual frustration, and offers a means of self-affirmation. It is not passion or even the simple quest for sexual pleasure that motivates the woman; she is searching for an outlet for the accumulated tensions of her daily routine. Thus her lover becomes a confidant who will listen to her complaints about her husband—that filthy, despicable, impotent, drunken oaf that she would leave in a minute if it weren't for the children. . . . Her soul relieved, even though her body always remains somewhat unsatisfied, she can pick up her burden and carry on again.

In conclusion, we might consider the attitude of the authorities toward premarital and extramarital sex, the increase in illegitimate births, and the cynicism that appears to be so prevalent among young people today—an attitude which seems to me to be highly ambivalent. On the one hand, the authorities continue to insist that the Soviet family is the happiest in the world and thus that adultery simply does not exist. For example, in *Love, Marriage, and the Family* (1951), by the sociologist Kolbanovsky, the author points out that in the USSR:

> . . . the strength and the beauty of love depends upon the ideological bond between man and woman. . . . For many decades in the West the children of millionaires have only been allowed to "marry for money." The sole purpose of this practice is to consolidate two sums of capital into one. And, to be sure, such marriages invariably lead to extramarital adventures. In the USSR, however,

since private property and capital have been abolished, love is free of all such material considerations, and adultery no longer exists.

I have not subjected the reader to this grotesque piece of reasoning simply because I want to fix the blame for the sexual misery of the Soviet people (once again) on the authorities. My aim is primarily to reveal the curious thought processes which can lead Soviet ideologues to deny the existence of a problem outright, and with the greatest possible complacency. In their eyes there is no such thing as human nature: if a married man runs after other women, it can only be for economic reasons, and it is society that is at fault. And since the Soviet regime is the most equitable in the world, and since it has decreed that henceforth it will be the duty of every couple to be happy, then how could things possibly be otherwise? Traditional morality did not deny the existence of adultery; it frankly condemned it in the name of a system of values which held the individual responsible for his own actions. Soviet morality is not morality at all; it is nothing more than a blind affirmation of an allegedly "objective" reality, which is actually much more restrictive, since it does not allow him to plot his own destiny. It is more frightening to be told—with total disregard for the truth—that adultery does not and cannot exist in the USSR than it is to be told that one has committed a sin.

This personality split exists on every level of Soviet society: the individual is forced to maintain an uneasy compromise between his normal behavior and the ideological image he is expected to emulate—whether he actually believes in it or not. The regime itself is affected by the same contradiction, for although it continues to proclaim the superiority of the Soviet family, the propositions with which it defends this claim are much more cynical. I believe that there are two reasons for this. First, Soviet officialdom cannot discount reality altogether, and as with the twist, jazz, and the Beatles, it is obliged to dissemble its true reactions when the shouts of protest are too loud to ignore. Second, we should not lose sight of the fact (though such a thing could never be admitted openly) that the present climate of unrestrained sexuality may succeed in reversing the catastrophic decline in the birthrate, which the government itself has repeatedly failed to do. I need only cite the legal code of 1944, which released men from the obligation of making child-support payments on behalf of illegitimate children—clearly a tacit encouragement of premarital or extramarital sex. In return, unmarried mothers were entitled to receive a stipend from the state. An even more surprising piece of evidence, in that it concerns the sacred printed word rather than the dead letter of the law, which is the usual priority in the USSR, is an article which appeared in *Literaturnaya Gazeta* in 1977. Its author, a certain Shukovitsky, states explicitly that even *more* illegitimate children should be born:

> If the majority of single women do not reproduce, then society will be the worse for it, since children are the future of our country.

Proposals of this sort are not only crass and cynical but perfectly gratuitous, since the only really effective incentive that could induce single women to have children would be a tenfold increase in state subsidies to unmarried mothers. However, they are altogether typical of Soviet officialdom's "other face," which is willing to accommodate itself to certain social aberrations in the singleminded pursuit of a specific goal (in this case, increasing the birthrate). Naturally, all other considerations fall by the wayside; the social implications of such a policy are completely ignored, and the authorities simply set about the task with the same narrow-minded brutality with which they attempt to solve all such problems.

CHAPTER 9
The Gardeners' Desertion

THIS BOOK was not intended as a criminal dossier or as an indictment of the parties responsible for the sexual misery of the Soviet people. In any case, such an exercise would be merely academic, since the magnitude of the problem far outstrips the ability of any government to solve it. Here the government can only play the role of enlightened legislator, or perhaps organize educational campaigns or programs in public health or preventative medicine. This chapter will examine the problems of contraception and abortion, two areas which are most directly affected by government policy and in which the regime has almost completely abdicated its responsibilities. There is an extraordinary inertia deeply ingrained in the character of the regime which resists any sort of fundamental change, even when there are those who are actually willing to carry out the necessary reforms. Since the sixties there have been sporadic attempts to promote sex education programs in the schools and for the general public; but all these feeble sparks were quickly extinguished by official apathy, red-tape, and the dogged opposition of an entrenched bureaucracy. Moreover, since these proposals originated within the bureaucracy itself and not with the public, they were extremely tentative, hedged in with administrative restrictions, and carefully picked over by the censors; even had they been pursued, they would not have extended any freedom of operation to those doctors and teachers who might have succeeded in putting them to good purpose.

Sex Education

The appalling ignorance of the Soviet people in sexual matters affects young people as well as adults. This is not simply because the State has not implemented a program of sex education, since this in itself is only an incidental consequence of the more general ban on all public discussion of sexuality. The barrier of silence, shame, and profound uneasiness which surrounds all such questions has meant that the subject of sexuality has been neglected and misunderstood, even dismissed as unimportant.

I could cite an infinite number of examples of this ignorance. A young student, Olya Polozova, found some packets of contraceptive douche in her mother's dresser and decided to try them out. After her third pregnancy and her third abortion—her faith in the efficacy of the little packets was apparently unshaken—she suffered an inflammation of the uterus which threatened to become malignant. It was only when she was brought to me for treatment that the whole story finally came out. Instead of dissolving the powder and using it as a douche, she had been simply swallowing it. What is almost incredible about this story is not that she could have made such a mistake in the first place, which seems entirely natural, but that it was only after three abortions and the serious medical complications which ensued that her mistake was finally discovered. Not only is this a sign of a truly shocking lack of information on the part of young people, but also of an equally disturbing failure of communication between young people and their parents.

A similar example was related to me by a Hungarian student, Oldar Dierd, who had attended the Institute of Precision Engineering in Leningrad. He was astonished to encounter an eighteen-year old student who was seized by an irrational panic when she kissed a boy for the first time: she was terrified that a single kiss would be enough to make her pregnant. The story really did not surprise me. Neither schools nor parents take the trouble to explain these delicate matters to young people. Parents are still trying to beguile their children with the conventional fables. I do not know of a single case in which a child's parents actually attempted to explain the physical process which brought him into the world. To the question, "Where do babies come from?" parents still predictably respond, "We got you at the store," "We found you inside a cabbage," or "The stork brought you."

This combination of parental dishonesty and precocious sexual experimentation on the part of their children can have catastrophic consequences. The medical journal *Health* reported the case of a fifteen-year old girl who came home from school every day with her math notebook decorated with such inscriptions as "Tania & Borris [sic] = Love." This was a subject that her parents had never dared discuss with her, and nothing was said until shortly afterward, when they discovered that Tania would have to have an abortion.

A recent survey of young people gives some evidence of how they acquire such sexual information as they do: 75 percent replied that they had been told by their friends, as opposed to 3 percent who had been told by their parents and another 3 percent by their teachers. The role of books, the press, and the other media is entirely negligible.

When we begin to consider the sexual ignorance of adults, even those who have been married for ten or twenty years, we are crossing the line which separates tragedy from burlesque, and I will confine myself to mentioning a few particularly striking cases which I became aware of personally.

One of my patients, a peasant, was accustomed to "stimulating" his wife's navel, in the belief that this was where her clitoris was located. Another patient, a summer-camp director, exhibited the sexual development of a five year old; when I began to explain this to him, he interrupted, "But I have a child, you know!" He seemed to be so firmly convinced that he had fathered a child that I restrained myself from trying to persuade him otherwise or from questioning him about how his wife got along with his neighbors. This case is far from unique: I have treated hundreds of patients who suffered from arrested or incomplete sexual development. One of them once came to see me and told me that he had tried to make love to a woman for the first time in his life; since he had no idea what to do, he ended up using his nose. Another patient, a woman who was equally ignorant of the physiology of lovemaking, had married a man who was a complete eunuch. Her husband succeeded in breaking her hymen with his finger, and he acquired the habit of satisfying her with his thumb. It was only after some years had passed that she learned what a man's penis could be used for, but she was so accustomed to the thumb technique by then that she was unable to change over. Finally there was the lusty young man of twenty-two who sought me out shortly before his wedding and asked, "Where are you supposed to put it?"

But here I must interrupt this catalogue of misfortunes to return to the problem of sex education in the stricter sense. It goes without saying that such a thing would have been unthinkable during the Stalinist era, and today the old ideological strictures are still in force. When one speaks, for example, of the sex education in Western countries, it is only to criticize it as an attempt on the part of the bourgeoisie to "use sex to seduce young people's attention away from the problems of the class struggle, politics, and ideology." The Soviet consensus, among both the authorities and the population at large, is that the less young people find out about sex the more likely it is that they will behave themselves. Whenever circumstances seem to warrant it, opinions such as this one, from a letter written by a high-school teacher, suddenly receive a great deal of play in the press:

> Frankness is all very well, except where sexual problems are concerned. Modesty is not only a natural emotion, it is also the best form of sex education.

In 1966, *Komsomolskaya Pravda* printed a letter from a gentleman called Lynev in the city of Tyumen to the effect that anyone who gave a lecture or organized a discussion about sex was "attempting the mass seduction of the young people in his audience." As far as he was concerned, "sexual problems are not a fit subject for a public meeting. They should be thought over in private, with the help of an intelligently written book." This last reference is simply ludicrous, since the idea that the shelves of Soviet libraries are liberally stocked with books on sex education is pure science fiction. It is true that an East German marriage manual, *A New Book on Married Life* by Neubert, made a brief appearance on the library shelves, in

1968. Although the information it presented was quite elementary, this book very shortly became unobtainable and today can only be read by librarians. The publication of *The Problems of Sex*, by Dr. Stankov, was delayed for several years. The book was to be issued under the imprint of the Soviet Academy of Sciences, and the editorial committee had given the go ahead. The book was already set up in type when the committee was obliged to reverse its decision; the pretext was that the Academy was not currently sponsoring any research projects in this field.

As for the lectures on sexual problems which Comrade Lynev found so disturbing, there have been certain attempts made in this direction since the sixties. In 1966, for example, Dr. Gutkovich gave a lecture on "the compatible couple" in Kislovodsk. He made every attempt to speak frankly and honestly about physical relations between the sexes. After he finished speaking, he was met with an avalanche of questions, each one more provocative than the last. Each question and answer was greeted with nervous laughter and knowing winks. Subsequently *Komsomolskaya Pravda*, ever vigilant in the defense of the purity of Soviet youth, printed this letter from a high-school teacher called Khorolsky, who had also attended the lecture:

> As I was leaving the auditorium I heard a young man joking loudly with a young woman about the possible applications of the theoretical knowledge he had just acquired. I am convinced that before he attended this lecture he would never have had the audacity to address a young woman in this preposterous fashion.
>
> Lest my fellow readers be too quick to accuse me of hypocrisy, I should point out that I am not opposed to sex education for our young people. But there are certain intimate topics which should not be discussed collectively. I propose that young people should acquire this knowledge under better supervised conditions, perhaps by organizing separate lectures for men and women, particularly for young men and young women. Perhaps it would also be worthwhile to organize separate lectures for younger people and adults. . . . But the best method would be to distribute pamphlets which could be read privately. . . . It would be unacceptable to present this information to a mixed audience, an audience which would include many young lovers, since this kind of propaganda only promotes cynicism and is destructive of every form of modesty.

The fact that such a lecture could take place shows that there have been some attempts in the last fifteen years to make this sort of information available and that these attempts have met with rather contradictory reactions. Clearly, the organizers of these lectures were given the green light, sometimes as a result of a decision on the highest level. But the newspapers still continued to print letters from indignant workers to prove that "public opinion" was opposed to sex education. I would like to attempt to explain this contradiction.

If the authorities are inclined to tolerate some form of sex education, it is only because of the disturbing increase in all sorts of deviant behavior, particularly among young people. The increased incidence of illegitimate births, divorce, abortion, and sexual offenses could well prompt them to take the population in hand. But the measures available to them are limited. They could reinstitute the old system of education, with its stern prohibitions and its stifling morality, but this system has shown itself to be less and less effective, and the more intelligent officials (who are not always true believers any more than ordinary citizens are) are beginning to realize this. And the application of pure and simple repression would no doubt be more difficult in this area than in any other. Besides, one characteristic of the regime is its need to be constantly educating and improving the people. All this explains why the authorities are so hesitant about implementing sex education, and why it remains subject to the strictest forms of control and supervision.

The late sixties witnessed the birth of a more liberal attitude toward sex education and even the word *sex* itself, long forbidden by the censors, began to appear in the press with increasing frequency. A brief sampling of newspaper articles will give some idea of this progression: in 1966, an article entitled "Obscenities"; in 1968, "Teaching Methods and Intimate Personal Problems"; in 1969, "We Should Not Hesitate to Discuss Intimate Personal Subjects." Even if young people were still being sheltered by the veil of modesty, some information was being made available to adults. Medical journals, which are read by laymen as well as doctors, published articles which discussed sexual techniques, although their tone was rather dry. Newlyweds were warned that it takes a woman longer to become aroused than a man but that the man should not allow this to discourage him. The bridegroom was advised to be especially gentle if his bride was still a virgin. Husbands were enjoined not to speak sharply to their wives, not to try to make love when they were drunk, and not to be too rough. But when it came to more practical advice, these writers were usually less inspired. They recommended, for example, that readers who felt sexually unfulfilled should consult a urologist or a gynecologist. Today, at last, there are sex-therapy clinics for married people in Riga, Leningrad, and Moscow; they are still in the experimental stage and very limited in their scope, but their very existence can be considered as a revolutionary breakthrough.

More and more often, people request sex-education programs for both young people and adults, and especially when some particularly lurid sex crime has just come to light. When a roving gang of fifteen boys began systematically raping schoolgirls in Kuybyshev, the reaction in Moscow was that such a thing could never have occurred if they had adequate sex-education programs in the Kuybyshev schools. The same explanation has been offered for the rising divorce rate. In the early sixties a book called *Young Men and Women* was published in Moscow. The word *sex* did not appear once in this book, even though it claimed to be a popular treatment of the subject of "intimate relations." More to the point, however, the author attributes the runaway increase in the divorce rate (.6 per 1000 inhabitants in 1955, 1.3 per 1000 in 1961) to the fact that so little information on this intimate subject is available to young people. In 1970, the alarm was sounded again, and with increasing frequency, this time over the teenage pregnancy and venereal disease statistics. Seminars of doctors, teachers, and representatives of the Union of Soviet Youth were organized, and these in turn proposed that new departments be set up in the universities and that sex-education handbooks be distributed to doctors and teachers. However, these proposals have rarely been followed by any sort of action; as with the question of economic reform, it has become fashionable to discuss the urgent need for sex-education programs, but so far no significant steps have been taken in either of these directions.

In 1975, the journal *Health* devoted a series of issues to the subject of sex-education. Though the concrete details are still rather sketchily filled in and the VD menace is still exaggerated out of all proportion, one of the articles does contain this sentence: "Some women have erogenous zones where others do not, and these erogenous zones may be located in different areas of the body." This seems commonplace enough, but I assure you that I am not exaggerating in the slightest when I say that by Soviet standards this is an extremely daring passage, in terms of both the vocabulary and the writer's implicit attitude toward sexuality—namely, that the act of love should not be treated as an urgent public duty to be accomplished as quickly and expeditiously as possible. But after this unprecedented endorsement of foreplay and sexual stimulation, the level of sophistication of the rest of these articles is rather disappointing: "The idea that a man's sexual capabilities are determined by his physical makeup is a myth." The discerning reader should be able to translate "physical makeup" as "the size of his penis." Another cautionary word, from Dr. Belkin: "The new husband may be disagreeably surprised by his young wife's apparent coldness, whereas in fact this is perfectly natural."

Thus, most of the available information on sexual matters has been so thoroughly compromised by the censors and vitiated by the usual taboos that it has totally lost its credibility with the Soviet people. Sexual technique, the physiology of orgasm, and reliable methods of contraception are almost never discussed. In their place, however, we find a wealth of solemn triviality. "If a young man notices that a young woman's slip is showing, he should ask another young woman to call this to her attention." (It would be bad form for him to mention this to her directly.)

But the same official policies which produce such inconsequential results as these also have their harsher side. In 1964, when the authorities were deeply concerned with the various manifestations of the adolescent sexual revolution, *Isvestia* denounced parents and teachers for instructing children in the basic facts of human physiology, which, it claimed, could only result in an increase in the number of teenage pregnancies. Baskov, the Moscow chief prosecutor, demanded stricter penalties for statutory rape. He cited the case of a fifteen year old schoolgirl called Vera, who had met her "dream lover" at a skating rink. Her teachers knew full well that she was having an affair, yet they did nothing about it, and soon Vera's mother was presented with a grandchild. The tone of all this is extremely callous, in that adults are automatically expected to exercise the crudest sort of interference in young people's private lives. Here is another case, reported by a Soviet writer, in which decisive intervention of this sort did occur:

> A seventh-grade girl wrote a note to a boy in which she told him that she was in love with him. The note fell into the hands of her teacher, who showed it to the principal. . . . Her mother was sent

> for, and in front of the entire school she was told that her daughter was engaging in "intolerable misconduct" with a boy in her class. The girl's mother slapped her across the face. Some of the students laughed; others began to cry. The girl broke free and ran out of the school, but only as far as the railroad tracks nearby, where she threw herself under a train.

Another characteristic of Soviet sex-education which I have already illustrated is that almost every attempt at reform or innovation is followed by a barrage of indignant letters in the press. As usual, the regime giveth and the regime taketh away. For example, in 1968 an article by the journalist Ada Baskina entitled "Neither a Beast nor an Angel" appeared in *Literaturnaya Gazeta*. This was in effect the first swallow that seemed to signal the end of the long, gloomy winter of official puritanism. Baskina called things by their proper names and, among other heresies propounded in this article, even suggested that a wife should not just be a dutiful housewife but a "seductive lover" as well. She related the story of a young man whose wife had left him because, as she had explained, "He was more of an animal than a man." The young man told the author quite simply, "But after all I'm her husband and I love her," and his wife had been no less straightforward: "With him it was all quite simple, and quite disgusting."

The author cited another anecdote: a married couple went to a photographic studio to sit for a portrait.

"Pay no attention to me," said the photographer. "Just pretend that I'm not here. Go ahead and kiss each other and don't let me bother you."

The wife sprang up indignantly. "How dare you! We're not just lovers, after all—we're married! Kiss each other, indeed! Perhaps you've forgotten that we have children!"

Referring to the prohibitions of the Stalinist period (although not explicitly of course), Baskina remarked that "our latest research into human sexual behavior was suddenly forgotten exactly thirty years ago." Man, she went on, is neither a beast nor an angel, and love between a man and a woman should not be like the mating of animals, nor should it be purely platonic; it should simply be human. To demonstrate the urgent need for modern sex therapy in the USSR she asserted that half of all divorces were the result of simple ignorance of the basic facts of human sexuality, and thus:

> It is absolutely critical that the practical means of disseminating this information be provided immediately and that courses in sexual pathology be included in the medical-school curricula . . . perhaps it will even be necessary to establish a research institute for the study of human sexual behavior.

I have quoted freely from this article because its tone of refreshing candor, which at the time seemed almost shocking, was virtually unknown in the USSR. Ada Baskina's proposals were echoed by Professor Kolbanovsky, who wrote that there were hundreds of thousands of adults and young people who stood to profit from such a program of information and counseling and that accordingly sex-therapy centers should be set up "in every major city and in the principal towns of each district."

The editors of *Literaturnaya Gazeta* had no sooner allowed these opinions to appear in print than they hastened to subject them to a withering barrage of criticism in their correspondence pages—which was presumably their chief intention from the beginning. This included a letter from Dresden, written by Neubert, author of the East German marriage manual that was mentioned a few pages earlier:

> Communism should not foster the practice of asceticism but rather a spirit of joyful exuberance which gives rise in turn to a deeply fulfilled emotional life. We should not rely chiefly on sex therapy or the study of sexual pathology. . . . What we need are preventative measures, since our goal is to see millions of healthy families who are free from pathology of any kind.

This was followed by a letter from a woman by the name of Sergeyeva, which bore the caption "A Return to Decency":

> I am writing on behalf of a group of teachers in Tyumen who have read the article "Neither a Beast nor an Angel" and were very distressed by it. The author seems to have failed to realize that many of our youth have already had an early initiation into the subject of sex education! To some extent the responsibility for this must be borne by those so-called educators who would still prefer to deal with such things on a "scientific basis." We are firm believers in decency and discretion in books, films, and magazines, and we categorically reject the idea that sexual problems should be discussed in the way that they were in this article. We are absolutely opposed to this kind of "education." We deplore the fact

> that your paper allowed such an article to be published. Therefore, let us have more discretion and less of this gross interference in the most intimate sphere of human existence!

Another reader, a woman called Poylova from Nikolayevsk in the Far East, wrote: "If we allow books on sexology to become freely available, their most avid readers will surely be adolescents, and such books can only have an unhealthy effect on them." Thus, in practically no time at all, a reasonable and perfectly workable set of proposals was buried under a mountain of rubble—smothered by hypocrisy, narrow-mindedness, and pure hatred.

I myself was involved in an ill-fated experiment of this kind from 1971 to 1972. I had been invited by a group of school doctors to give a course in sex education to the upper grades of one of the Vinnitsa schools. It must be said that this was an extraordinary innovation; the only other such course in the entire USSR was being offered in certain experimental schools in Latvia, twelve class hours per year. At any rate, I began my lectures. The principal of the school went to a great deal of trouble to segregate the girls from the boys. Then, because this subject seemed to be attracting too much interest—a great deal more than all the other subjects, the appropriate administrative response was not long in coming, and the course was instantly dropped from the curriculum.

To be sure, the implementation of a sex-education program in the schools would not be a panacea, as many of its proponents seem to believe. But this might at least help to dispel some of the lies and signal the accession of a simpler, more candid and more courageous approach to sexual problems. At present, however, we have a long way to go before we can be released from this vicious cycle of ignorance and hypocrisy.

I would say then that, at least, in comparison to the vast emptiness of the Stalinist period, a form of sex education does exist in the USSR today. However, it is limited to the sort of uplifting "advice" that is lavished on adults and young people alike, advice that is dispensed by the regime in order to help it attain certain objectives of its own, or to help restore people's beliefs in its ideology and its official code of morality. This has nothing to do with the state or educating the people but simply with the state reasserting its control over them.

And what are the principal themes of this campaign? It is made up in part of the same sort of patronizing and irrelevant recommendations I have already illustrated, recommendations which are merely laughable. But the other, far greater part of this literature is simply an endless reiteration of the dangers of venereal infections. Scores of writers have advised parents to speak of sexual matters "only indirectly"—a marvelous notion guaranteed to put their relationship with their children on a solid basis of trust and understanding. In particular, the parents' role is to alert their children against the threat of VD. I have already given several examples of this national phobia, which is no more than a morbid fear of germs and infection in its most hysterical form. As early as the twenties the satirists Ilf and Petrov observed that the subtlety and tact of this brand of advice was exemplified by posters warning that "Kissing Spreads Contagion!" Things have not really progressed much since then. Imagine the effect it must have on a thirteen or fourteen year old girl, who is just beginning to discover her own emotions, when her parents and teachers suddenly take it upon themselves to threaten her with the horrors of venereal disease! And as I have indicated, this morbid fear of germs is the principal theme of Soviet books which purport to deal with sex. In 1965, a book entitled *From Little Girl to Woman* was published, which described the process of sexual maturation from puberty to menopause. But what is not generally known is that the real purpose of this book was to help combat a serious outbreak of syphilis, gonorrhea, and, especially, trichomonas infection. In a special chapter devoted to the dangers of venereal disease parents were warned to pay particular attention to personal hygiene and to be careful to use separate towels to eliminate the risk of infecting their children.

The essential purpose of these books is to provide young people with a lurid catalogue of all the dangers that lie in wait for anyone who is sexually active. Granted that the dangers of venereal infection are very real—though the cunning and malevolence of the spirochete is certainly exaggerated, and the entire subject is handled with a total lack of sensitivity—is it actually necessary to forbid the entire population to make love except under certain conditions that are rigorously supervised by the Ministry of Public Health? On the other hand, there are "dangers" which are inspired by nothing more than simple charlatanism. What are we to make, for example, of Dr.

Svyadoshch's observation that "premarital sex can lead to serious psychiatric problems." Either this is a truism—since we might say the same of any other activity that we engage in in this problematic world—or it is a piece of lying demagoguery, intended merely to terrorize young people into toeing the official line. Here is another example, from the same series on sex education in the journal *Health:*

> Premarital sex does not contribute to marital harmony; on the contrary it makes it more difficult to achieve. . . . The young woman who loses her virginity before marriage loses her charm at the same time, and she especially loses all her faith in the nobler and deeper emotions, and in herself as well.

If this sanctimonious drivel had at least been served up honestly, that is, in the guise of a lecture on morality, that would still have been less misleading and pernicious than its masquerading as a "scientific" article with the full sanction of the editors of a respected medical journal.

Sexuality seems to be surrounded on all sides by so many dangers, at least if we are to believe these publications, that we can only wonder how the human race has managed to survive for so long:

> It is very dangerous to try to expose the intimate details of married life to public scrutiny or to discuss the relations between husband and wife openly. This approach leads inevitably to the devaluation of the emotions involved.

I will conclude with a few official pronouncements on the act of love and "sexual technique." Several years ago, after reaffirming the hidden consequences of premarital sex—neuroses, impotence, and frigidity—*Health* also gave its opinion on the ideal duration of the sexual act—two minutes! And this is not merely the quirk of a single whimsical doctor; it is a dogma which all medical students have had drummed into their heads for decades. If the man restrains his ejaculation with the idea of giving his partner greater pleasure, this is something "terribly injurious, which can result in the gravest consequences: impotence, neurosis, psychosis."

The sexual act should be as brief as possible and, no doubt, devoted exclusively to the fulfillment of the couple's demographic duty to the nation. It should not be performed too often. Dr. Svyadoshch recommends a maximum of once in twenty-four hours, at night or during the day according to preference, just so long as it is possible to get a good rest before going off to work. Even better still, perhaps, would be to abstain altogether, or to engage in sexual activity for the sole purpose of propagating children. Recently *Health* published an article advocating sexual abstinence, a great boon to health, whereas sexual intercourse can only be harmful.

This is the sexual mythology in which young people are indoctrinated, without, as we have seen, any notable degree of success. The various experimental attempts to provide sex education in the last fifteen years have all been short-lived, most of them smothered in their cradles at the behest of the state. Only the future can tell whether conditions will ever be more favorable; at present the outlook for "liberalization" in this area seems scarcely more hopeful than it is on the economic and cultural fronts.

Contraception and Abortion

Family planning programs or any other public health programs designed to make contraception widely available are virtually nonexistent in the USSR. In this respect the situation bears comparison with that of the so-called underdeveloped countries or of prerevolutionary Russia. One might even conclude that modern contraceptive methods are not widely in use simply because the need for them has not yet made itself felt—and why force it on the population if they neither need nor want it? This, of course, is not the case at all. If we recall the demographic statistics, it will be clear that the Soviet people have already entered the era of zero population growth, since most Soviet couples have no more than two children. This leaves the USSR in a unique position, then, in comparison with the rest of the world. There are countries where population control is desired by the people themselves and encouraged by the state, others where the state attempts to impose it on the people, or at least to encourage it, and still others where legislation and medical practice have been responsive to social change and where contraception is freely available. But in the Soviet Union, where contraception has been an accepted part of everyday life for decades, events have not taken such a rational course—yet another paradox in a country which calls itself progressive, which claims to be in the world vanguard of social change, but might more truthfully claim to lead the world in social paralysis and stagnation.

Contraception was unknown in Russia until the end of the nineteenth century, and even then was only practiced by a tiny fraction of the population. In the twenties, the free-love movement familiarized a great many people with the idea of contraception, though it was probably just as rarely practiced as before the revolution, especially among the peasant masses. With the dawn of Stalinist virtue, it was heard of no more until our own day, when it enjoyed an extremely discreet revival; no medical or social organization has publicly endorsed any form of contraception.

In the Soviet Union the most prevalent contraceptive device is the condom. They are manufactured in Bakovka, not far from Moscow, and are commonly referred to as "galoshes," since they are made of very thick, low-grade rubber and are extremely erratic in their other dimensions, generally either too long or too short—a commentary on both the official indifference toward all sexual matters and the deficiencies of Soviet light industry. Although they do provide a fair measure of protection, most men only use them reluctantly, since they are unpleasant to the touch, a kind of sickly whitish color, and dusted with talc, which gives them an extremely disagreeable smell. For all of that, though, they are still very fragile and tear easily, so that some men prefer to put on two or three at once. Needless to say, this does little to enhance the pleasures of lovemaking, and even with these precautions, they are still not absolutely reliable. The wife of one of my patients was diabetic, and her doctor had strictly forbidden her to become pregnant. Accordingly her husband began to use four condoms every time they made love. Since this couple was not rich, they decided to economize by reusing the condoms afterward. This proved to be a fatal error, since the simple process of washing and drying them out was enough to render them totally ineffective.

There is a lively black market in Western-made condoms, obtained from foreign tourists or Soviet functionaries who have traveled abroad, but these are five or six times more expensive than the local product. Once a couple has gotten accustomed to the imported model, however, they experience a great deal of difficulty when the supply runs out. A female patient of mine told me that she had become completely frigid after her husband was compelled to resort to the Soviet "galoshes" once again. Another patient was astonished to discover that Western condoms were specially lubricated and sold in hermetically sealed packets, since "galoshes" are simply wrapped in ordinary paper or in flimsy cellophane, which is usually full of holes.

Thus, the Soviet people are beginning to be aware of the contraceptive techniques that are practiced in the West, and what is worse, they are even beginning to acquire a taste for this forbidden fruit. As long as the benefits of Western technological progress remain tantalizingly out of reach, the substitutes which are available in their own country will continue to be seen as profoundly unsatisfactory. This situation, essentially the same where all consumer goods are concerned (clothing especially), is one which the Soviet people cannot be expected to endure indefinitely.

The diaphragm, the only other commercially available form of contraception, is even less popular than the condom, and not nearly as reliable. The IUD is as yet practically unknown. In any case, men as well as women find it very difficult to ask for such things at the pharmacy; it was the custom of one of my patients to send his son on this distasteful errand with a letter explaining that he was ill and asking the clerks to give the condoms to his son but to wrap them up in such a way that the boy wouldn't know what was in the package.

But after we have exhausted the resources of the pharmacy, we are left with an entire catalogue of folk remedies, of which I will only give one example—lemon juice applied locally immediately after intercourse. Younger people seem to favor oral and anal sex, which avoids the question altogether, and although coitus interruptus is a primitive and haphazard contraceptive technique (which sometimes has harmful physical effects as well), my observations indicate that it is practiced by over 60 percent of Soviet men. The only remaining medical alternative—vasectomy—is rarely resorted to except by the power elite.

It should be clear from this why abortion remains the principal and only really effective method of contraception in the USSR. In Moscow, Leningrad, and other large cities 80 percent of pregnancies are terminated voluntarily, and in Leningrad in 1963, 80 percent of legal abortions were performed on married women—which shows that this has as much to do with the unavailability of the less drastic methods of contraception as with adolescent sexual ignorance.

This truly appalling state of affairs is well known and even publicly acknowledged in the USSR. In a collection of articles on population growth published in 1976 abortion was damned with faint praise as "a primitive but reliable and accessible method of contraception," yet no rational attempt has been made to improve this situation. Instead of promoting a more effective form of contraception, the government regularly entertains proposals that abortion once again be made illegal.

Let us review the history of abortion in the Soviet Union. First legalized in 1920, though only under strict medical supervision, it was made illegal again in 1936; performing an abortion under any circumstances was punishable by two years' imprisonment. Although there are no statistics available for this period, women continued to seek clandestine abortions, often at the risk of their lives, as was officially acknowledged some years after "the period of the cult." Finally, in 1955, two years after Stalin's death, abortion was legalized once more; the cost of the operation was fixed at five rubles for city dwellers and two rubles for peasants. In 1965, and again in 1971 and 1972, the authorities' anxiety over the declining birthrate impelled them to impose new restrictions, but at present it would be difficult to turn back the clock to the time of Stalin.

Today abortion has become a routine fact of life, though it is still just as closely supervised by "society" as ever. And although the procedure itself is practically free, it still requires an imposing amount of red tape to be unraveled, a whole series of painful and humiliating encounters with unsympathetic bureaucrats. Thus, despite the increased risk of post-operative complications, many women still prefer to have private (that is, illegal) abortions—the risk involved for the abortionist is considerable as well, since the penal code prescribes a maximum penalty of eight years' hard labor. But whether the abortion is performed privately or in a hospital or clinic, the technique is crudely mechanical (dilation and currettage, without anesthesia, though sometimes the patient is given a shot of novocaine). Nevertheless, there are women who have had literally dozens of abortions (I once treated a woman who had twenty-two), since, as

I have said, this is the most "convenient" form of contraception. And often these women no longer require the help of any external agency; the usual recipe calls for a glass of vodka, a soak in a hot tub, then jumping up and down until a miscarriage ensues. In such cases the muscles of the uterus become so weak that the simple effort of walking may cause spontaneous abortion.

As we have seen, there is no clear demarcation between the subjects of abortion and contraception. The idea of population control has been firmly established as official policy in the Soviet Union. But the implementation of this policy has fallen far short of its logical conclusion—the development of an accessible and reliable form of contraception. It is as if only the negative aspect of contraception (the termination of pregnancy) has been retained, when contraception might have become a permanent means of assuring individual happiness and allowing women to have some control over their lives. Repeated abortions cannot possibly promote a balanced and harmonious emotional life, particularly for the woman. As in the realms of "women's liberation" and love and sexuality in general, the situation as far as contraception is concerned remains unhealthy and ultimately untenable; modern ideas and newly awakened aspirations are confronted by entrenched routine and the negligence and indifference of the state. The only real outcome of this confrontation has been an increase in the abortion rate. However, it would be difficult to tax the state with the responsibility for all this; in fact it would be more accurate to speak of the irresponsibility of the state. Whatever else we may say, the regime has totally transformed the country; it has created a modern, industrialized state which stands in the front rank of the so-called developed countries. And in so doing, it has awakened new aspirations among the people, and at the same time totally destroyed their traditional ways of life and thought. But as soon as the regime is called upon to provide a concrete solution to a precise problem—such as the disturbing increase in the abortion rate or the urgent need to provide sex-education for adults and young people—it retreats to its own ideological fastnesses and leaves the situation to deteriorate. Yet there exists an even more serious contradiction: since the state has suppressed all forms of private initiative, it alone can provide the motive force for any progress that is to occur, at least in the immediate future; but it seems that this is a responsibility that the state will not or perhaps even cannot undertake. I am not so naive as to think that a few courses in sex education and a few clinics dispensing contraceptives would be enough to solve all the sexual problems of the Soviet people. But at least these small acts of courage would be a first step toward dispelling the poisonous atmosphere that permeates every aspect of sexuality in the Soviet Union.

III

FORBIDDEN PRACTICES

THE SOVIET penal code contains seven articles that prescribe criminal penalties for sexual offenses:

1. Transmitting a venereal disease: maximum sentence, three years' imprisonment.
2. Performing an illegal abortion: maximum sentence, eight years.
3. Rape: maximum sentence, death.
4. Forcible seduction: maximum sentence, three years.
5. Abduction of a minor: maximum sentence, six years.
6. Sodomy: * maximum sentence, three years.
7. Pederasty: * maximum sentence, eight years.

This list gives a fairly good idea of what is forbidden, at least as far as sex is concerned, in the Soviet Union. In practice, of course, the list would be much longer; it goes without saying, for example, that the article dealing with sodomy can be construed as a prohibition of almost anything that seems worth prohibiting. Similarly, the legal definition of pornography (which is strictly suppressed) is flexible enough to bring an indictment against an artist who paints a single nude figure.

The important thing to realize here is that sexual problems in the Soviet Union are almost automatically classified as "abnormal," "pathological," or "perverse." Lovers kissing in the street are committing an "obscenity"; the most diffident attempt to act out their private sexual fantasies immediately brands a couple as disciples of the Marquis de Sade. To prolong the sexual act is really playing with fire—not only psychologically very risky but totally depraved as well. And if we take Stalinist morality to be the current Soviet norm, then any kind of sexual activity that is indulged in for nonprocreative purposes is by definition perverse.

* "Sodomy" includes any heterosexual act that is defined as "perverse"; "pederasty" includes all forms of male homosexuality, irrespective of the partners' ages. [Translators' note]

This will help us in distinguishing what is considered "normal" and "abnormal" by Soviet standards. Of course, as soon as we try to establish objective standards of our own, we will find ourselves on very dangerous ground, since this would involve both a cultural evaluation of what sort of behavior is considered acceptable or unacceptable in a given society, as well as a scientific evaluation based on some sort of medical criterion. Homosexuality, for example, has come to be less and less commonly regarded as "abnormal" in the West, whereas in the Soviet Union it is still forthrightly condemned. Even incest is not considered a crime everywhere in the world. Clearly, then, it would be impossible to establish any such cultural standard that would be universally recognized as valid, and the medical criteria would have to be essentially empirical. A doctor treats people who have come to him because they are "ill," in other words, because they themselves feel that they are in some way "abnormal." So, since I have no intention of trying to resolve this question conclusively in a paragraph or two, I will simply try to present this problem in the same terms in which it is posed in reality in the Soviet Union.

It seems quite clear that there is a very fine line between "normal" and "abnormal" behavior in the Soviet Union. This may seem paradoxical, in light of the ferocious punishments provided for all manner of sexual offenses. But in fact everything is abnormal, or nothing is abnormal, depending on one's point of view. After all, is it normal for a man and wife to make love just three or four times a year, and only then when they are drunk? And yet is it abnormal for a mature man to continue to masturbate because the conditions under which he lives, or his wife's frigidity, prevents him from experiencing the pleasures of "normal" heterosexual intercourse? At this point, I would like to return to the idea of prison sexuality, which has been the central image of this book. In prison the libido is so repressed that it might be compared to a heavy steel spring which has been so forcefully compressed that when the pressure is released, it snaps back with such violence that its original structure is deformed. In such a case "deviance" is a natural reaction to the unnatural tensions and enormous external pressures of the prisoner's world. These deviations may take such an exaggerated form—which is no more than proportional to the strength of the forces that have repressed them—that they appear in reality to be no less than pathological crimes. And if rape, adult masturbation, and exhibitionism are so common in the USSR, this is at least in part because ordinary relations between men and women are so difficult and because their sex lives are so unsatisfying.

In the third part of this book I am not going to try to provide a complete inventory of all the more or less exotic forms of "deviance" that abound in the Soviet Union, for this would quickly become very tiresome for even the most avid reader. Instead, I intend to discuss only those forms of behavior which are the most strictly repressed (such as homosexuality), and which are the most typical of the Soviet Union (exhibitionism and masturbation), at least to judge from their statistical importance, and finally those which are manifested under very specific conditions (such as prostitution).

CHAPTER 10
Masturbation

FORBID MASTURBATION? The idea is enough to make any enlightened Western parent cringe. Nevertheless, it is true that masturbation, as far as children and adolescents are concerned, is still regarded as a pathological aberration by almost everyone in the Soviet Union.

Officially infant sexuality does not exist—children are innocent, sexually neutral creatures. This pre-Freudian view of childhood was first accepted as dogma in the thirties and has not been modified. We have already seen how the Russian psychoanalytic movement was suppressed in the late twenties when the publication and the study of the works of Freud were abruptly discontinued, as was all research on childhood and adolescent sexual development. The current Soviet position on Freud is reflected in this extract from a recent work by Mikhailov and Tsaregorodtsev, *Beyond the Conscious Mind:*

> Freudianism originated as a product of the bourgeois mentality at the height of its decadence, and today it still serves as a justification for sexual license, debauchery, pornography, and every form of moral degeneracy that is practiced in the capitalist countries.

> . . . More than any other theory, Freudianism contributes to the climate of moral degeneracy which is constantly growing more pronounced in imperialist countries. Freudian therapy plays no small role in the moral corruption of children and young people: Its emphasis on sexual problems only leads to the corruption of their moral character, and is a major factor in the development of a premature interest in sexual matters.

There is a great deal that might be said about the Soviet regime's rejection of psychoanalysis. I wish to stress only the essential point: Freud postulates the existence of an unconscious self which cannot be educated or socialized, of a libido that cannot be "domesticated" by the techniques of Communist education. Such a hypothesis is fundamentally incompatible with Soviet ideology, which views the child as a "hothouse plant" that springs up by spontaneous generation into this best of all possible worlds, as the raw material, in other words, from which the state can create its "new man." For all its vaunted materialism, Soviet ideology has always been the implacable enemy of nature. Or rather, which is even more pernicious, it simply denies the existence of nature altogether. If the "normal" child does not show a "premature interest in sexual matters," as he definitely should not, then children who are unfortunate enough to be curious about such matters must certainly be "sick." In the USSR, masturbation is considered to be shameful evidence of moral degeneracy, a vestige of bourgeois decadence. This prejudice is not confined to psychologists and doctors, which would certainly be a lesser evil; it is also shared by the great majority of the Soviet people, which, as we might suspect, is the source of a great deal of absurd and tragic conflict.

One of my patients asked for a divorce when he found out that his wife masturbated—when she was a little girl. If there is any sign of pathology here, it is certainly to be found in the husband's reaction. When I asked him if *he* has ever masturbated, he finally admitted, "Yes, but I'm allowed to—I'm a man."

As a rule children are punished if they are caught masturbating, which may have a very damaging effect on them, as almost everyone has come to realize in the West. If he is lucky, the child's parents will be so concerned that they will consult a doctor. But this rarely happens (and is usually quite ineffective in any case); the more usual remedy is a sound thrashing. I once had to deal with an unforgettable case in which a little boy's mother had actually uttered the classic threat: "If you do that again, I'll take a razor and cut it off." This didn't prevent the boy from masturbating, but he began to have recurring nightmares of an airplane which had the blade of a straight razor as one of its wings. These terrifying dreams continued for three years and only ended after he was taken to a psychiatric hospital for treatment.

With all due deference to Soviet medical propaganda, masturbation is very commonly practiced in the USSR, and not merely by oversexed degenerates but by perfectly normal children, who are accordingly condemned as vicious brutes and incorrigible little sinners. According to the official statistics, 8 percent of girls and 20 percent of boys habitually masturbate, but in my experience these figures have been grossly understated, and I can at least confirm that almost all my male patients have resorted to the practice at one time or another in their lives. As for women, I always found it more difficult to get them to "confess"; as the remarkable reaction of my divorced patient shows, masturbation is considered much more reprehensible for women. Nevertheless, since this question has always been of particular interest to me, I am prepared to offer the results of my own clinical observation, which include the curious fact that masturbation seems to have become increasingly common among young girls.

During the war years I only encountered a single patient who admitted that she had ever done such a thing—when she was thirteen years old. But between 1953 and 1964 out of a total of 430 female patients I questioned 81 (18.5 percent) replied that they had masturbated at least once, to which we might add an indefinite number of other women who were not being entirely truthful. The situation changed radically between 1964 and 1973. My colleague Professor Mizrukhin and I each surveyed 500 women patients. In my group 43 percent currently engaged in masturbation or had done so at some time between the ages of nine and nineteen. The figure for the other group was 55 percent, yielding an average of 49 percent for the entire sampling.

I don't know whether or not this change in women's attitudes was produced by the general relaxation of discipline as the tensions of the Stalinist era began to subside, but it does amount to a fairly startling change. And not only are more and more young women engaging in masturbation, they are beginning to have their first orgasms at an earlier age. Though I am not in a position to provide any precise statistics, I can at least point out that in my own practice, in 1961, I came across only two girls between the ages of four and nine who had already experienced orgasm, but in 1970 to 1971 there were twelve.

It is curious that sexual precocity seems to be directly related to the repressiveness of the child's family life. The case of three year old Lena S. is typical in this respect, both as an illustration of parents' reactions to sexual precocity and of the child's reactions to an anti-sexual upbringing.

Here is the story as Lena's parents first told it to me: Lena would go to the public toilets in the park, not far from her house. She would hide in one of the booths so that she could spy on everyone who walked by and wait for a man to show up. Whenever someone came into the toilets, she would start to masturbate; she had already discovered how to give herself pleasure by touching herself in the appropriate place. Panting with excitement, she would be cruelly disappointed if a man walked by and didn't go into one of the booths, or if it was a boy who did: "A boy's thing is too little. I want a grown-up man," she had said. She sometimes spent several hours at a time in the toilets, "touching herself" until she reached orgasm every time she caught sight of a man urinating in one of the booths. Sometimes, when she managed to evade her mother's surveillance, these sessions would continue until she was totally exhausted.

I had already come across many cases of precocious masturbation in little girls, but when Lena's parents brought her to see me and told me what she had been up to—which they had discovered quite by chance—I was totally dumbfounded. At the time, Lena was three and a half, but the problem had started earlier, when she was three. Her parents had sometimes noticed that when she lay down on their bed, or on the beach or on the grass in their courtyard, she would squeeze her legs together tightly and seem to grow chilly and pale. They began to worry about this and decided to keep a very close watch on her, which is how they discovered her observation post in the public toilets.

At first, I was inclined to think that this was a case of precocious sexual development (I had already encountered several in my practice). But when I examined Lena, I found no physical evidence of this. It is perfectly natural for children to masturbate, of course, but Lena's age, the fact that she was already having orgasms, the intensity of her precocious sexual life, and especially her habit of spying on men while they were urinating—all these made her case seem completely out of the ordinary. Clearly I had a great deal to discuss with her parents.

"Your daughter is in perfect physical health," I told them. "The origins of her problem are psychological, and if we want to help her, we will have to bring them to light."

Her parents were overwhelmed. They had wanted very much to have a child, and Lena's mother had suffered three miscarriages before Lena was born. As far as they were concerned, Lena was seriously ill, and they felt as if all their hopes had turned to ashes. Her mother began to cry.

"Doctor, how can you possibly say she's in perfectly good health after what's happened? It's like something out of a bad dream."

"But I promise you that physically there is absolutely nothing wrong with her."

"But how can she be having these *problems*, as you call it, if there's nothing wrong with her?"

This conversation shows very well what a doctor is up against in the USSR. Masturbation is regarded with such horror that a child like Lena is automatically assumed to be sick. If her case was actually somewhat disturbing, it certainly did not justify the doomsday prophecies of her parents. But her parents seemed completely incapable of understanding the psychological dimension of their daughter's problem; they simply assumed that her troubling behavior could only be caused by some physical disorder. This naive and simplistic "materialism," which is shared by the official ideologues and population in general, often prevents patients from answering the doctor's questions at all. In this case, Lena's parents were both unable and unwilling to understand what I was trying to tell them, nor could they be much help in locating the real origins of the little girl's behavior. No matter what sort of questions I asked, they persisted in talking about "muscular spasms," alleged to be the aftermath of an early bout with pneumonia.

Finally, after a long discussion, I did manage to discover the cause of Lena's behavior. One day she had burst into the apartment while her father was undressed. She pointed at his genitals and asked, "What's that sausage thing, Papa?" Her childish curiosity was rewarded with a terrible beating, after which she was locked in the kitchen and told that if she ever spied on her parents like that again or said such wicked things, she could expect to get more of the same.

It was only then that Lena set out to discover the truth on her own, from her outpost in the public toilets in the park. The "cure" was not very difficult, except when it came to convincing Lena's parents that they should not be so concerned about hiding their nakedness from a three year old child—for only an atmosphere of trust and understanding could dissipate the neurotic tensions that had taken hold of the entire family, to the extent that it would have been difficult to say whether this "sickness" resided primarily in the child's behavior or in her parents' reaction to it.

It has become a commonplace of our times to point out how dangerous it can be to forbid children to masturbate, or to react violently against anything that has to do with sex. But I am repeating it here for two reasons. First, because far from being regarded as a cliché in the Soviet Union, it is an idea that still smacks of heresy. Second, because the consequences of this approach to child-rearing can be catastrophic. I once treated a young man of twenty-five, a technical draftsman, who suffered from impotence and a persecution complex so severe that he had finally become convinced that he was being followed by the KGB. This young man appeared to be quite innocuous however, even by the rather exacting standards of the KGB, and it was also apparent that his impotence was completely psychological in its origins. When he was a child, he had been cruelly beaten by his father whenever he was caught masturbating. The last time that this happened, when he was fifteen years old, his father had bloodied his nose, and it was some time before he could stanch the bleeding. Afterward he not only stopped masturbating, he also lost all sexual desire and soon became totally impotent and began to suffer from paranoid delusions.

I have already mentioned the general tendency toward sexual precocity in the Soviet Union. In extreme cases a young girl may experience spontaneous orgasms with little or no physical stimulation at all, a phenomenon that is becoming more and more common. For instance, I encountered a patient who had an orgasm the moment the slightest pressure was applied to her clitoris. This probably can be explained by the stifling and restrictive atmosphere of the child's family life, which so thoroughly shields her from the outside world and especially from any awareness of sex that she becomes hypersensitive to any external stimulus. One of my patients, an airline stewardess, had to quit her job because the plane's vibrations in flight kept her in a constant state of sexual excitation. As a girl she had stopped going out with boys when she discovered that a simple kiss was enough to bring about an almost instantaneous orgasm. She had masturbated nearly every day from the time she was twelve years old, until her job with Aeroflot made this entirely superfluous. Another example: one of my colleagues took his five year old daughter to the traditional May Day parade. With the little girl riding on his shoulders and waving her tiny red flag, he and his wife set off for the center of town. Suddenly the flag fell to the ground and the little girl cried out.

"What's the matter, Vera?"

"It makes me feel hot all over."

Her father thought nothing of this incident at the time, but from that day on Vera began to experience repeated spontaneous orgasms, especially whenever she found herself in the middle of a crowd. Then she discovered the source of these pleasurable sensations and began to masturbate frantically several times a day. (The only advice I could give her parents was not to take Vera to the movies, or the May Day parade.)

Sexual precocity may go hand in hand with innocence and naiveté, but sometimes children are perfectly aware of what they are up to. A patient of mine received a rude shock when she happened to pick up the telephone while her nine year old daughter was talking to her best friend:

"Nothing happens, you know? I keep touching myself there, but I just can't get it to happen. It's nice, of course, and I kept rubbing between my legs for a long time, but it was nothing like you said. . . . We both ought to try it together sometime when my parents are at the movies. . . ."

Here the "cynicism" of the younger generation is still quite innocent. It may be considerably less so and a good deal more aggressive, as this incident, which took place in School Number 25 in Vinnitsa in 1958, bears out. A group of boys, all of them around thirteen, would gather, ten or twenty at a time, for a communal masturbation session. (On one occasion they collected their semen in a glass and poured it into the inkwells in the classroom next door.) This pastime became so popular that its enthusiasts began to refer to themselves as the Manual Arts Club, a derisive allusion to the workshops and hobby clubs that are organized in every Palace of Young Pioneers. Teenagers have a similar game, called Give and Take, which is played like this: two or three twelve or thirteen year old girls will walk along Lenin Street in Vinnitsa or Gorky Street in Moscow until they run into a group of boys their own age. "Give and take," say the girls, and then they go off with the boys to find a secluded spot where they can masturbate until they reach orgasm. Afterward boys and girls go their separate ways, preferably without speaking another word unless it is necessary to arrange a second meeting. This is a fairly recent phenomenon which, I should emphasize, would be unimaginable without the great changes that have occurred in young people's attitudes in the past decade or so. Perhaps the most remarkable aspect of this game is that it is always played with strangers, casual pickups, who may never be seen again. This seems to heighten the pleasure of the game, as an additional challenge to the adult world, an ever more provocative way of claiming the sexual freedom that young people are so eager to enjoy. An extreme case of this rather hard-bitten and defiant attitude is presented by the story of Ginger, a young girl from Vinnitsa. Ginger was a model student, an orphan who lived with her grandfather; she never played with the other girls, since she far preferred the company of boys. She had been on a trip to Leningrad when her parents were still alive, and there, at the age of ten, she had been initiated into the mysteries of Give and Take. She quickly collected a circle of young admirers in Vinnitsa, and by the time she was eleven, there was a group of ten teenage and preteenage boys whom she masturbated regularly. At thirteen she began to go off on excursions to Moscow, Leningrad, and Kiev, though no one knew where she got the money to pay for them. It was common knowledge that she performed her sexual services for boys and even men completely free of charge; she did it only because "she liked to." And none of them ever paid much attention to the curious questions she asked about their political opinions and their private lives, even though this was not the sort of thing one would expect a young girl to be interested in. It was only later when some of her friends began to have trouble with the police that it became apparent that Ginger had been working as a paid KGB informer for several years—not unlike the prostitutes who are employed by the KGB.

My own clinical observations indicate that masturbation is equally widespread among children of all backgrounds and that it would be futile to try to identify any one social group in which it is more prevalent than another, although young athletes perhaps deserve special mention. A sixteen year old gymnast, a patient of mine for two years, described how she discovered masturbation while she was climbing a rope: "One day when I was coming down the rope, I started to feel very strange . . . a very pleasant sort of trembly feeling. I tried it a few more times, and every time I slid down the rope, I had the same feeling, until I finally figured out that it was coming from down there. . . . I hope it's not something dangerous, doctor. I want to become a champion gymnast, but I'm afraid that something might be the matter with me." I assured her that this was far from being abnormal, that it was simply a part of becoming a woman.

For adolescents, as for adults, it is often difficult to find a secluded spot in which to masturbate. In Leningrad the doorways of old houses are preferred; in Odessa the public toilets on the beach, and in Moscow, the elevators, are often made to serve this purpose.

The masturbatory technique that most women and girls seem to prefer is clitoral stimulation (direct vaginal stimulation is rather rare), usually with the fingers of the right hand. Some women masturbate while reading an erotic book, in the classic manner, though in the Soviet Union this is usually nothing more explicit than one of Zola's novels, unless it is a work in *samizdat* edition; boys sometimes resort to gynecological textbooks. Masturbation may also be associated with voyeurism, as we shall see in the next chapter.

Young girls are often afraid to touch their vaginas, though the reasons for this may not be all that clear to them—in some cases they are afraid of becoming pregnant. But it often happens that after several years of clitoral masturbation, a young girl will overcome her reluctance and end up by breaking her hymen. This happened, at any rate, to a fifteen year old Vinnitsa girl who was spending the evening with some friends at the time. She took one of her girlfriends aside and told her what she had done. When she returned home, her mother happened to notice a spot of blood on her leg and discovered, upon examining her, that she was no longer a virgin. Her mother happened to be a judge, and she immediately set out to salvage what she could of her daughter's honor. "Who were you with tonight?" she demanded. Frightened, the girl gave the names of some of the girls she had spent the evening with, and finally, more or less at random, mentioned the name of one of the boys. As a result the boy was sentenced to eight years' detention in a camp for the rape of a minor, even though there was not a shred of evidence to support this trumped-up accusation, and despite the fact that the boy's parents made it clear that he was willing to marry the girl. The boy's parents appealed the judgment in a higher court, but by the time the "rapist" was released from the camp, both his physical and mental health had been seriously impaired; he remained my patient for two years after that, since his experience had left him totally impotent.

There are also various techniques of anal masturbation that are practiced by women and girls, though it would be difficult to say whether a preference for this erogenous zone is innate or acquired. I once treated a young woman, Lilya K., from the city of Bobruysk. When she was eighteen, it was her ambition to become a film actress, and with this goal in mind, she embarked on an affair with a director from Moscow, who was a devotee of anal intercourse. Subsequently, she discovered that this was the only way she could reach orgasm, and she quickly lost interest in men who were unprepared to satisfy this particular craving. She turned instead to anal masturbation, in which she engaged habitually, and later became a lesbian.

If the habit of masturbation is prolonged for some time, or if it is severely repressed or the girl or woman herself becomes seriously inhibited, this can result in some rather curious practices. A young girl was brought in an ambulance to a clinic in Leningrad; her vagina had been severely lacerated by splinters of broken glass, some of which had penetrated as far as the neck of the uterus. When the doctors tried to find out what had happened, she refused to answer and insisted simply that they tell her whether she was going to die. It turned out that she had come across a cylindrical lamp imported from Czechoslovakia, which she had immediately realized would serve very well as an artificial phallus. One evening she had failed to notice that the lamp had cracked, though happily she had not switched it on as she usually did, having realized quite early on that the heat from the lamp enhanced the pleasure of masturbation.

I came across a similar case which involved a twelve year old schoolgirl from Vinnitsa, Sveta R. She had read accounts in the popular science magazines, *The Young Technician* and *Applied Science for Young People*, of a series of experiments performed by the English scientist James Olds. Olds had implanted electrodes in the brains of rats and devised a system whereby the rats could be taught to stimulate their own "pleasure centers" by pushing a lever which would trigger a mild electrical impulse in their brain. The rats responded by pushing the lever as many as seven thousand times in an hour before they collapsed from exhaustion. Accordingly, Sveta rigged up an electrical circuit, and while her parents were away on vacation she attached an electrode to her clitoris—contriving to experience for herself the pure joys of scientific research.

When her parents returned home, Sveta proudly informed them of the results of her experiments. She had no idea that sex came into it at all and simply thought of herself as a disciple of James Olds. However, her parents were horrified when they discovered that she had lost fifteen pounds and brought her to me immediately. The therapy was not very difficult once she had dismantled her experimental apparatus and stopped frequenting the Palace of the Young Pioneers and the Manual Arts Club. It was more difficult for her to gain back the weight she had lost. A year later, I was happy to learn that Sveta had been admitted to the celebrated high school of science and mathematics in Novosibirsk, which selects only the most gifted students from all over the Soviet Union.

If Sveta's case provides evidence of nothing more than harmless scientific curiosity, I have certainly come across others in which the imagination has taken a morbid, even grotesquely sadistic turn. For example, Alik T. was a fourteen year old boy from a perfectly "normal" family. His masturbatory fantasies followed a highly stylized ritual. First, he would catch a stray cat, then, stroking and soothing it, he would take it into a shed, where he had prepared an arrangement of string and nails with which he could immobilize the animal—crucifying it, in effect, with its feet splayed out against one wall of the shed. Next he would take a knife and drive it through the cat's heart and deep into the wall. As soon as the animal was dead, Alik would begin to masturbate, taking sadistic pleasure in the sight of the blood draining from its body. Afterward, he would take the cat's body down from the wall and throw it behind the shed, and then wash the knife. He would end the ritual by reading a few pages of *The Three Musketeers.* The remains of more than thirty cats were later discovered behind the shed, and inside it, a pool of dried blood along one wall, and on a bench, his copy of *The Three Musketeers,* with the knife still marking his place.

Here of course we are dealing not merely with forbidden sexual practices but with out-and-out pathology. However, for the most part adolescent masturbation represents nothing more than a kind of sexual awakening, and if it elicits a reaction of horror and outrage from Soviet society, it is no less natural for all that. The fact that this awakening sexuality is sometimes expressed in strange, or even disturbing ways can be explained by the nature of the prohibitions that seek to suppress it; abnormal behavior may be the normal response to an abnormal situation. An instructor at the Institute of Steel and Ferrous Alloys in Vinnitsa who was a patient of mine told me that in the compulsory course on the history of the Communist Party the students in the back rows of the auditorium would sit quietly masturbating throughout the entire lecture. This may at first seem rather perverse, but it makes a great deal more sense when one understands how deeply students despise these compulsory courses, which are inflicted on them several times a week for five or six years and which consist of equal parts of pure propaganda and historical falsification which neither the lecturer nor the students can take seriously for a moment.

What happens when adolescents who masturbate become adults? Some readers may be surprised to learn that they rarely give up the habit of masturbation altogether, if my observations and those of my colleagues are any indication. This constitutes a serious problem, since, although masturbation may be interpreted as a sign of awakening sexuality even in an adult, it is just as likely to be a sign of a disturbed and unsatisfying sexual life—of the sort produced by the profound anomalies of Soviet life. Here, for example, is a conversation I once had with a woman who came to see me because she was worried about her husband:

"Everything seems fine, except that there's one thing that bothers me. Every time we make love, he starts to cry as soon as it's over. He didn't want to come with me today because he's so ashamed, but he doesn't seem to know what's going on himself."

"How long have you been married?"

"Four years—we got married as soon as he was discharged from the army."

"Does he drink?"

"Oh, no, I should say not! I've been lucky—not like one of my friends. Her husband drinks, he beats her, he won't go to work and on top of that their kids are turning into real degenerates. . . ."

As so often happens in interviews of this kind, she went on to tell me about everything except the problem that had brought her to me in the first place. But when I had spoken with her husband (I finally managed to get him to my office in spite of his "shame"), I realized that his story was not all that unusual. As a child he had been severely beaten by his parents whenever he was caught masturbating, which left him with profound feelings of guilt and inferiority, which persisted into adulthood. Sex, for him, was synonymous with evil, with danger, and his crying simply signified that he felt guilty about yielding to "temptation." In addition, unbeknownst to his wife, he had continued to masturbate regularly during the four years of their marriage, always with the result of more tears and feelings of deep remorse. For this man masturbation was not a prologue to adult sexuality but his sole means of achieving genuine sexual gratification, although it had remained a forbidden activity which he could only experience in secret.

I often observed this kind of postcoital depression in my patients. Some of them were very severely affected by it without understanding why, since they had not made the connection between their feelings of depression and the sexual repression they had been subjected to as children. Others seemed to regard masturbation as a sort of refuge, a means of reestablishing a connection with their past; however, this proves to be false comfort indeed, since only masturbation can give them real pleasure and often this kind of self-therapy only leads to divorce.

Is masturbation an important sexual outlet for adults? Between 15 and 20 percent of my male patients and 60 and 70 percent of my female patients engaged in masturbation regularly or sporadically. Fifteen percent of the women had never experienced orgasm in any other way, and the practice sometimes persisted until—or made a startling reappearance at—a very advanced age. Thus a senile eighty-four year old patient of mine discovered a new source of pleasure only a few months before her death: every time a man came into the house, even her son or one of her grandsons, she began to rub her crotch vigorously with one of her slippers, all the while laughing, crying, and calling to the men in the house—and to her dead husband. She could no longer distinguish them as individuals; it was enough that they were men, and their identities blended together into a single object of overwhelming desire. After she had reached orgasm—at least to all appearances—she would place both her slippers on the table. If anyone tried to put them back in their usual place by the side of her bed, she would retrieve them and set them back on the table, or even start to masturbate again. And if anyone tried to take the slippers away from her, she would begin to scream hysterically. These episodes continued until her death.

For adults masturbation often serves as a kind of substitute for an extramarital affair. One of my patients, whose wife was beautiful but frigid, was too diffident to take up with another woman, and in any case he loved his wife very much. Every night before he went to bed he would go into the bathroom and masturbate, for this was the only way that he could sleep in the same bed with his wife without tossing and turning all night.

"When I do make love to her, I feel lower than an animal. She doesn't even try to respond to me physically. She just lies there like a log and waits for me to get it over with. Sometimes she even tells me to hurry up, because it isn't the least bit enjoyable for her. I think it's better to masturbate than to have a sex life like that."

"But it would be better still if you tried to help your wife achieve a normal sexual response."

"Yes, but how do I do that?"

This problem finally resolved itself when, after the birth of their first child, his wife began to respond to him spontaneously without any special prompting on his part.

In general, however, the real problem is not male masturbation as a response to frigidity but masturbation among women whose husbands are impotent. As the statistics I have cited indicate, masturbation is extremely common among women; in fact, it has become a very real social problem in its own right, a problem that I was confronted with almost every day in my practice.

One of my patients, a construction worker, was married to a man who was impotent and an alcoholic as well. In fifteen years of marriage she had never experienced any kind of pleasure during intercourse. She had three children, all of whom suffered from some sort of disability as a result of her husband's alcoholism. I discovered, however, that for the past ten years she had actually been engaging in an involuntary form of masturbation without being aware of it. Simply by pressing her lower belly against the vibrating handle of the jackhammer that she often operated at work, she could have as many as ten orgasms in a single day. But when she was reassigned to another job—unloading bricks—she became so seriously depressed that she began to drink heavily, without having a clue of the real cause of her depression.

Another of my patients was the wife of the manager of a confectionery factory in a provincial town. One day she came to my consulting room in tears, crying, "Lisa's dead! My poor little darling is dead!" She produced a tear-stained photograph for my inspection—

Lisa was a little dog. The woman's husband was impotent and he treated her brutally even when he was sober. They had no children, and apart from a few inconclusive attempts, no sex life at all. Such an outpouring of grief over the death of a pet dog may seem ridiculous, but I can assure you that I was not in the least inclined to laugh when this woman began to speak of Lisa's death as if it had been the death of her only child, and then went on to describe her "perverse" relationship—if one can truly call it that—with the only living creature she had ever really loved. Lisa had meant so much to her that she was able to confide in me with the kind of sincerity that is born of despair. For many years the little dog had been even more than the object of her affection; she had also been her "sexual partner"—licking her mistress' genitals and breasts while she engaged in masturbation.

The wives of members of the Party elite often resort to masturbation when their husbands become impotent, for this is the only alternative to divorce—which would hardly be profitable considering the privileges which are theirs by virtue of their husbands' positions—or extramarital affairs, which involve considerable risk. This is particularly true of the wives of diplomats, who pick up all sorts of exotic knick-knacks in their travels and who think of sex as a kind of sport; they keep detailed records of their orgasms, compare notes on the relative merits of the vibrator, the dildo, and other erotic appliances that are easily obtainable in the "sex-shops" of the West.

One of these diplomatic wives returned to Leningrad with a brand-new Volga sedan, which, thanks to the privileges of her rank, had cost her a mere 1400 rubles instead of the standard 9150, and a collection of thirty rubber dildos. She lent the Volga to one of my patients until she could find a buyer for it, then finally sold it for 30,000 rubles to a wealthy Georgian black-market profiteer.* Some time later she asked my patient if he knew anyone who might be interested in buying a rubber dildo.

"Of course I do," he replied eagerly.

"They're five hundred rubles apiece."

He managed to suppress his astonishment long enough to carry out the simple multiplication—30 dildos × 500 rubles = 15,000 rubles. (The average salary in the Soviet Union is 140 rubles a

* Cars are so scarce in the USSR that they often sell on the black market for a great deal more than the official price. [Translator's note]

month.) The combined attraction of sex and the West is so great that well-heeled Soviets are willing to pay the most ridiculous sums for a lump of molded rubber. I suppose that the dildo is regarded as a symbol of Western "sexual freedom," of pornography, of everything that is taboo in the USSR and is thus believed to be the passport to the furthest realms of sexual ecstasy.

Adult masturbation, as well as this preposterous fad of erotic gadgetry, seem to be the inevitable consequences of the disruption of normal sexual relations. Men and women are strangers to one another, physically as well as emotionally alienated, and so they resort to masturbation—and, as we shall see, to other sexual practices which are essentially onanistic, such as exhibitionism, voyeurism, and casual sex in public places. This sexual alienation may even dictate the choice of a heterosexual partner. Just as adolescents seek out nameless strangers to join in their masturbatory games, there are certain sexual relationships which seem to be little more than an extension of the search for exotic devices that will deliver the ultimate orgasm. Thus, Danya S., a forty year old woman from Vinnitsa, took a nineteen year old lover; her choice was dictated solely by the fact that the young man suffered from Parhon's syndrome, a disorder of the hypothalamus which results in the precocious and abnormal development of the male sexual organs. Here sexuality has been dehumanized, has become no more than a variant form of masturbation.

Chapter 11
Exhibitionism and Voyeurism

Exhibitionism is so common in the USSR that, like impotence, it has become a nationwide epidemic. Very few of the many thousands of women I have treated had never seen a man exposing himself. And of course, this aberration is especially common among men, although female exhibitionists are far from rare. Because of the general prudishness of the culture and the fact that men rarely witness these displays, they are often unaware of how prevalent they really are. A couple once arrived in my consulting room; the husband was anxious for me to examine his wife, since he was convinced that she was suffering from sexual hallucinations. He found it incredible that she should see men exposing themselves to her everywhere, in the park, in the subway, in the streets. "How can it be, when *I* never see them?" he demanded. It came as quite a revelation when I explained, "After all, you're a man, you know, and exhibitionists only perform for women."

A woman patient who had studied at the Leningrad conservatory related how she and her roommate had devised a game which they called the Little Pigeons. This was a competition to see which of them had seen more male sexual organs that day. They would tote up the score every evening when they came home; the loser would buy dinner at the university dining hall. Her roommate held the all-time record—eight little pigeons in a single day.

A number of jokes on this subject have recently been making the rounds in Moscow. There is the story of a girl student, for example, who sees a man exposing himself on a bus. She indignantly asks one of her instructors,

"Why don't they take people like that and lock them up?"

"If they did, you'd have to ride to school on a camel."

"Why a camel?"

"Because if people like that were all locked up, then Moscow would be a desert."

This anecdote is slightly inaccurate in one respect. Exhibitionists are indeed locked up—sometimes on a drunk and disorderly charge. The unlucky perpetrator is trundled off to the precinct station and sobered up in the regulation manner, with a cold shower. The exhibitionist is also regarded as a troublemaker and a public nuisance—a "hooligan" in Soviet parlance. Nevertheless exhibitionism is sometimes thought of less as an antisocial act deserving of the most stringent punishment than as a kind of practical joke.

Several years ago my family and I were driving back from a vacation in the Caucasus. Suddenly the car in front of us began to swerve wildly. I stepped on the brakes and honked, but the other driver paid no attention; he and his passengers seemed to be fascinated by something in the road ahead. Then I caught sight of a policeman at the next intersection. His technique was very original, to say the least—he had unbuttoned his trousers and was directing traffic with his penis, beet-red and fully erect, which he was holding with one hand and waving about like a baton. The other motorists were splitting their sides with laughter; some stuck their heads out their windows to shout encouragements, insults, and amiable obscenities. The policeman ignored all this and solemnly carried on—stopping every car with a woman in it, waving on the rest. We were not required to stop; he presumably recognized me as a doctor by my "medical" Van Dyke beard. The policeman appeared to have been drinking, but he may have only been feigning drunkenness as a cover for his other activities, since in Russia a drunkard is considered an irresponsible creature who is capable of anything. This is why one often sees exhibitionists pretending to be drunk so that they can urinate in the streets with impunity.

Every exhibitionist has his own individual style. The more cautious conduct their performances in their apartments, which requires only that the house across the street be amply provided with windows. Thus anyone in it who is so inclined can witness a display of exhibitionism and masturbation which might well be the envy of a pornographic film director in the West. This is the usual technique of the urban exhibitionist, and for many invalids it is the only sexual outlet that is available to them. The spectators of these house-to-house performances include men, old women, even children, and the street theater of the exhibitionists and voyeurs creates a tacit understanding, sometimes a kind of permanent bond, which has something of the character of a genuine sexual relationship. As one of my patients jokingly complained to me about his neighbor, who spent a great deal of his time spying through a hole in the window shade, "That guy's watched my wife getting undressed more often than I have."

There was another patient whom I treated by proxy, a twelve year old schoolgirl whom I never actually met. Her parents had first come to me in a state of near panic. It seemed that she locked herself in her room, allegedly to devote more time to her schoolwork. She spent hours studying, but to her parents' astonishment her grades showed no improvement. One day her mother decided to take a peek through the keyhole to see how she was getting on with her schoolwork. The girl was standing next to the window with her back to the wall, one hand under her skirt, masturbating and sneaking surreptitious glances out the window. Her mother gasped as she caught sight of a stark-naked man in the opposite window, who seemed to be oblivious of the fact that he was beginning to collect an audience in the house across the way.

What surprised me here was not the girl's behavior, which was scarcely out of the ordinary (voyeurism in adolescents is fairly normal, as long as it does not become an obsession which persists in later life). What I found unusual was her parents' restraint. Most parents would have disciplined the girl in the usual heavy-handed way, starting, of course, with a good beating. This girl's parents did not make a fuss of any kind, and even more remarkably, they did not let their daughter know that they had discovered the reason for her new enthusiasm for her schoolwork. Quite sensibly they sought the advice of a doctor instead.

What are the causes of exhibitionism and why is it so prevalent in the USSR? Clearly it would be difficult to provide a simple explanation of what is, after all, a complex psychological problem. But it is equally clear that exhibitionism is essentially a way of asserting oneself as an individual, a way of quite literally showing off one's virility and one's sexuality. The exhibitionist is too inhibited to approach a woman in the ordinary way; he is often a vulnerable creature, unsure of himself. In a country where serious sexual disorders are common and normal sexuality is subject to so many restrictions, it is not surprising that men should take refuge in a perversion which is, to some extent, an unconscious appeal for sexual freedom. There is a point at which the statistical prevalence of what is essentially an individual psychological problem transforms it into a social problem. I would tentatively submit that if exhibitionism is a nationwide sickness in the USSR, this is because the country itself is in a sense exhibitionistic, with its perpetual public boasting, its constantly reiterated claims that it "leads the world" in sports, in music, in industrial production. This national character trait has even been given a name—*pokazukha,* the compulsion to put on a show, to put up a bold front. But all this bluff and bluster does not always successfully conceal a certain feeling of inadequacy—a national inferiority complex, if you will.

As in all other countries, exhibitionism in the USSR is primarily an urban phenomenon; however, for reasons which remain mysterious to me, it is no less common in the sub-Arctic northern regions of the Soviet Union than in the south.

I have often encountered more than one case of exhibitionism in the same family, which at first led me to the naive conclusion that it might be a hereditary affliction, at least in the male line. In fact, the real causes may be found in certain types of particularly unhealthy family situations. The man who habitually exposes himself in public is a model of discretion at home; he never allows his children to catch sight of his sexual organs or any other part of his uncovered body. His own sexuality is so inhibited that he reacts to any sign of sexual curiosity on the part of his children with shame and anger.

I have treated exhibitionists whose sexual drives were abnormally high as well as abnormally low. Among the latter group are those who are partially impotent, who are afraid that they will not be able to perform adequately with a woman. These men are often alcoholics.

Senile exhibitionism is particularly pathetic, since it often occurs in women who have been alone all their lives or who have raised illegitimate children, frustrated women who sense the approach of the inevitable. It is as if these women were crying out in desperation, "Look at me! I may be old and ugly, but I'm still a woman!" No learned psychiatric commentary on senile dementia could ever do justice to the real meaning of these words.

Adolescent exhibitionism is not uncommon, but it is often a transitory phenomenon. It is more typical, however, for a child or an adolescent to be victimized by an adult exhibitionist. The following incident, which took place in a Vinnitsa school, involves not only exhibitionism but a pronounced streak of sadism as well: a drawing teacher made his students keep their hands on top of their desks at all times so that he could bring his pointer down across their fingers without warning. When he felt particularly vicious, he would strike them on the back of the neck. The terrified children scarcely dared to breathe until he walked back to the dais, sat down at his desk, and began his lectures on the mysteries of art. They could hardly fail to notice that he always sat at his desk with his knees spread and his fly gaping open, but so great was the terror that he inspired in them, none of his students ever dared to denounce him to the school administration.

Voyeurism is as common as exhibitionism, and its causes range from simple curiosity to pathological obsession. One of my patients was a lesbian who spent her evenings wandering around the city, peering through windows in the hope of seeing a naked woman. She spent her summers at the beach, loitering by the women's dressing rooms treating herself to the sight of young girls taking off their clothes and trying diffidently to find a partner, and then risking a tentative caress.

When patients with sexual problems consult a therapist, shame and false modesty often prevent them from being completely frank about what is really bothering them. Thus it is left for the doctor to enter into the patient's secret world and to arrive at an understanding of the particular laws that govern it. On one occasion it was a drawing made by one of my patients, a twenty-three year old woman, that allowed me to diagnose a rather complex case of voyeurism, in spite of all the obstacles which the patient herself had placed in my path to prevent me from discovering the real cause of her distress. This woman was an amateur artist, and she had arranged a private consultation at my house. Her problem was simple enough as she stated it—she had never experienced sexual pleasure, even after a year of marriage, and she also indicated that she had been suffering periodic attacks of tachycardia. Had she not happened to bring her sketchbook along with her, and had it not occurred to me that it might be helpful to glance through it, I very much doubt that I would have arrived at a correct diagnosis. Prompted by my questions, and quite unaware that one of her drawings had already presented me with the essential facts, she recounted her voyeuristic experiences in detail. In fact, her frigidity was confined to her relationship with her husband; although she had never masturbated, she had experienced sexual excitation and even orgasm while watching exhibitionists masturbate in the city park. It was her custom to sit in the park for hours with her sketchbook in her lap waiting for a man to expose himself. She became aroused very quickly and reached orgasm long before her "partner" had finished masturbating. This was her only sexual outlet, and as far as I could tell, her complex had developed in childhood. However, she had come to consult me about her attacks of tachycardia, which occurred not only during her moments of sexual excitation in the park but at other times as well and for no apparent reason. In general, tachycardia may be caused by any number of psychological or physiological factors; in her case it was purely sexual in origin. I told her that I would treat her for the tachycardia, but the actual treatment was primarily psychiatric, and quite successful inasmuch as the young woman was cured of both her voyeurism and her supposed frigidity.

This case opened my eyes to something which I had not properly understood until then. Men and women whom we imagine to be "totally" impotent or frigid are often no such thing in reality. They may still be capable of experiencing orgasms, even if the experience itself takes a completely unexpected and highly specific form which is often "abnormal" but sometimes much more intense than in a "normal" individual.

This brings to mind another case history—actually a case of episodic or "circumstantial" impotence. This patient was an exhibitionist who could only make love to his wife if there was a third person watching them. He explained that it made no difference to him whether this concealed observer was a man or a woman; in either case his virility was instantly restored. His friends imagined that he asked them to spy on him as a sort of erotic diversion, scarcely realizing that he was incapable of any sort of performance unless an audience was present.

One often hears of exhibitionist "attacks" on women in movie theaters or on trains. A female patient of mine was once riding on the night train from Vinnitsa to Moscow. She had gone to sleep in her compartment but was awakened suddenly at dawn as the train was approaching Moscow by a curious sensation in one of her legs. When she opened her eyes, she realized that the man who was sharing her compartment was standing in front of her, completely naked, and vigorously flicking his erect penis at her, presumably in a kind of early morning exercise session. Horrified, she shut her eyes immediately.

"I beg of you, don't shut your eyes," the exhibitionist said plaintively.

"Stop it at once! Have you no sense of shame?" She sprang from her seat and made for the door of the compartment.

"Please, don't go away," said the exhibitionist, by now almost in tears. But in spite of all his supplications she went out and stood in the corridor until they reached Moscow.

Since exhibitionists naturally expect that their quarry will try to flee from them, they are careful to choose enclosed places which make it more difficult for a woman to escape. They also prefer to operate when it is raining (at least in Leningrad, or so I have been informed), since a sudden shower will clear the streets of undesirable third parties. When it is raining in Kazan, the exhibitionists tend to congregate next to the public toilets near the cathedral; many of them are alcoholics or even drug addicts.

Some of my female patients seemed to be genuinely outraged by the "sick" behavior of exhibitionists, but most were simply perplexed: "Why do they do it? What can they possibly get out of it?" One of my patients, an attractive young student called Galina Kosotrova, told me of an encounter she had had with an exhibitionist which she found highly disturbing and disagreeable. First, I should explain that in the Soviet Union private automobiles often pick up pedestrians and carry them to their destinations for a modest sum; these unofficial taxis are referred to as "specials." On this particular occasion Galina decided to ride home in a "special." She noticed immediately that the driver was wearing a fur coat and a sable cap—not the ordinary outfit of a gypsy cabdriver—but the significance of this did not dawn on her until several moments later, when he flung open his coat and revealed that he was wearing nothing underneath. Galina was terrified by the sight of his erect penis and convinced that the man was about to rape her. "Stop the car!" she screamed, but the exhibitionist calmly drove on, both hands on the wheel; he laughed pleasantly as she began to threaten him with all manner of awful punishments and reprisals. Finally, as he drove up in front of her house, he announced, "You're such an attractive girl, I'd gladly take you to the ends of the earth if you asked me to." Galina was still trembling and on the verge of tears as she flung open the door and scrambled out of the car.

Her reaction was perfectly natural, of course, and was essentially shared by the majority of my female patients who had been subjected to exhibitionists' "attacks." However, it was also indicative of the pervasive ignorance which surrounds all sexual matters, exhibitionism included. For, paradoxically, in a country where sexual aberrations are so numerous as to be almost past counting, people as a rule know almost nothing about them. Of course, some women are aroused by exhibitionism, but they will only watch such a performance if they are certain that no one will catch them at it, especially the exhibitionist himself. Conversely, if it is a woman who is the exhibitionist, men feel free to satisfy their curiosity openly.

I should mention another variety of exhibitionists and voyeurs which I prefer to call "mental masturbators." These are repressed, often partially impotent people, and their pathology only manifests itself in the realm of words. The professional duties of judges, policemen, and high officials are especially compatible with this perversion, and the best example I could give can be found in the transcript of my trial, which has already been published in the West.* There is a single prurient refrain that runs through the entire text, a single charge that is repeated over and over—that I forced teenage boys to undress in front of their mothers! This accusation appeared in the prosecutor's summation and the tribunal's verdict, and it was pursued with the liveliest interest in almost every session. "Making a son strip naked in the presence of his mother, and making her look at his sexual organs"—this was the formula with which the prosecutor began his address to the bench on a good many occasions, and here is the court itself questioning a witness:

> JUDGE: Did it bother you that he undressed your son right in front of you?
> WITNESS: No, since it must have been necessary.
> JUDGE: But it must have been unpleasant when he took your son's clothes off right in front of you.
> WITNESS: He's a doctor.
> JUDGE (getting angry): Did the doctor in fact make you look at your son's sexual organs?

* August Stern, ed., *The U.S.S.R. vs. Dr. Mikhail Stern,* translated by Marco Carynnyk, New York, 1977.

This lunacy does not require any further comment. In a show trial, of course, the prosecution will seize on any available pretext to trump up an indictment, but surely only a diseased mind would try to interpret an ordinary medical examination as some sort of incestuous orgy.

It is not difficult to find traces of this verbal exhibitionism in the Russian language itself. I mean by this simply that every language has a considerable stock of obscenities and sexual invective, and the Russian language is particularly rich in this respect. The generic name for these obscene insults in Russian is *mat;* some refer to homosexuality, others, even more offensive, imply that the speaker has had sexual relations with the mother of the person he wishes to insult.* At any rate, the various applications of *mat* seem to enjoy a remarkably wide currency in the Soviet Union today. It has become an indispensable part of the everyday language of the professor as well as the ordinary worker. There are those, in fact, whose speech seems to contain a greater proportion of *mat* than of "dictionary" words. Khrushchev himself, as you may recall, often allowed such pungent colloquialisms to slip into his speeches, which would have to be edited out in the published transcript.

But here I have just touched lightly on a problem which certainly deserves fuller treatment. Though I don't know whether other languages have experienced a similar mass infiltration of obscene words into ordinary speech, I can't help wondering if this might not represent an unconscious form of exhibitionism.

In prisons and labor camps exhibitionism is prevalent and, if I may say so, a necessary sexual outlet. I recall one occasion when I was an inmate of the transit prison in Kharkov. First, I heard voices shouting, "Come on—show it to us! Turn around! Bend over! I'm beating off up here, so let's see your ass!" The voices were coming from the windows which overlooked an interior courtyard that prisoners were permitted to walk around in during their exercise period. The windows were barred and fitted with overhanging metal panels which prevented the inmates from looking into the windows on the opposite wall, though they could still see into the courtyard below. The prisoner in the exercise yard was a woman. She was bending over with her skirt pulled up and her underclothes pulled down, oblig-

* In fact, the word *mat* itself is a derisive mispronunciation of the Russian word for mother, and it may also have the incestuous connotations of the word *motherfucker* in the United States. There is also a verb derived from *mat* which means something like "to go around calling everybody a motherfucker." [Translators' note]

ingly trying to point her buttocks in the direction the voices were coming from. The men in the cellblock were masturbating furiously, trying to make the most of this rare glimpse of naked female flesh. I don't know what the woman could have been feeling through all this—sexual excitement perhaps, the unaccustomed thrill of putting something over on the authorities, or perhaps a sense of solidarity, of sympathy for her fellow prisoners, deprived of all contact with women. This scene has always struck me as the perfect, tragic symbol of the perversion of normal sexuality—normal men and women, separated by iron bars, transformed into voyeurs and exhibitionists.

I later came to learn that the cry of "Show it to us!" is a watchword of prison life. I will return to the subject of sexuality in the camps, but suffice it to say here that exhibitionism is merely a way in which women try to relieve the suffering of their fellow prisoners, by offering them the sight, at least, of their naked bodies, simply and unashamedly. The guards make few attempts to discourage this practice, and even join in as curious spectators. A camp veteran called Vtorenko described to me how, in the transit prison where he was held while awaiting trial, a dozen inmates regularly masturbated to orgasm while a female thief exposed herself to them.

In the Gulag there are exhibitionists who seek out male victims. I will also return later to the subject of homosexuality in the camps, but there is one case from my own experience that seems worthy of mention here. At the beginning of September 1974, I was unexpectedly transferred from an individual cell in the Vinnitsa prison to a "tank" with three tiers of bunks and thirty-five inmates in all. The heat was intolerable, and the inmates usually took off their clothes during their half-hour exercise period. The air was scarcely breathable, and one of the pipes had burst, so that we were forced to go without water for two days.

One of my cellmates was sick, almost on the point of collapse; he went over to the hatch through which our food was passed to us and began to hammer on it with his fists, shouting at the top of his lungs, "Water! Water!" A noncom opened the hatch, "You're thirsty?" he asked sardonically. "Then how would you like to suck my cock?" (This, of course, is a common catchphrase in the *mat* repertory.) At that, he produced his erect penis with a flourish and began laughing uproariously. In the camp to which I was subsequently sent, another KGB noncom called Ivaniak amused himself by strolling around with his fly undone and seemed to derive particular pleasure from urinating in front of the inmates.

For a woman, an encounter with an exhibitionist may prove traumatic; I will only mention two of the most serious disorders which this trauma may produce—vaginismus (painful spasms of the vaginal wall which make intercourse difficult if not impossible) and genitalophobia (a morbid fear of the male sexual organs). These disorders may have a number of other causes, of course, but I will only discuss them here as they relate to exhibitionism.

Since we already have ample evidence of the sexual naiveté and ignorance of so many young women in the Soviet Union, it is not difficult to imagine the sort of emotional shock that the sight of a strange man exposing himself might have on a susceptible teenage girl. I have treated a great many women who suffered from vaginismus, and many were already aware that this disorder was linked to a particular incident in the past in which they had been the target of some sort of sexual aggression. The most difficult cases to treat were those in which the vaginal spasms caused such severe contractions of the vagina that intercourse became impossible. One of my patients had tried repeatedly and unsuccessfully to have intercourse with her husband. He had absolutely no idea of what she was going through, and he reacted violently, calling her an "idiot" and a "madwoman." He was her first man, and she never succeeded in having intercourse with him. On my advice she divorced him. She told me that when she was fifteen an exhibitionist had chased her through the park, holding his erect penis in his hand, and that she believed that her affliction could be traced back to this incident.

Another patient was a colleague at the clinic in Vinnitsa, a nurse who suffered from a serious psychosomatic disorder which I could only treat effectively with hypnosis. The very thought of sex was out of the question for her, since whenever she started going out with a man she began to suffer from acute vaginal pains, which disappeared immediately when she broke off the relationship.

An encounter with a particularly aggressive exhibitionist may also cause a morbid fear of the male sexual organs. One of my patients, a young married student, was so strongly affected by this phobia that whenever her husband began to make love to her, her hands would tremble uncontrollably for fear that she might touch his penis. As might be expected, she was completely frigid. She explained that when she first came to the university she had lived in a student residence. There were two bathrooms, one for men, one for women, and the seasoned residents were always careful to check all the stalls in the women's bathroom before they undressed, since an exhibitionist might be lurking in ambush. My patient, however, was still quite naive and unacquainted with these student customs; she simply closed the bathroom door and got undressed whereupon an exhibitionist sprang out of one of the stalls. Terrified, she ran naked and screaming down the corridor; the other women students took up the cry, retreated into their rooms, and locked their doors, assuming that she was being pursued by a rapist. From that day on, and even after her marriage, she suffered from this phobia—which proved to be incurable.

Chapter 12
Sex in Public Places

When sexuality is as severely repressed as it is in the Soviet Union, it usually finds a refuge in those rare moments of existence which are free from society's control. I have already described the difficulties that lovers encounter in searching for a private place in the cities, which seem to be especially hostile to any kind of intimacy. But there is one other way to escape society's prying eye—to lose oneself in the crowd, where the individual is at once isolated and anonymous. This form of escape represents a retreat from normal sexuality in the case of the exhibitionist, or the man or woman who seeks out sexual contact with strangers in public places. This is a common practice in all the great cities of the world; however, it appears to be a more significant phenomenon in the Soviet Union, simply because of the furtive, clandestine character of sexuality in general. In addition, this search for sexual contact with strangers seems to be something quite different in the Soviet Union. In the West, this may be dismissed as a handful of "perverts" taking advantage of a crowded subway at rush hour, fondling and groping with impunity; in the Soviet Union, however, it has evolved into a truly anonymous and clandestine sexual subculture.

In 1969, I treated a young man of twenty who told me the following story: when he was fourteen, his family had lived in Kazan. One day while he was riding on a crowded bus he realized that the woman next to him, who appeared to be in her thirties, had opened his fly, slid her hand into his trousers, and grasped his penis, which immediately became erect. He felt "an electric current" passing through his body; something had "caught fire" inside him, and he ejaculated for the first time in his life. By the time he returned to his senses, she was already making her way through the crowd toward the door. He never saw her again, and shortly afterward his family moved to Odessa; but six years later he was still setting out to "look for her," especially during rush hour on buses and streetcars and in the long lines of people waiting outside stores.

I am not claiming that such things happen every day, and it is certainly possible to take the bus or the subway in the USSR without meeting with an adventure of this kind. However, far from being a complete anomaly or a perversion which is only practiced by a few disturbed individuals who are incapable of having normal sex lives, this is a common sexual outlet for a relatively large number of people. The most curious aspect of this clandestine sexuality is exactly that—two people may make sexual contact in the middle of a crowd without anyone else being aware of it. Russians hardly seem "forward" or importunate; in fact, their public demeanor is singularly sexless; even the men's eyes are carefully averted, so that a foreigner inevitably gets the impression of a modest and reserved people. But this apparent reserve can be an effective camouflage for all sorts of small indiscretions which are taking place on the same bus or in the same subway car without his knowing it. As a foreigner, and always identifiable as such, he will inevitably be deprived of this kind of "intimate" contact with the Soviet people.

And naturally the privileged sanctuary of this curious form of sexuality is the public transportation system. Only one Soviet family in seventy has a car, so that every day at rush hour there is an incredible melee in the buses, trolleys, trams, and subways of even the smallest cities, conditions that are especially propitious to the sort of escapades I am referring to. In 1966, 640 workers addressed a circular letter to Alexei Kosygin complaining about conditions in the Leningrad subways; this letter was later widely reproduced in *samizdat:*

> For us the so-called rush hour is really several hours of shame and indignation, the perfect setting for every kind of rude and inde-

> cent conduct. In those glorified tin cans stuffed full of human bodies that dare to call themselves our mass transit system, it is human dignity that is really being trampled underfoot, particularly where women are concerned. . . .

Thus the harried Soviet commuter may have all sorts of unexpected sights in store for him: two students caressing each other's genitals; a young woman lifting her skirt to make it easier for men to get their hands underneath it; or, more rarely, a cruising homosexual. In Leningrad perfect strangers may actually succeed in having intercourse on the bus—the woman stands on a kind of platform that runs along the sides of Soviet buses, and the man enters her from behind, which requires a maximum of dexterity if the act is to be accomplished without attracting the attention of the other passengers. The woman will not even turn around—the partners "recognize" each other immédiately, although they have never seen each other before, and there is a tacit understanding that throughout the entire encounter they will behave as though absolutely nothing out of the ordinary was happening. Even so, there is a code governing these clandestine meetings which dictates that certain barriers cannot be crossed. Thus a patient of mine from Vinnitsa once tried to strike up an acquaintance with a young woman who had grabbed hold of his penis a minute or two before. At first, her only reply was a string of crude insults; then she added that she was shocked by such an indecent proposal. In fact, the most important aspect of these encounters is their anonymity—the partners must be strangers to each other; moments later they will not even be able to see each other's faces.

This is why the buses and subways seem to exercise a sort of magnetic attraction, as if they were the ultimate haunts of debauchery and pleasure. In 1967, a twenty-six year old painter, Tatiana A., came to ask me to save her from "going mad." She was convinced that she was losing her grip on reality because she was always seized by an irresistible sexual desire whenever she rode a streetcar, as if in the very next moment she might throw herself on a strange man. In fact, she often experienced spontaneous orgasms when she was riding a streetcar, although she was usually unresponsive in bed. Her therapy sessions with me were not very helpful. She actually had to give up riding on any kind of public transportation, but even when she started getting around on a bicycle, it was still no use. I finally had to refer her to a psychiatrist.

The raised platform on Soviet buses can also serve as a kind of runway for a female exhibitionist. A colleague of mine from Odessa told me about the case of a fifteen year old schoolgirl who used to wear a short skirt and no underwear; she always took a platform seat. On one occasion she was so preoccupied with her own performance that she neglected to notice that one of the spectators was a friend of her parents, who immediately informed them what she was up to. Like good Soviet citizens, the girl's parents took it upon themselves to inform the school authorities—since they apparently felt that the real responsibility for their daughter's upbringing fell to the schools and the state. In turn, the school informed the police, the police informed the people's tribunal, and several years later the girl was exiled as a social parasite.

Another incident, which took place in Vinnitsa: a soldier and his wife were riding on a streetcar; as the car gave a violent lurch, he noticed that his wife had grabbed hold of the penis of a fellow passenger who was pressing up against her in the crush. He slapped them both across the face and summarily ordered them off the car, to the astonishment of the other passengers.

Incidents that will seem less exotic to a Westerner involve some kind of sexual aggression against women or young girls. A Leningrad schoolgirl was riding on a subway when a strange man approached her, opened his fly, and thrust his erect penis almost under her nose while he held his raincoat open in such a way as to be unobserved by the other passengers—although they may have suspected what was going on when she began to vomit uncontrollably.

A young girl called Natasha Semashko was riding a bus when she was set upon by four men at the same time. One tried to force her to grab his penis, another thrust his hand under her skirt, a third pressed himself against her from the front, and a fourth from behind. She started to scream, and the four men immediately told her not to be a hysterical little idiot, that she had simply imagined the whole thing and that if she was afraid of riding a crowded bus, all she had to do was get out and walk. None of the other passengers came to her defense.

Trains are primarily the preserve of exhibitionists, rapists, and "inventors"—men and women who, when they find themselves sitting across from each other in a crowded compartment, cover their legs with a coat and masturbate each other with their feet. Casual sexual encounters often take place in the toilets on a train, especially over the long hauls between Moscow and Vladivostok or Novosibirsk, which may take as long as a week. The female attendants in the sleeping cars who take tickets, serve tea, and make up the beds often have to fend off aggressive passengers. A patient of mine who had worked as a train attendant once told me how she and her coworkers had taken to wearing chastity belts—two leather triangles sewn into the crotch of their underwear with heavy thread—that protected them from attack both fore and aft.

As everyone knows, the Soviet people spend an enormous amount of time waiting in line to buy clothes, bread, or vodka. This is an essential fact of Soviet life, which must be borne with resignation, but it has also become a popular rendezvous for those in search of casual sexual contact. Whether intended to relieve the interminable boredom or to gratify some curious personal preference, such contacts are, as usual, perfectly anonymous. People who grope and fondle each other while standing in line don't need to introduce (or seduce) each other or even to talk. You stand in line, you buy what you want, and you have a little fun while you're waiting. In Moscow the giant GUM department store is notorious; some of the miscreants who are caught red-handed by store security, instead of being turned over to the police, are taken to the provisions department on the ground floor, where they are given the opportunity to ransom themselves by buying their captors a bottle of vodka.

Such public caresses are only possible of course in the anonymity of a crowd. Kiril Mifodyevich, the athletic coach of a Ukrainian-language school in Vinnitsa, was remarkably free with his hands during practice sessions of the girls' athletic teams; every exercise was a convenient pretext for sliding his hand between the girls' legs. They were certainly not unaware of what he was up to, and they began to tell tales out of school. Fearing a public scandal, Kiril Mifodyevich slashed his throat.

Chapter 13
Eroticism and Pornography

Nowhere is the official "ban" on sex more apparent than in Soviet art and literature. As you probably know, the creative process is entirely supervised by the state, which supplies the artist not only with a readymade ideological orientation but with a very precise list of acceptable subjects and styles, along with the correct solution to all formal problems and a canon of official esthetics. Soviet art and literature are still preaching Socialist Realism, but I think it would be difficult to find a less realistic body of work in the entire history of art, since a process of systematic falsification is always required to transmute Soviet reality into Socialist Realism. The denial of the erotic element in art and literature is a critical part of this enormous project of mystification, and this brand of realism has always thrown a discreet veil over anything that so much as hints at sexuality, or even nudity. I find it all too easy to imagine how the foundations of the Soviet state would crumble overnight if the Crazy Horse * ever sent a troupe of its naked showgirls on a tour of the USSR (though it is very difficult to imagine how they would ever get into the country in the first place). In fact, a colleague from Moscow, a psychologist,

* A Paris nightclub, famous for its erotic floorshow. [Translators' note]

once told me in all seriousness that he was developing plans for a Soviet "sex bomb" which he hoped to submit to the appropriate authorities—the basic idea was that the NATO aggressors would be showered with little packets of pornographic photographs. The poor man seems to have had a fairly shaky grasp of comparative psychology, since it doesn't seem very likely that Western soldiers are ever seriously demoralized by the pornographic magazines displayed in every newsstand in London and Paris.

Thus, erotic or pornographic books and pictures are not banned because they are morally offensive but because they are subversive. It was scarcely accidental that the writer Sinyavsky ("Abram Tertz") was tried for the crime of writing books that were both pornographic *and* anti-Soviet and having them published abroad. (I should mention, of course, that the love scenes in Sinyavsky's writings are not the slightest bit pornographic by any other standards.) Similarly, Soviet propaganda still equates "bourgeois ideology" with "pornography," both clear symptoms of the "decadence of the West" and, by the same token, both intolerable in the Soviet Union.

This form of censorship has been a permanent part of Soviet life since the late twenties, and I should clarify that it is not just a matter of a film-review board, for example, deciding whether a certain film is suitable for public screening. Censorship is already present at the moment of conception, and the creative process involves not just the author but the editorial committee and all sorts of ideological consultants and Party vigilantes, to say nothing of the censors themselves. The net is drawn so fine that it is a miracle if so much as a lingering kiss or caress manages somehow to slip through the mesh. A short sketch entitled "Savanarylo" * by the humorists Ilf and Petrov, which appeared in 1932, gives a very good description of this kind of attitude in its infancy. An artist is supposed to design an advertising poster for a cafeteria; here he presents his preliminary sketch in a private audience with his art director:

ART DIRECTOR: And what's that supposed to be?
ARTIST: That's a waitress.
ART DIRECTOR: Not that—*that!* (Points with his finger.)
ARTIST: She's wearing a blouse.

* The title is meant to suggest Savonarola, the Florentine preacher whose disciples consigned "indecent" works of art to the bonfires, as well as the Russian words *savan* ("shroud") and *rylo* ("mug" or "snout"), hence, "corpseface." [Translators' note]

ART DIRECTOR (glancing nervously at the door): Don't play innocent with me—I want to know what that thing is *under* the blouse.

ARTIST: A breast?

ART DIRECTOR: There you have it! And a good thing I noticed, too, because it's got to go.

ARTIST: I don't get you.

ART DIRECTOR (impatiently): Too obtrusive, my dear comrade—in fact I would say it's *enormous.*

ARTIST: Not at all—just a regulation-sized breast.

ART DIRECTOR: Now you mustn't start losing your head over a mere matter of a breast. It's not so big that we can't still do something about it. And don't forget that women and children are going to be looking at this poster of yours—married men even.

ARTIST (wearily): All right, all right. Just tell me what, in your considered opinion, are the correct dimensions of a waitress' breast?

ART DIRECTOR: As small as you can make 'em. . . . (wistfully) If only they didn't have any at all!

ARTIST: How about a waiter then?

ART DIRECTOR: No, no need to go quite that far. Besides, we're supposed to be encouraging women to play a more productive role in our economy.

ARTIST (struck by a happy inspiration): How about an *old* waitress?

ART DIRECTOR: No, better stick with a young one—only not nearly so . . . well developed, if you get my meaning. . . . So, I can rely on you to erase it then?

ARTIST: Consider it done—since I don't seem to have a whole lot of choice in the matter.

Ilf and Petrov have shown us that there were still a few hardy spirits around who remained unaffected by the suffocating atmosphere of Year Fourteen of the Revolution—an atmosphere that has not dissipated perceptibly since then. The authors clearly understood one essential aspect of Soviet censorship which has survived unchanged since the beginning. For their art director, the problem was not so much concealing the waitress' breast as doing away with it altogether. The dictates of modesty, or even prudery, which prevailed in the West until the liberalization of the past few decades never completely banished the erotic element from art or literature; it was simply portrayed more indirectly and allusively than it is today. And it is certainly possible for a writer to create an erotic scene without having his characters cavorting about in the nude. However, the Soviet censorship has ruthlessly obliterated all traces of the erotic, along with nudity and physical love, and in this attempt to strip all men and women of their sexuality, the regime has shown once again that its real intentions are not simply to transform nature but to destroy it.

Thus censorship has become a collective enterprise, a firmly established tradition, and an indispensable complement of the creative process. Stalin, and later Khrushchev tried to establish themselves as arbiters of literary and artistic taste, as they felt they had every right to do. During the Khrushchev era a Vinnitsa sculptor was commissioned to provide a statue of a soccer player for the city park. After he submitted a plaster model for approval, he was obliged to make the statue's shorts an inch or two longer. Another statue, of a female athlete, was also found wanting, on purely ethical grounds, and she had to be provided with a slightly sturdier bra. Representations of the nude in painting or in sculpture are still almost unknown—the only exception that I am aware of in the last thirty years was a female nude by the Lithuanian sculptor Kedanis, exhibited in Moscow, in 1966, and later reproduced in the magazine *Soviet Culture*. But this was, after all, a unique exception, which only means that the censorship had momentarily relaxed and allowed itself to slip back a few notches, and nothing more.

Exhibitions of foreign works of art are subjected to special scrutiny, of course. In 1977, there was a show of recent American paintings at the Pushkin Museum in Moscow; the authorities were highly displeased by one of Philip Pearlstein's paintings of two female nudes lying on a bed—the censors were convinced that they could only be lesbians. Finally, after a great deal of diplomatic maneuvering by the American organizers of the show, the authorities allowed themselves to be persuaded that this was not necessarily the case, and the painting was exhibited.

The situation in the theater and films is hardly different. In 1971, a Moscow theater presented a play called *Valentin and Valentina,* in which the hero and heroine appeared partially clothed for a brief moment in a frozen tableau and in semidarkness. Kosygin himself attended the premiere, and insisted that the "nude scene" be cut.

Intellectuals, who are more susceptible to the lure of the West, have naturally had great hopes for the relaxation of censorship, but most unofficial attempts in this direction have been sternly rebuffed.

In 1973, a Leningrad theater put on a play which, for the first time in the history of Soviet drama, included a character who was a homosexual. To be sure, the play was only presented to a carefully selected audience, and the play itself was set in the West, but nevertheless this bold experiment soon fell under the ban.

For many years Soviet film directors were forbidden to show even a friendly kiss on the screen; some time later cinematic lovers were allowed to hold hands, and finally even kiss each other, on the understanding that things would go no further. And there, with the usual rare and fairly modest exceptions, the situation has remained. And as the director of Mosfilm, Kiril Shirayev, recently explained in an interview with several Western journalists, "Speaking as a member of the public, I really don't see why it should be necessary to depict sexual acts on the screen." This sort of response is typical of all Soviet officials whose duty it is "to maintain relations with the West." Just as the average Soviet citizen "doesn't need" freedom of the press or the right to belong to a different political party, at least according to these self-appointed spokesmen for the inarticulate Soviet masses, he also doesn't need sex in the cinema. As one of Shirayev's young assistants remarked, in a facetious attempt to drive home the excellent point just made by his boss, "You gentlemen are over eighteen, so you don't need it either."

However, younger directors have been trying for several years to undermine or break through the barrier of censorship. If they try to make a film that is an ideologically correct and personally and artistically meaningful statement that is still expected to attract an audience . . . obviously something has to be sacrificed, and the Party severely criticized Mosfilm in the early seventies for releasing films of dubious political merit.

Tartovsky's *Andrei Rublëv*, which has been widely shown in the West, did contain a number of erotic sequences which were totally unprecedented by Soviet standards. However, this film was banned in the USSR for several years, and it was more or less by accident that a print found its way to the Cannes Film Festival, where it was hailed as a masterpiece. In *The Mirror*, another Tartovsky film, there is a brief shot, which only lasts for a second or so, of the heroine taking a shower—an astonishing spectacle for the Soviet moviegoer which his Western counterpart might almost have overlooked.

Soviet producers are not entirely immune to commercial considerations either. As a rule, the public stays away from Soviet films unless they have something new and tantalizing to offer, and even the less distinguished foreign imports tend to draw larger audiences. Consequently, there have been some attempts to copy successful Western formulas, sufficiently diluted to satisfy the censors. The censors are equally ruthless with foreign films, by the way; when *A Man and a Woman* was first shown in the Soviet Union, it had an extraordinary impact on the women in the audience—because of a scene in which the hero's naked back and shoulders were clearly visible. One of my patients went back to see it several times.

Even the most routine Western commercial films seem bold and innovative to Soviet audiences, since they give the impression of great artistic freedom by comparison with the stodgy, derivative, and politically standardized Soviet product. A few passionate kisses and extramarital adventures have been portrayed on the screen—like the few timid allusions to the Stalinist past that have crept into films and books; these are no more than placebos, substitutes for real sexual and artistic freedom, administered with a sly wink to the audience, as if to say, "Look how liberated we are!"

Stalin, according to his daughter's memoirs, forbade her to wear short skirts when she was a little girl, and the majority of his compatriots still have a morbid and puritanical reaction to nudity. One of my colleagues, the director of a clinic in the Caucasus, owned a valuable antique clock; the dial was supported by a bronze figure of a naked boy. But since cherubs, even bronze ones, are supposed to be sexless, my colleague actually sawed off the figure's phallus and crudely filed down the spot where it had been. He explained that he had done this to keep his family from being "corrupted"; however, when I met him, his daughter was twenty, and whenever the conversation turned to the mutilated figure on the clock, she denounced her father as a "barbarian," and rightly so, in my opinion. Her father still didn't seem to comprehend—"You see, it didn't work after all. My daughter was corrupted just the same."

Yet at the same time the effect of all these prohibitions and taboos has been to erase all distinctions between physical love and pornography, just as the words which describe the sexual organs and sexual acts in ordinary speech are used as crude insults. To be sure, it is a serious crime to possess and especially to distribute pornography of any kind, and, as I mentioned earlier, the legal definition of pornography is almost infinitely elastic. After I was arrested, for example, a photograph of a former patient, which I used to illustrate my medical lectures, was discovered among my papers. (The subject was a five year old boy who suffered from a hormonal imbalance which had resulted in hypertrophy of the penis.) The examining magistrate seized on this photograph gleefully, and was about to add a new article to my indictment—"illicit possession of pornographic materials." Fortunately my son Victor, who was present at the hearing, was so openly scornful of this proposal that our provincial Sherlock Holmes was dissuaded from pressing this new charge any further.

In less formal situations, however, the Soviet attitude toward pornography is somewhat less clearcut. In 1968, I found myself in a train with a group of military officers who had just returned from Czechoslovakia. One of them, a lieutenant, started to explain why "our people" had been forced to take such drastic action in stamping out socialism with a human face.

"They wanted more freedom, can you imagine that? But all they got was hippies and pornography."

"And what have you got there?" I asked, noticing that one of his pockets was bulging with postcards.

"Just a sample of that pornography I was just telling you about. They're completely depraved over there, you know." He showed me the postcards—fairly ordinary photographs of naked women.

"You're going to take them home with you?"

"That's right, back home to Rostov. The beaver shots are presents for my buddies." The corners of his mouth turned up in a distinctly unorthodox smile.

This sort of behavior is typical of the human contradictions that abound in any puritanical society. And this is why I believe that a disinterested policy of laissez-faire would be the best one for the authorities to adopt if the Soviet people are ever to be cured of this national malaise. When pornography is publicly condemned and then greedily devoured in private, the consequences are bound to be unhealthy. Far better to treat the disease than to attempt to suppress the symptoms and in other words, to lift the restrictions altogether. But such a proposal for the free circulation of pornography is no more realistic than the demand for a free, uncensored press, probably less so, though at present the question is entirely academic.

In any case, the pornography which circulates clandestinely in the Soviet Union only finds its way to a very limited audience, essentially among the privileged and the powerful—the only sectors of the population which have the wherewithal and the social influence which is necessary to get hold of films or other material of this kind. These are also the most intellectually "liberated" and the most cynical, and thus the most likely to embrace this sort of hypocritical doublethink with enthusiasm.

There are private screenings of Western films, for example, in government dachas and other exclusive haunts, such as the House of Film in Moscow. In the latter case, the films that are shown are not pornographic as such; they simply contain scenes that the censors have found unacceptable. The subject of Antonioni's *Zabriskie Point*, for example—a band of young American revolutionaries—may have been very much to their taste; however, there is a fairly explicit sex scene near the end of the film that made it unsuitable for mass consumption, though it could still be savored by a more select audience. And the Party higher-ups can see any film they want, since they are responsible for maintaining ideological vigilance over the arts.

The same elite circles have access to pornographic books and magazines, like those that I have encountered in the libraries of Vinnitsa Party leaders and academicians in Kiev and Moscow. Most of this "pornography"—whether or not deserving of the name—comes from the West and consists of magazines, which seem to breed like rabbits in the photocopy machine. An original or a photocopy may go for fifty or one hundred rubles—the price is not based on what the magazine shows but on what the customer can pay—which makes this an important source of revenue. If a Western tourist arrives in the USSR with a copy of *Playboy* in his luggage, he can be sure that it will not be sacrificed in vain. The customs officer who confiscates it is sure to pass it on, at the best price he can get. Also, the very existence of such magazines serves as a convenient pretext for evading the provisions for the free exchange of information and ideas in the Helsinki Accords. As *Literaturnaya Gazeta* explained in November 1975:

> It has become fashionable in the West to speak of the free exchange of information, an exchange which is said to be seriously hampered by the recalcitrance of the Soviet Union. However, the sort of literature which these devotees of "cultural exchange" seem to have in mind is nothing more than pornography.

Again we have this curious mingling of sex and politics, the equation of individuality and nonconformity with anarchy, which recalls the reaction of many Soviet citizens to their first sight of a Paris street demonstration—they are astonished that the republic does not instantly topple.

Apart from members of the diplomatic corps and other Soviet officials who are stationed abroad, sailors have become the greatest champions of this form of cultural exchange. As with many other Soviet travelers, as soon as they set foot on Western soil, they head straight for the "sex-shop" or the pornographic bookstore. But they are often surprised to find that there are not many other customers in these establishments—since to them this display of forbidden fruit represents the complementary pleasures of Paradise and perdition. Their next surprise is that the faces of the people in the pictures are so unexpressive, even sullen or morose, and completely devoid of passion. They naively imagine that these photographs were taken from life, though not in the usual humdrum setting, and it is almost as if someone had shown them the flesh-and-blood reality of something that ordinarily they would not even dare to dream of.

Though the faces of the actors and models in Western pornography may be expressionless, the amateur participants in Soviet pornography are quite literally faceless—to protect them from being identified by the police. Photography buffs arrange real or staged orgies, usually in private apartments (another sign that we are dealing with a privileged sector of the population) and primarily for the purpose of taking pornographic photographs. A young man called Tikhomirov, a cadet at the Military Academy and the son of a ranking Party leader, would invite a group of compliant young women up to his apartment; most of the evening's diversions were preserved on film. This idyll was finally interrupted by the police, and Tikhomirov was expelled from the Military Academy, though his father's position saved him from criminal prosecution.

This pornographic cottage industry is not very widespread because of the obvious risks involved, and extremely primitive from a technical and "esthetic" standpoint, if the word even applies in this context. The slides that are sold by the black-market vendor—which he produces from inside his coat in the classic manner—often are more reminiscent of the illustrations in medical school texts than the stuff that dreams are made of. A few eight millimeter pornographic films have also been made in the Soviet Union, but they can very rarely be shown, since few Russians have access to a movie projector.

Erotic literature, though, is quite another matter, since it is simple enough to photocopy a book or crank a mimeograph machine; also in the minds of the Soviet people, especially the intelligentsia, the printed word has traditionally been considered the primary refuge of political nonconformity and intellectual freedom. The result is the well known *samizdat* ("self-publishing") network, which distributes banned or unpublishable material on a fairly large scale. And apart from the political *samizdat*, there is also an erotic *samizdat*, which serves more or less the same function.

There are satirical pamphlets with provocative titles, such as, *One Hundred Ways of Making Love* and *Questions and Answers about Sex*, dispensing tongue-and-cheek "advice" like:

> Q. What should a thoughtful husband do when he catches his wife naked with another man?
> A. Throw a blanket over her so she doesn't catch cold.

All sorts of literary and scientific contraband is available on the black market: Freud, microfilm copies of the Kinsey Report, the *Kama Sutra*, Western sex manuals (the price of these may be the equivalent of a month's salary for an office worker), and classics of Russian erotica, such as "Luka Mudishchëv," "Vengeance" (a short story by Alexei Tolstoy), suppressed works by Polezhayev and Pushkin, and poems by Sergei Yesenin that were never published officially because of their obscene language and frank imagery.

But the majority of the Soviet people, who do not have access to *samizdat* or such black-market treasures from the West, have to make do with dirty jokes and obscene graffiti, though the latter also entails a certain risk. A worker in Kharkov was sent to prison for drawing an enormous phallus on a wall of the woman's dormitory of a technical institute, along with the inscription "Dear Virgins: My member is completely at your disposal, any time, day or night."

With pornography in such short supply in the USSR, it is scarcely surprising that some people have to resort to improvisation. All sexuality involves a certain element of voyeurism and exhibitionism, and in any kind of group sex this tendency is especially pronounced. A group of bright young people in Leningrad, for example, organized parties at which everyone would do a great deal of drinking to get into the proper mood; then, they would gather around a large table by candlelight, and one of the couples would shuck off their clothes, hop onto the table, and set to it while the others looked on.

A less convivial example: one of my patients, Galina Stetsenko, once told me that she and other women who applied at the Vinnitsa pension bureau were obliged to strip naked and to assume all sorts of ridiculous and humiliating poses, a spectacle that their bureaucratic audience found highly diverting. Of course they could only refuse to cooperate at the risk of losing their pensions.

We have already seen how pornography is suppressed in the Soviet Union and other Communist states as a potential threat to political stability—and not in the name of morality or religion, as it is in most other societies. And conversely, protest against the system often takes on an erotic dimension. As is well known, Soviet elections are a complete sham; not only is there only one slate of candidates, but a voter who stays away from the polls or turns in a blank ballot is likely to find himself in serious trouble. It is not generally known, however, that the ballot urns are often stuffed with such things as pornographic drawings, photographs, and torn-out pages from a gynecology text. A country schoolteacher once told me that in every election he defaced his ballot with a drawing of a pair of buttocks, since, as he perceptively explained, "our elections are nothing but pornography."

A worker from Kharkov that I met in the camp had been arrested for putting up a homemade placard at the entrance to the polls on which he had drawn a phallus in red pencil, with the legend, "Here's what we get from Soviet power." Even though he was drunk at the time, he was given a four-year sentence—not for anti-Soviet agitation but for "hooliganism." The same sentiment appears in a popular Soviet jingle:

> The hammer and the sickle is the emblem of our land,
> 'Cause the worker wields the hammer and the farmer grows our food.
> But no matter what you do, or what you've got in your hand,
> They treat us all the same—we all get screwed.

And among the innumerable anecdotes debunking the great Lenin, there are quite a few that picture him in bed with Krupskaya, trying out a problematical position and getting into difficulties.

This kind of iconoclastic humor can be found in every country, but in the Soviet Union it seems to have a sharper edge, and it is more directly political. Peter Sadecky, a Czech journalist who was posted to Kiev in 1961, discovered a group called P.P.P. (Progressive

Political Pornography), who published their own homemade erotic comic strip; they clearly thought of themselves as part of an oppositionist underground, since, as they informed their readers, "by reading these pages, you become a saboteur, an internal enemy of the system." In fact, their heroine Oktyabryana is a kind of Marxist version of Barbarella, and the strip is a satirical pastiche of her erotic and revolutionary adventures.

It was only in the camp, however, that I actually saw how pornography could express violent political protest against the regime. Since I will be discussing sexuality in the camps in a later chapter, I will only give a single example here: an inmate had tatooed the words *Slave of the USSR* on the soles of his feet; each letter was represented by a drawing of a mutilated penis—a startling and unexpected symbol of this man's despair that seems to go far beyond any conventional definition of pornography.

Chapter 14
Prostitution

Prostitution has a long history in Russia. Illicit brothels first appeared in St. Petersburg in 1718 (just fifteen years after the city was founded), and after 1843 brothels were licensed and inspected by the authorities, and prostitutes were obliged to register with the police. They also made their first appearance in Russian literature, notably in the works of Tolstoy and Dostoevsky, although the subject was treated almost from the first with a heavy admixture of sentimentality—the conscience-stricken hero is overwhelmed by the misfortunes of his fallen sisters. The popular writer Alexander Kuprin (1870 to 1938) provides this bathetic commentary:

> What a pitiful, absurd, and tragic path the history of Russian prostitution has taken! It is all mingled together—Russian faith and Russian indifference, the greatness and the despair of the Russian soul, the simplicity, the backwardness, the moral degeneracy of the Russian character, the liberality and the baseness of the Russian peoples themselves.

But this view of sentimentality was quickly played out after the revolution. The regime undertook to stamp out prostitution altogether, and it has effectively eliminated all obvious traces of it—which has nonetheless not prevented it from flourishing underground.

The Soviet penal code has more or less deliberately perpetuated this charade. Strict penalties are prescribed for procuring (five years at hard labor, followed by internal exile), but prostitution as such is not even mentioned. The official line is that prostitution automatically "withers away" when pimps are no longer allowed to exploit their victims; prostitution was a congenital vice of the old bourgeois society, but in the workers' state it is inconceivable that women would voluntarily submit to such a fate. This does not imply that prostitutes are immune from prosecution. In 1971, in Azerbaijan alone, seven brothels were raided by the police; 1221 women were tried and sentenced—not for prostitution but for "vagrancy" or "parasitism" (the Soviet equivalent of "no visible means of support").

The Soviet people find nothing strange in this kind of judicial illogic, since they have become accustomed to a legal system that is often merely another conduit for official propaganda. And this two-faced official attitude toward prostitution does nothing to promote a sense of social responsibility for a serious problem that Soviet society has not succeeded in solving. The people's tribunals seem to find it all too easy to dispatch these "vagrants" and "parasites" off to the camps to be "re-educated," but the public is rarely aware of the brutal repression that is concealed behind these slogans.

In the mid-sixties a group of students from the Institute of Highway and Bridge Construction were brought before the Moscow Tribunal (which is a standard "people's tribunal" on a somewhat grander scale). The case attracted a great deal of attention because all the defendants were the sons of Soviet dignitaries—a KGB general, a judge, a top Party official, a well known writer, and a famous composer. The nature of the offense was this: one of the defendants had thrown a party to celebrate his parents' departure for their country retreat; since the family apartment was now liberated territory, he and his friends decided to invite six prostitutes over for a collective orgy. Everything went according to plan until some neighbors, who heard the noise and suspected worse, called the police. As a result, the young women were condemned for "parasitism." One was sent to Kilometer 101 (one of the best known rehabilitation colonies for teenage prostitutes); another was exiled from Moscow for five years. As for the young men, it was thought to be enough that they had

had a good scare thrown into them, so they were merely expelled from the institute (which in no way jeopardized their chances of being accepted in any other professional school).

This story demonstrates the ease with which the privileged classes are able to flout the law. In fact, if one is on very good terms with the authorities who are responsible for suppressing prostitution, one can even enjoy the luxury of frequenting a clandestine brothel with minimal risks of being arrested.

Prostitution is organized in quite a different way than it is in the West. In the Soviet Union a prostitute usually acts as her own pimp. And since, as I have said, prostitution is not technically a crime, prostitutes must be treated as "dissidents" rather than criminals, and thus they encounter many of the tactics of administrative harassment to which political dissidents are subjected. For example, a prostitute may be exiled from a city as an "economic parasite." Her only safeguard is to take an ordinary job that will provide her with legal cover—as a bus conductor, cleaning woman, nurse, saleswoman, hairdresser, secretary, or waitress.

Quite naturally certain locales are more suitable for the prostitute's trade than others—the Odessa waterfront, the permanent Industrial and Agricultural Exhibition in Moscow (which attracts crowds of tourists from the provinces), railway stations, and, in general, the center of any large city. Overt soliciting is more or less out of the question—there are too many uniformed and plainclothes policemen patrolling the streets and too many informers, paid or *pro bono.* In fact, Russians often profess to be astonished that Westerners can tell the difference between prostitutes and other women, since prostitutes in the Soviet Union make every effort not to attract attention to themselves—they dress as unprovocatively and as shabbily as possible, they are careful not to even smoke in public, and they certainly never display too much skin. The only sign that they are prostitutes at all—the going price, five, ten, or fifteen rubles, chalked on the sole of one shoe—is kept well hidden from the police. Another difference between Soviet prostitutes and their Western counterparts is that they are more generous with their time. Since the customer is expected to provide the vodka, a prostitute can often see her way clear to spending the entire night with him at no additional charge. In fact, a great many prostitutes are alcoholics—this was apparently true even in prerevolutionary times.

Most prostitutes have had little education, their notions of hygiene are extremely primitive, and they are extremely neglectful of their personal health. Thus, they often contract and transmit venereal disease, and illegal abortion is the standard method of contraception—either performed by helpful friends or self-administered.

As an exception to the general rule I proposed earlier, there are certain cases in which prostitutes are still exploited by pimps. Occasionally these are alcoholic drifters who live on the fringes of the underworld, or even alcoholic husbands who force their wives to sell themselves for the daily ration of vodka. But it is far more common for a cabdriver to act as a pimp, and in Leningrad this was a common "second occupation" among shoeshine boys for many years. However, the severe criminal penalties for procuring have proved a fairly effective deterrent (though, as always, those who cater to the sexual appetites of highly placed individuals are exempt from prosecution). Nearly everyone in the Soviet Union recalls the notorious Ladnov case: an album containing the photographs of 521 women, with their ages, addresses, and physical descriptions, was produced at Ladnov's trial. The court and the prosecution agreed that these women were innocent victims of an inadequate political education which had rendered them incapable of distinguishing "the higher emotions from mere animal desires." Ladnov himself was sent to a labor camp for ten years.

What are the real reasons that women become prostitutes in the Soviet Union? Apart from the boredom of daily existence, which is particularly acute in the USSR, it is mostly a question of material incentives, even though Soviet propaganda still asserts that the material conditions that contribute to prostitution have long since disappeared. The government maintains that a subsistence level income is ninety-two rubles, fifty kopecks a month; the average per capita income is about sixty-five rubles a month. Thus a prostitute can take on only a handful of customers a month and still get by. Even so, since most of her potential customers are not so far above the poverty level themselves, business is not always easy to come by. In addition, Russian men are often reluctant to avail themselves of the services of prostitutes. All this imposes certain limitations on the practice of the world's oldest profession. There are prostitutes in Moscow who only accept payment in dollars; some in Odessa prefer chewing gum, which is not normally available in the USSR. The emigré magazine *Continent* printed a story about a young woman who took a man up to her room, and afterward presented him with a bill for exactly twelve rubles, seventy-five kopecks. When he expressed astonishment that the price of such a thing could be worked out so exactly, she explained that she was a student and showed him a list of her weekly expenses for groceries, stationery supplies, carfare, etc.

A trusted patron of a Moscow, Leningrad, or Odessa hotel may be able to buy an address or a telephone number from the hotel manager for a modest sum. The Karl Marx Monument in Moscow was a favorite haunt for some time, and Muscovites naturally referred to the prostitutes that gathered there as "Marxists." In Odessa there are at least five brothels along the Passazh, Pasteur Street, and Karl Marx Street. The rates are very reasonable—three, five or seven rubles, depending on the generosity of the client. Some clients prefer to be satisfied orally, because of the risk of venereal disease, and the prostitutes who specialize in fellatio often attend to several clients at once (three rubles each, with intercourse extra). Sometimes the patrons sit down for a hand or two of *duraki** while twelve or thirteen year old prostitutes set to work beneath the table; loser pays for all.

There is even a kind of state-subsidized prostitution, at least in the sense that it is the state that ultimately foots the bill. For example, a factory manager may hire a secretary whose only duty is to sleep with her boss; her salary is paid by the state, and when he tires of her, she can readily be replaced. There is a popular joke about a secretary who walks into her boss's office one morning and notices that the couch has been removed: "What's going on? Does this mean I've been fired?" The word *sekretutka (sekretarsha + prostitutka)* has been coined to describe this phenomenon; the *sekretutka*'s fringe benefits may include extra vacations, bonuses, and travel with all expenses paid. Sometimes, of course, the arrangement is less permanent; sexual favors are demanded simply as a condition of employment. Thus the singers at the Vinnitsa philharmonic hall were always teasing the artistic director about his "casting couch"; "How can you hold auditions out here? The couch is back in your office."

Prostitutes in provincial towns often develop a regular clientele of as many as twenty men. They never solicit in the streets; they simply receive their patrons at an appointed time. Sometimes they are even paid on a monthly basis, like salaried employees, though a patient of mine told me that she preferred to have her clients take her out to dinner in lieu of cash.

* A popular cardgame, roughly equivalent to the American game of Hearts. [Translators' note]

A prostitute who has a room in a communal apartment has to take special precautions, since a rowdy parade of clients trooping in and out is certain to arouse the indignation of her neighbors, followed swiftly by a visit from several gentlemen in uniform. Thus she has to make sure that her clients behave quietly and discreetly—which cannot be any too stimulating for them. A patient of mine who lived in a communal apartment was once walking down the hall to the toilet in the middle of the night when she caught sight of a strange man creeping up the stairs in his stocking feet, holding his shoes in his hand. At first she was terrified, thinking that he was a burglar, but a moment later she realized that he was one of her neighbor's customers, who was simply following the house rules.

A prostitute who is unable to find an indulgent employer, a patron, or an apartment may find herself plying her trade in the back seat of a taxi. The reasons for this original choice of venue are basically economic. Even taxi drivers have not escaped the national mania for central planning; they are expected to meet a daily quota, a certain number of kilometers and rubles ticked off on the meter. But it is usually rather difficult to meet this quota, especially since fares were doubled in 1977, and it is common to see a long line of empty cabs waiting at a taxi stand. Of course, if the driver has a woman sitting in the back seat, this makes it somewhat easier to meet his quota—and make an extra ten, twenty, or thirty rubles a day besides. This more than compensates him for his trouble—and for his long aimless walks in the snow while the cab is parked in a secluded spot and his partner and her client are left to themselves.

Sometimes the fare may prefer to keep moving at a comfortable speed down a quiet, dimly lit street, though this is a somewhat more costly diversion since he has to pay the meter, plus five or ten rubles for the driver, and five or ten more for services rendered. And if he finds the vibrations of the engine disturbing, the driver usually knows of an unlit doorway or a quiet spot where he can park the cab. In Moscow, for example, he will usually head for the Izmaylovski or the Sokolniki park. When there is snow on the ground and a car driving through the park would be too conspicuous, he may head further out to the suburbs of Cherkisovo or Bogorodskoye; the entire excursion takes about two hours.

The taxi driver is thus an indispensable part of the Soviet scene, as he is always able to answer at any hour of the day the two key questions: "Where can I get a drink?" and "Where can I find a woman?" The bottle of vodka he customarily keeps hidden under the driver's seat, and he will gladly offer it at only twice the normal price. If the fare seems especially trustworthy, an address or a telephone number may be forthcoming as well; being a call girl is a risky business, and he must screen his protegees' clients with particular care. On the other hand, as residents of Moscow, Kiev, and Leningrad are well aware, there are also taxidrivers on the police payroll who report conversations between "suspicious" persons, and if they seem particularly suspicious, may even deliver them straight to the precinct station so their documents can be checked.

The more enterprising prostitute can simply buy a train ticket from Moscow to Baku or Tiflis and, sleeping with occasional clients who get on and off at stations along the way, arrive at her destination with enough money for a pleasant vacation in the Caucasus. Here there is practically no risk of arrest, and in addition the Caucasus is a favorite hunting ground for prostitutes from all over the Soviet Union. For one thing, life is supposed to be easier there, and with good reason; it has the reputation of being (all other things being equal!) the Soviet California. For another, the inhabitants of the Caucasus are said to prefer blondes, whether natural or artificial, which means that visitors from the north can fix their rates accordingly (far above the average in the rest of the USSR) and still never lack for clients. I remember one occasion in the Black Sea resort of Sukhumi when three Georgians caught sight of a blonde walking toward them, grabbed hold of her, and unceremoniously dragged her into their car. She put up a feeble protest for the sake of appearances, but none of the other onlookers seemed to find the incident at all remarkable. The hotels and guest houses in the Caucasus often harbor prostitutes from Tallin, Moscow, Leningrad, and especially (though I have no idea why) Odessa. This calls to mind a satirical poem by Yevtushenko which circulated briefly in *samizdat:* I remember that it contained the line, "The little blond chickens are going to see the tawny cocks." At any rate, this remarkable influx of young women in search of easy money and an easy life has become a great source of revenue for the underground economy of the Caucasus. When the daughter of a well known scientist was raped in Baku, the resulting investigation led the police to a clandestine brothel which numbered a whole contingent of local Party leaders, and even three ministers of the Azerbaijani government, among its best customers.

Another common form of prostitution involves payment in kind rather than in cash. A woman may occasionally sell herself for a taxi ride or a few hundred grams of meat in a foodstore. One of my patients told me that she often flew to Moscow without paying a kopeck (I should mention, though, that airline tickets are not very expensive in the USSR); the exchange of favors took place in mid-flight. Prostitutes from lower classes have equally good prospects of hitching rides with truckdrivers.

The patient who told me about her airplane trips spoke quite openly, without the slightest bit of embarrassment. This is significant because, though sex may be a taboo subject among "respectable" people in the Soviet Union, those people who live on the fringes of society, who think of themselves as belonging to "the lower depths," talk about sex very openly and naturally. This is particularly true of prisoners and camp inmates, but once again, this is a subject which I will return to later. It might be appropriate to mention here, though, that prostitution also exists in the camps. Free women workers sometimes sell themselves to inmates and their prices are naturally very inflated, as much as twenty-five rubles, which makes this a luxury that very few inmates can afford unless they receive money from the outside or run an illicit operation of their own inside the camp.

The most pathetic class of prostitutes are those who congregate in the railroad station; their customers are mostly transit passengers between trains—ordinary workers or collective farmers from the provinces—or railroad workers. Most of them are young girls or older women, uneducated, shabby, and none too clean; many are alcoholics who are simply trying to make the price of a bottle, and a fair number are also pickpockets and petty thieves. Though their appearance may inspire nothing more than pity or revulsion, any man who rebuffs their advances is likely to be repaid with a stream of obscenities. Like their sisters on the streets, they mark their price on the soles of their shoes or on the palms of their hands—no more than three rubles, perhaps only one. Some will sell themselves for a glass of vodka or a chocolate bar (in Odessa there are even women who will prostitute themselves for a glass of lemonade). But when a woman gives herself away, she is no longer considered a prostitute *(prostitutka)* but merely a whore *(blyad')*.

There are also prostitutes who work the subway stations; they usually appear shortly before midnight, when the trains stop running. Their clients are lonely soldiers and the occasional student, and the price is the standard half-liter bottle of vodka. Their services are especially sought out by government clerks and low-level bureaucrats who have been sent to Moscow from remote cities such as Novosibirsk, Tomsk, and Archangelsk; for them this represents an economy measure, for a night spent with a prostitute costs less than a good hotel room.

On a somewhat less utilitarian level there are the Moskva River excursion boats that leave from the quay at Khimki. The trip lasts four hours, the cabins are no more expensive than hotel rooms, and more important, it is possible for a couple to book a cabin without producing their passports and a marriage certificate. There is also an inexpensive seafood restaurant on board, and the client will have time for a good meal after his pleasurable outing on the river. (The excursion boats continue to run until late fall, when the Moskva freezes over.)

Apart from the documentary requirements just mentioned, another problem with hotels, as far as prostitutes and their clients are concerned, is that a Soviet citizen cannot get a hotel room in the same city in which he is registered as a resident. But travelers to Moscow are allowed to rent hotel rooms, a loophole which permits prostitutes to infiltrate these supposedly inviolate sanctuaries, usually at the invitation of military officers, workers from the north who intend to fritter away their paychecks in the capital, and rich Georgian "profiteers" who specialize in selling out-of-season fruits, flowers, and vegetables on the black market.

A woman visitor in a guest's room is automatically suspect (particularly if the guest is a Georgian), and she may be summarily ejected from the hotel at any time after eleven o'clock at night. Thus a prostitute must be careful not to arouse the suspicions of the matrons who hand out the room keys and patrol the corridors on every floor. But even if one of the matrons catches her in the act, she may be able to buy her off with a couple of rubles, and some floor matrons have been so thoroughly corrupted that they have taken to procuring on their own.

In the Soviet Union there are no real nightclubs or cabarets, so that the night life of the big cities comes to an end around midnight. Apart from the theaters and the movies, people gather in cafés and restaurants, where they go to spend the entire evening, not just to have dinner. Unfortunately certain restaurants are notorious as places where prostitutes come to pick up men; in Moscow, for example, there is the National, the Metropol, the Rossiya, and the cafés on Kalinin Avenue, and in Leningrad the cafés on the Nevsky Prospekt. Consequently, many restaurants refused until quite recently to serve unescorted women. Since the prostitute's usual haunts are closely watched by the police, she is forced to change her base of operations regularly, or even to retreat to a less fashionable locale, such as the subway stations or the underground walkways beneath Sverdlov and Mayakovsky squares.

Foreigners are the prostitute's most attractive and most dangerous clients. Attractive, of course, because they may offer to pay with American cigarettes, stylish clothes, or any of the foreign trinkets that most Soviet people think of not just as luxury goods but as the symbols of an unattainable bliss. But on the other hand, any kind of trafficking with foreigners is likely to attract the attention of the police.

The widespread notion that any woman who sleeps with a foreigner is also working for the KGB is not totally unfounded but merely somewhat exaggerated. Intourist hotels are kept under tight surveillance, and if a young woman does manage to spend the night with a foreign guest on a regular basis, then it seems safe to assume that she is a KGB agent. Similarly, if a foreigner answers the phone in his hotel room and finds himself talking to a young woman who apologizes charmingly in broken English for having dialed a "wrong number," this too can be laid at the KGB's doorstep. When she calls back a minute or two later, the foreigner may decide that it would be foolish to pass up an opportunity like this, but the young woman's visit, if he invites her to his room, may be recorded on tape—or even on film if the KGB decides to give him the full James Bond treatment. This, then, is the only "legal" form of prostitution in the Soviet Union; the prostitute can operate with complete impunity if she agrees to fatten the dossiers of the KGB with full reports on all her conversations with her clients.

The Maritime Club for foreign merchant seamen is located in Bebel Street (Bebel * is celebrated in the USSR for his sympathetic views on the women's question) and is much frequented by both "real" prostitutes and KGB protégées, a role which may also be played by women guides and interpreters. These employees of the KGB take great pride not so much in their professional ties with the police as in their expert knowledge of the West, which certainly far surpasses that of the average Soviet woman.

* August Bebel (1840 to 1913) was one of the founders of the German Social Democratic Party. [Translators' note]

Unfortunately, this account of prostitution in the USSR must remain incomplete, since any statistical data that might have been compiled on this subject remains a jealously guarded state secret. Still I think the evidence I have presented is enough to invalidate the official claim that prostitution no longer exists in the Soviet Union. Though I am certainly not about to claim that this particular form of "dissidence" is an unmixed blessing to society, I do believe that the survival of prostitution in the USSR is quite significant, given the confident reports of its demise and the many attempts to suppress it by means more severe than any that have been used in other countries. In trying to change human nature, the Soviet regime has only succeeded in brutalizing and distorting it. But we should not allow ourselves to be deceived by appearances. Though prostitution may appear to be no more than another face of human misery, I prefer to think of it differently—as part of a secret campaign in which the Soviet people are trying to recover a lost territory within themselves that has been ravaged by the state; quite simply, they are trying to recover their rights. The common picture of the Soviet Union is that of a "successful" totalitarian society, everyone marching in lockstep beneath the banner of the omnipotent police state. Again I propose a different picture, this one of two societies—or rather, of an alternative, human society that exists within the rusty framework of the state machine, and an entire system of antirules and nonregulations that allows the people to evade the rules and regulations laid down by the state. Just consider those Moscow hotels, every door carefully watched, where the prostitutes still slip by all the same, and often with the complicity of the guardians themselves.

CHAPTER 15
Sex Crimes

CRIMINALS, PARTICULARLY sexual offenders, can be found in every society, and the Soviet Union certainly has its fair share—just another of those unpleasant facts of life which the authorities take great pains to minimize or conceal. Accurate crime statistics are almost nonexistent, and those that are usually cited are fragmentary and not very plausible, since their sole purpose is to demonstrate that crime has almost disappeared in the Soviet Union. Thus, any independent assertion that crime is increasing or decreasing in the USSR can only be supported by subjective impressions based on everyday experience, which are always deceptive. So I will simply try to present the evidence as judiciously as possible, all of it drawn from recent publications on the subject * or from my own conversations with fellow inmates in the labor camp at Kharkov.

RAPE

Rape is certainly the most common of all sexual offenses. According to one Soviet source, rapists accounted for 1.7 percent of felony

* Notably a study by the Soviet dissident Valery Chalidze, *Crime in the Soviet Union.*

convictions in 1966. If we follow Chalidze in assuming that there were a million criminal convictions in that year, this implies that there were almost 20,000 rapes, and the true figure is undoubtedly much greater—even though a convicted rapist may be sentenced to three to seven years' hard labor, and with aggravating circumstances (second conviction, gang rape, physical harm sustained by the victim) he may be sentenced to death.

But in fact rape is no more than the logical consequence of sexual frustration and of the way men behave toward women in the Soviet Union. The cult of *machismo,* the prevailing ignorance of foreplay and of the possibility of sexual pleasure for both partners—these are the "natural" preconditions, in a sense, for this act of pure violence. I have already described several cases in which husbands raped their wives. A patient of mine was reluctant to divorce her husband because of their children, but she also did not want to go on sleeping with him. He raped her whenever he felt the urge, and without fear of prosecution, since no court would have taken an accusation of this kind very seriously.

The nature of the crime itself may vary. A young woman may be raped after an evening of drinking or dancing; on the other hand, a rape victim may be accidentally killed in a struggle or deliberately murdered to prevent her from identifying her attacker. I knew a young man in the camp who was already serving his second term at hard labor; he had raped and murdered a young woman in Petrozavodsk when he was only twenty-two years old. Gang rape is very frequent; in the Vinnitsa prison I met three inmates—Igor Kuznetsov, Victor Elki, and Alexander Zaviazun—who had raped a twenty year old woman called Gureyva; Kuznetsov was also involved in the rape of an eighty year old woman, and we shall hear more of him later.

It is important to note here that such crimes are not the work of psychopathic killers; they are usually committed by ordinary men who are otherwise perfectly "normal." This does not make their crimes any less horrible, of course. I am thinking now of sexual assaults on very young girls, or in particular of the young schizophrenic who was brought to our clinic every year from her home in Litin when she became pregnant once again. Sexual assaults on old women are rare but certainly not unknown. Here is a first-hand account of one such crime, as it was related to me by a fellow inmate in the Kharkov camp.

An old Ukrainian woman was making her way home at dusk; it was already dark by the time the houses of her village came in sight. Suddenly a group of drunken young men appeared on the path ahead of her. They immediately threw themselves upon her, stifled her cries, and dragged her into a nearby grove of birch trees. She continued to struggle until one of them punched her in the face and knocked her unconscious. They pulled up her long peasant skirt and knotted it over her head, tore off her underclothes, and spread-eagled her on top of a pile of hay. Her attackers took turns raping her, then turned her over on her back, and all nine of them raped her again before they finally left her lying in a pool of blood.

One of the rapists—the narrator of this story—was almost sober when he returned home, where a horrifying sight awaited him. His mother was lying on her bed, covered with blood.

"What's happened?"

"I was raped . . . I'm going to die."

"Where did it happen? Who did this to you?"

"My son . . . you were the last of them. I could see your face."

At this the young man fainted. "When I came to, she was dead. She hung herself right there in the room with me, right in front of my eyes. I can't bear to go on like this, and sooner or later I'm going to kill myself. A filthy bastard like me doesn't deserve to live." He always ended his confession with the same words, and this was not an idle threat, for he had already made two attempts at suicide.

Igor Kuznetsov, the convicted gang rapist whom I mentioned earlier, far from feeling any kind of remorse, seemed to take a genuine delight in recounting the details of his crimes. On this occasion he had gone out mushroom picking with four friends from his village of Nestevarka, but before too long they filled their baskets and decided to head back to the village for a drink.* They came to a house that was somewhat isolated from the rest of the village, where an eighty year old woman lived.

"Well, lads," Igor shouted, "here's another one for our collection!" They tied the old woman's hands and held a knife to her throat while all five of them took turns raping her; then Igor picked up a stick of kindling that was lying on the floor and thrust it into the old woman's vagina.

Such horrible crimes are very much in the Russian tradition—senseless, brutal, and irrational acts of violence which are by no

* Mushrooms are customarily eaten raw and as fresh as possible, washed down with vodka. [Translators' note]

means the exclusive preserve of gangsters and psychopaths, but which may be committed impulsively and without warning by the ordinary "little man," the honest *muzhik.*

According to one Soviet study, more than half of all rapes are unpremeditated and committed while the rapist is under the influence of alcohol. Chalidze cites an even more revealing statistic: 55 percent of all rape victims are drunk when the crime is committed, 30 percent have actually been drinking with the man who subsequently rapes them. This seems entirely plausible, since in the Soviet Union alcohol is a kind of magic potion whose effects are completely unpredictable, and Russian women seem to enjoy behaving as provocatively as possible when they are drunk. In fact, this provocative behavior is only part of a "social game," a collective display of high spirits, and is in no way intended as an overt sexual invitation.

Rape is regarded by some as one of the privileges of power, and the police, as in many other countries, are often in a position to engage in this form of sexual extortion. A certain Sergeant Medyanik, for example, was in the habit of picking up young women, bringing them down to the station, and threatening to write them up on the police blotter for some imagined offense if they refused him. He had accounted for several dozen victims before he was discovered.

But the most extraordinary cases of rape are those in which the victims are men. This sometimes occurs when women are sexually deprived and live in isolated or self-enclosed communities. In Vinnitsa, for example, a group of women raped a young man in the dormitory of Armaments Factory Number 54; they had tied a sort of tourniquet around the base of his penis to keep him from losing his erection, which ultimately resulted in his death. In the Kurile Islands the captains of fishing boats are afraid to let their men go ashore; there are thousands of women working in the canneries there who may go for years without seeing a man, and any sailor who ventures ashore is truly taking his life in his hands.

Sadism

Violence, aggression, and sadism seem to be highly characteristic of Soviet sexuality. (I should mention here that although sadism is very common, masochism is very rare. I have practically never encountered a true masochist, either male or female, and I have only heard of a few isolated cases from my colleagues.) In any case, we should attempt to identify the social and historical reasons for this strongly sadistic component of the national personality.

There are two such reasons that immediately spring to mind. The first is the sadistic atmosphere of the prisons and the camps, a brand of sadism which became an instrument of national policy under Stalin (who was notorious for the macabre "pranks" he played on friend and enemy alike); there are still substantial traces of this sadism in the ways that suspects are interrogated and prisoners are treated today. Captain Samedok, the commandant of a camp in the Caucasus, was very proud of the updated version of the rack he had devised, which he called the "easy chair." An inmate who had committed some infraction of camp discipline was suspended between two metal chairs by means of leather straps, and the chairs would be moved progressively farther apart. A certain Major Zeinalov found it amusing to crush tomatoes on the inmates' genitals. The prevalence of such practices is both symptomatic of a serious national sickness and at the same time one of its causes: overt, quasi-legal sadism can only serve as an irresistible example to many people who in other circumstances would keep their impulses in check.

The second reason is part of the legacy of the war against Nazi Germany. As the Red Army advanced into enemy territory, atrocities against the local population were regarded as perfectly natural, the usual reaction of an army drunk with victory. The same soldier who used to recite poetry to his girlfriend before the war was now just as likely to rape any girl or woman who fell into his hands. There were even extraordinary incidents in which Russian women prisoners in German slave-labor camps were raped by their Red Army liberators. A patient of mine called Chustov, from Kharkov, once told me that when a Soviet detachment captured one small town in eastern Germany, they discovered that all the inhabitants had fled, and so they threw themselves on the still-warm bodies of the women who had been killed in the latest shelling.

We have already encountered the ancient Russian tradition of wife-beating, and it is clear that in Russian folklore the maxim "Spare the rod . . ." does not only apply to children; since wife-beating is inherently sadistic, the differences between individual cases can only be differences of degree. Unfortunately, there are too many cases in which the real nature of this practice is only revealed when the husband (or wife) is brought to trial. In Moscow, a pipefitter called Merzlyakov was charged with the murder of his wife

Nadezhda. It appeared that he had beaten her regularly, or rather worked her over systematically with his fists before he began kicking her, then striking her with a hammer or a screwdriver until she lost consciousness. Then he would plunge her in a cold bath to revive her, so he could pick up where he left off. One of these sessions ended in her death.

In Ivanovo, a twenty-seven year old woman called Elizaveta Sindryakova, the mother of two children, was tried for murder. Her husband Evgeny, an office worker, had beaten her so brutally that she had to be taken to the hospital immediately in serious condition. When she recovered from her injuries, she was determined to leave him; she wandered around the city for two days, but found that no one would rent a room to a woman with two children. She returned home and killed her husband by striking him repeatedly with an ax.

I am convinced that this phenomenon of the battered wife exists on a scale that simply cannot be compared with anything in the experience of such countries as France or the United States (although unfortunately I cannot produce any statistics that would document this claim). And the same half-buried sadistic impulses may emerge in even more monstrous aberrations—crimes of pure sexual sadism and incredible savagery. Chalidze mentions a case in which a rapist savaged his victim with his teeth and actually bit her nose off. Victor Astafyev, age thirty-five, found himself in the Vinnitsa prison after he had torn his wife's nose off during a quarrel. Another inmate's wife had sliced off his penis while he was dead drunk—apparently a friend of hers had been boasting that she had slept with him. When he came to his senses and realized what she had done, he killed her.

It seems that crimes of passion and revenge are often committed by impotent husbands; at any rate, I can testify that there were dozens of men in the Kharkov labor camp who had committed such crimes, and the majority of them were impotent. One of them told me that he had started to berate his wife one day for sleeping with other men; she replied that her sex was big enough to satisfy everyone, whereupon he picked up an ax and split her skull.

Sexual Attacks on Minors

The rape or the seduction of a young girl is a common occurrence. Perhaps this may be seen as one of the consequences of the last war and the indiscriminate sexual violence against civilians of all ages. In the camp with me there were as many as fifty men who had been convicted of statutory rape, sometimes of their own daughters. Boris Podpesny, leader of one of the camp work brigades, was serving an eighteen year sentence for the rape of a seven year old girl; there was also a boarding-school instructor who had forced himself on several of his young students. The case of the film director Roman Karmen was notorious. He was charged with having enticed a number of thirteen and fourteen year old girls into his car and then raped them. But it was not considered appropriate for a People's Artist of the Soviet Union * to be convicted on a charge of rape and the indictment was quashed.

There have been some truly monstrous cases in which the death penalty was invoked. A thirty-seven year old peasant in Vinnitsa was shot for the rape and murder of a five year old girl. In November 1977, a worker who had raped and murdered a seven year old girl was condemned to death in Moscow. A condemned man in the Vinnitsa prison who had raped an eight year old girl was so overcome with remorse that he castrated himself with the sharpened edge of a spoon (the inmates were forbidden to have knives); his testicles were preserved in alcohol and displayed in the prison "museum."

Sexual relations between father and daughter seem the most prevalent form of incest. I came across one truly extraordinary case: a patient of mine from the nearby village of Yakushentsy told me that she had seen her husband put his penis in the mouth of their two year old daughter. A man who had been sent to the camp for raping his daughter was still given to cynical remarks like, "Was I supposed to wait until everybody else was screwing her too? It's bad enough that I was doing it!"

Another of my fellow inmates at Kharkov was a peasant by the name of Pentyukh; it seemed that one day while he was drunk he had observed contemptuously to his wife that her vagina was much too big compared to Marka's—Marka was their little daughter. His wife denounced him immediately, and he got twelve years on the strength of this remark. The army newspaper *Red Flag* reported that an officer in Odessa was degraded to the ranks because he had slept with his fifteen year old daughter.

Incest between brother and sister is rarer, though I knew a man in

* The highest distinction that can be conferred on a creative artist, a performer, or an entertainer. [Translators' note]

the camp who had given his sister sleeping pills and then raped her. As a result she became pregnant; he drowned their newborn child in a bucket of water.

Sexual Psychopaths

Crimes committed by sexual psychopaths are actually fairly rare, but there have been occasions on which entire cities were terrorized by a psychopathic killer. For example, there was a series of psychopathic murders in Leningrad several years ago; the killer had surprised his victims in their doorways, stunned them with a hammer, and raped them. All of these women had died of head injuries, and all of them were wearing red coats.

The "red-coat killer" turned out to be a young man from a good family who was declared to be insane after psychiatric examination and sent to a mental hospital for treatment—which did not prevent a court from imposing an additional sentence of fifteen years in a labor camp. Theoretically a criminal who is found incompetent to stand trial could never be sent to a camp, but in practice Soviet justice is not necessarily in the habit of making exceptions for the mentally ill.

I find this case particularly interesting because of the killer's (presumably unconscious) fixation on the color red, which I believe can only have one possible explanation: red flags, red stars, Red Army, Red family, and all the other clichés and visual symbols that are burned into the brains of Soviet citizens almost like an obsessional image. In addition, *red* has become more or less synonymous with *good.* Thus, if crime can really represent a kind of revolt against society and its moral standards (as I believe it can), it is entirely possible that the "red-coat killer's" obsessional hatred for women was strongly reinforced by his obsessional hatred for the color red.

An unsuccessful provincial tenor, Vladimir Yonessian, created a similar panic in Moscow before he was finally arrested. He had provided himself with a meter-reader's badge and a small woodsman's ax, and he gained admittance to the victims' apartments on the pretext that he had come to read the gas meter. In the course of his two-week psychopathic spree he raped and killed six women and girls (as well as making off with all the money he could find in their apartments). Rumor insisted that the actual number of his victims was many times greater; there was even talk of ritual murder, and naturally the genuine meter readers had to stop making their rounds while the killer was still at large. There was even an incident in which a waggish husband came home and called out "Meter reader" as an ill-advised practical joke. His wife started to scream hysterically, and thinking that he must have interrupted a tryst between his wife and her lover, he tried to batter the door down, which naturally elicited even more hysterical screaming from his wife. The authorities were unimpressed by the couple's attempts to explain this misunderstanding, and the husband was sentenced to fifteen days in jail for hooliganism. As for the killer himself, Yonessian maintained an air of cynical detachment throughout his interrogation and trial; he announced that he had simply intended to avenge himself on society because he had been thwarted in his chosen career. The tribunal held that he was mentally competent and later sentenced him to death. In addition, his family, friends, and colleagues were publicly taken to task—the collective had obviously not provided him with a good political education, since he had shown himself capable of committing such atrocious crimes even though he was not mentally ill. (I only mention this last as an example of what Soviet justice is sometimes capable of itself.)

Alcoholism and Crime

Someone who has never been to the Soviet Union may not be aware of the social importance of alcohol, vodka in particular, not as an accompaniment to other activities but simply as an end in itself. In fact, drinking often takes precedence over all other human activities, including sex. It is also an inexhaustible topic of conversation and the object of many curious rituals. For example, there is an unwritten commandment that once a bottle is opened, it must be finished off at one sitting, and everyone must always drain his glass—be it a vodka glass or an ordinary water glass—or even his bottle, as the case might be.

A number of very serious attempts have been made to measure the real extent of alcoholism in the USSR. A. Krasnikov has calculated the annual per capita consumption of vodka for the entire country at 10.8 liters. This figure does not include other alcoholic beverages—brandy, for example, is illicitly distilled in enormous quantities which the most vigilant statistician could never hope to measure.

The average intake increases every year, and the statistics already indicate that the average Russian consumes four times as much vodka as meat, and 15 percent of the money that Russians spend in stores is spent on vodka!

The consequences of this mass intoxication are innumerable, and no one can predict what they might be in the future. As far as the subject of this book is concerned, vodka contributes to the problems of impotence, sterility, sexual brutality, and crime. Some studies have cited alcoholism and drunkenness as a factor in 80 percent of all murders and 70 percent of all rapes—roughly in agreement with the study mentioned earlier which estimated that 55 percent of rapists are under the influence of alcohol at the time the crime is committed. Violence, alcohol, and sex make up an explosive mixture, even in the hands of the "ordinary" law-abiding Soviet citizen, since here again the barriers between "ordinary" behavior and criminal pathology may easily be thrown down.

I have seen many marriages in which alcohol was an essential preliminary to violence and to out-and-out rape. I once treated a woman from Gorky whose husband forced her to drink vodka—though certainly not by depriving himself of his fair share—since he thought this was the only proper way to set the scene for a night of love. In fact, his wife became completely frigid.

A male patient of mine always started drinking the moment he got home from the factory, and before long he would start in on his wife—kicking her, hitting her with his fists or even with a bottle, silencing their twelve year old daughter's tearful protests with a slap across the face. Their apartment was a shambles, since he had already broken most of the furniture. At last he would throw his wife down on the bed and rape her; this final scene would be concluded in a matter of seconds. Afterward he would fall asleep immediately, which at least would leave her with a few precious hours of tranquillity.

The drinking habits of the Soviet people suggest several parallels with drug abuse—which is not to say that drugs are unknown in the Soviet Union. Certain data released by the Prokuratura (Ministry of Justice) suggest that 1.8 percent of urban youth currently experiment with drugs. Of course, drugs in themselves are not an inducement to crime, but they can produce certain personality changes that make it impossible for the individual to resist his visceral impulses, and thus he may even become dangerous. On January 18, 1970, a young woman was strangled on Narimanov Avenue in Baku by a sadist who was under the influence of drugs. Finally, many camp inmates take drugs, when they can get them, as a stimulus to their erotic fantasies and a way of relieving sexual frustration. This remedy proved less than efficacious for a camp inmate called Novikov, who was relieved of about five ounces of marijuana during a spot inspection and had several years added onto his sentence as a result.

I cannot conclude this discussion without mentioning another particularly disturbing phenomenon—the dangerous increase in crimes committed by young people over the last few years. This is a trend that most Soviet citizens will freely acknowledge, and for once at least it is also supported by official evidence. The Prokuratura commissioned a secret investigation into the crime rate in twenty-four Soviet cities and forty-eight villages, the initial results of which were released to the local Party committees (though not to the public) in April 1972. Its conclusions were so alarming that the Central Committee quickly put a stop to the entire investigation. A 1971 study of twelve hundred Soviet cities had revealed that 49 percent of rapes and 12 percent of all murders were committed by young people under twenty. In 1974, 718,000 crimes were committed by teenagers younger than seventeen, and there is certainly no reason to assume that these young criminals spring from the "lower depths" of society. On the contrary, in 1970, in eighty-one selected trials of youthful offenders in Moscow, Kiev, Novosibirsk, and Baku, 62.8 percent of the defendants were the children of Party officials, researchers, scientists, intellectuals, and other members of the privileged classes or the more prestigious professions.

I am aware that these phenomena are very difficult to analyze, and moreover that a similar trend can be observed in many other countries. Still, I would like to return to an observation which I made earlier in connection with adolescent sexuality—young people are increasingly losing their faith in the moral and ideological standards in which the society is still attempting to indoctrinate them. And we have already seen how this has resulted in a clandestine sexual revolution, which may lead to the kind of violent excesses which accompany any kind of revolutionary social change.

Chapter 16
Homosexuality

Several years ago in Moscow the English defector Guy Burgess gave an interview to a Western journalist. He was asked if he had encountered any problems as a homosexual living in the Soviet Union. Burgess replied that in this respect the Soviet Union was no different from the West. In fact, nowhere in the Western world is homosexuality as despised or as strongly discouraged as it is in the Soviet Union. The Soviet penal code threatens male homosexuals with from three to eight years' imprisonment; you may already be familiar with the case of the film director Serge Paradzhanov, who spent several years in a labor camp after he was convicted of "pederasty" and "incitement to suicide" in 1974. In November 1977, a member of the Italian Chamber of Deputies, Angelo Pezzana, even held a press conference in Moscow to protest the Soviet government's treatment of homosexuals.

But homosexuals are still being sent to the camps, and neither the law nor the prevailing attitude toward homosexuality has changed, and there are no signs of any such change in the future. The word *homosexual* itself is used rarely, and then only as an insult or as a convenient way of indicating that someone is a social undesirable. I don't think that the Soviet press has ever discussed the problem of homosexuality, since it is not even considered a sickness, but rather the most sickening of all perversions, and thus a subject that is best passed over in silence. Those few books that attempt to deal with sexuality only provide a spare clinical definition of homosexuality—the Soviet Medical Encyclopedia makes no mention of lesbian sexuality as such, simply informing the reader that Lesbos is an island in the Aegean Sea.

Male Homosexuality

There is a deep-rooted popular prejudice against homosexuality, and the ordinary vocabulary of profanity and drunken banter is filled with homosexual allusions. As in many other languages, to accuse someone of passive homosexuality is an extremely powerful insult; *idi na khui* is a standard phrase, roughly equivalent to (but more explicit than) "up yours" or "get fucked." And as with all taboos, homosexuality has inspired a number of popular myths. For example, it is widely believed in Moscow that the durable Soviet politician Anastas Mikoyan, who died in 1978, actually served as a kind of male *sekretutka* to several of his colleagues in the Kremlin, which was how he managed to survive the reigns of both Stalin and Khrushchev and pass into peaceful retirement in 1965. In fact, this preposterous story was inspired by the racist canard that all Armenians have pronounced homosexual tendencies.

At any rate, it is clear that the repression of homosexuality is not just a matter of legislation. Rather than prison or the camps, the homosexual's primary risk is harassment and maltreatment. An actor who once came to Vinnitsa with a repertory company learned this to his sorrow, if he had not been aware of it already. He encountered a young man, a patient of mine, in the hotel restaurant and persuaded him to come to his room. The actor begged my patient to allow him a few caresses, and they arranged a meeting the next day. When the young man came back, though, he had brought three of his friends with him, one of them an amateur boxer; they beat up the actor and broke several of his ribs.

"Why did you do it?" I asked him later.

"But why not? They're criminals after all—they ought to be shot."

A straightforward reply, and a perfect illustration of the Soviet attitude toward homosexuals. And since the law offers them no protection, they are condemned to suffer this contempt and brutality in silence; they lead lives of perpetual terror, fragmented and beleaguered, and so it is hardly surprising that homosexuals often succumb to serious psychological disorders. In Vinnitsa, for example, the constant constraints of this existence proved too much for one man; one day he began to tear down the main street of the town, running up to the men and boys he met, reaching out a hand to touch them, and then running away. He finally grabbed a thirteen year old boy—who was completely stunned, of course—and took him under a porch, timidly stroked his crotch, and then fled, only to recover his courage and return again a few moments later. This continued until he was arrested.

Homosexuals can sometimes be identified simply by the sort of behavioral traits that are associated with perpetual fear—nervous laughter, furtive eye movements, and so forth. I recall an evening I spent at the house of a woman friend in Leningrad, where I met the assistant director of the Leningrad Conservatory. His extremely apprehensive manner made me suspect that he might be a homosexual, and in fact he was dismissed from his post a short time later for trying to seduce one of his students.

Homosexuals themselves often regard their sexual preference as a pathological disorder, an illness that has been inflicted on them by fate—an attitude very probably confirmed by the sort of treatment to which society subjects them. Few have come to me for treatment, since homosexuals are usually afraid of giving themselves away to anyone. In 1972, while I was giving a series of lectures at the Vinnitsa Pedagogical Institute, I received three letters from homosexual students who had heard me speak and who wanted me to help them. For example, one of them wrote that his sickness made him feel nothing but contempt for himself, but that he was powerless to do anything about it. He only felt sexual desire for men; women had ceased to attract him entirely. He ended his letter with the words "What should I do?" In other words, he had defined his homosexuality as an illness, and he was beginning to fear that it might prove incurable.

The totally clandestine way of life that is imposed on homosexuals presumably accounts for the fact that homosexual love is purely physical. They are condemned to seek out their partners surreptitiously, if they dare, and no emotion can be invested in these ephemeral relationships. In addition, homosexuals are extremely vulnerable to blackmail, and thus a prime target of the KGB, who are always eager to recruit new agents.

However, a homosexual underground still exists in every large city; at the present time in Moscow homosexuals know to look for one another in the small square near the Bolshoi Theater, opposite the Karl Marx Monument. In provincial cities the homosexual cruising grounds are somewhere near the public lavatories, which, as in other countries, are covered with obscene graffiti and sexual invitations.

How many homosexuals are there in the Soviet Union? The statistical breakdown of criminal convictions for 1966 (mentioned in the last chapter) gives the figure of 0.1 percent for the crime of "pederasty," or approximately a thousand out of a million convictions in that year. This is not a very useful index of the real extent of homosexuality in the USSR, though it is the only statistical evidence that I am aware of.

From my experience as a camp inmate, I can state without hesitation that the only place where homosexuality is allowed to flourish is in the prisons and especially in the camps. Though I had very few homosexual patients, 80 percent of them were former inmates, and I might add that approximately 15 percent of the inmates at Kharkov were active homosexuals by the time they were released.

I might also mention the army and the navy, and particularly the submarine service; there are also a great many homosexuals in the criminal underworld, which is simply a survival of the customs of the Gulag in the outside world. I remember hearing of an incident that occurred in Odessa in 1963—two professional criminals raped a thirty-eight year old man, murdered him, and cut his body into pieces, which they hid under a pile of coal.

I learned from some of my patients that homosexuality is also prevalent in the diplomatic corps. This may seem curious, but the reason for it is the strict surveillance exercised by the secret police over Soviet nationals who are stationed in foreign countries. They are categorically forbidden to enter into sexual liaisons with foreigners, so the KGB tolerates these homosexual relationships, since in their eyes it is better for good Soviet citizens to sleep with other Soviet citizens rather than decadent Westerners, irrespective of gender.

I have also heard of a number of incidents involving homosexual university professors. For example, a group of students at the Baku

Pedagogical Institute addressed a petition, dated June 12, 1972, to the scientific section of the Central Committee of Azerbaijan: "Professor Bairamov forces his male students to have sexual relations with him; otherwise he flunks them on his exams. What should we do?" In Novosibirsk one professor even took to knitting sweaters as a way of ingratiating himself with particularly needy students.

I treated a patient whose homosexual orientation was a direct consequence of his impotence, which in turn was caused by chronic alcoholism (even when he came to see me at the clinic, he was always drunk). He seduced young boys with the story that he was a wounded war hero—to be precise, that a grenade fragment had injured his penis—who was no longer able to enjoy a normal sex life.

Finally, I will mention an exceptional group of men whose homosexual orientation is the result of an endocrine insufficiency. When this has a marked effect on the man's physical appearance, he is referred to as a eunuchoid, since the resulting hormonal imbalance produces the same physical transformation that is observed in men whose testicles are actually removed before puberty: fine, fair skin, absence of facial hair, small bones, a wide pelvis, and other skeletal features that are normally characteristic of women: subcutaneous fat deposits on the breasts, hips, and buttocks, and atrophied development of the sexual organs.

Eunuchoidism may even manifest itself in adults, and it is accompanied by the same atrophying of the sexual organs and a similar alteration in the man's physical appearance. Such men may become passive homosexuals, since they are incapable of having a normal sex life and their extreme effeminacy may make them attractive to active homosexuals. Conversely, I once treated a man whose sexual organs were perfectly normal but whose breasts were as fully developed as a woman's—he was the active partner in a homosexual relationship with his own brother, evidently because he was afraid to confess (or reveal) his physiological ambivalence to any woman. However, after a successful operation—a mastectomy, in effect—he soon got married and abandoned his homosexual liaison with his brother.

Female Homosexuality

Although lesbianism is not explicitely mentioned in the penal code, it is equally condemned by popular morality, and given the extreme flexibility of Soviet justice (at least when it comes to discouraging any kind of deviant behavior), lesbians have as much to fear from the law as male homosexuals do.

As nearly as I can judge, lesbianism is much less prevalent than male homosexuality, though I should be cautious in making this claim, since it is equally likely that sexual relationships between women are carried on in even greater secrecy than is the case among men. And just as with men, the only place where it is really easy for a lesbian to find a partner is in the prisons and the camps. There was an extraordinary case in Kishinev of a young woman who became a habitual shoplifter, pilfering small staple items from stores; her only purpose in this was to be arrested, then get off with a relatively light sentence in the camps, for there at least she would be able to find a lover.

There is still another place that I know of where lesbianism is quite prevalent—the Ivanovo region, the traditional center of the textile industry, which has been constantly expanding since the revolution and where a disproportionate percentage of the population are women textile workers. We have already seen how a community's social relations are not evolved autonomously but in fact are totally subject to external policy considerations. And so, as we might imagine, the regime has shown itself to be completely indifferent to the problem of insuring that these women can still lead normal lives, or rather of *allowing* them to arrange these things for themselves. In fact, all social arrangements are dictated by the imperatives of industrial planning. Women textile workers rarely succeed in finding an apartment or a job, or obtaining a residence permit, in another locality; in effect, they are chained to their factory benches. And because of this artificial imbalance in the population, sexuality can only survive in an aberrant form—gang rape of men by women, incest between father and daughter, sexual relationships with young boys, and lesbianism.

I knew a man in the camp at Kharkov who had murdered his wife. During his military service he had been stationed in the Ivanovo region; after he was discharged, he met a woman who worked in the textile mills, fell in love with her, married her, and brought her home to his village. But he was astonished to discover that she had absolutely no interest in sex, and he began to hear reports that she had been seeking out the company of single women. When he asked her very bluntly to explain what all this was about, she admitted that since she had lived exclusively among women for so long, she had acquired a taste for lesbian sex. Her husband had never even heard the word before, so she explained that this meant that having sex with a man did not give her any pleasure. "And what does give you pleasure then?" he asked. In a burst of candor she tried to describe the sensations experienced when her lover stimulated her vagina with her breasts. "That was true happiness, and I don't think I could ever give it up. You know, it would be better for both of us if we got a divorce and I went back to live with her." Her husband was so stunned and appalled by this that he picked up a flatiron and killed her.

Apart from these exceptional situations—the camps and industrial enclaves such as Ivanovo—I have encountered very few lesbians in the course of my practice. Most of them were older women, presumably because their generation suffered most acutely from the demographic crises of the twenties, thirties, and forties. Still, I would like to quote a letter that I received in 1971 from a nineteen year old psychology student in Leningrad, which I was able to take with me when I left the USSR, and which I find so intriguing that I think it deserves to be given in its entirety:

> Dear Doctor Stern,
>
> Professor K.E. has suggested that I write to you, and that you might be able to help me. There isn't anyone here in Leningrad that I can trust not to tell someone at the university or even my family. I could even come to see you in July if you thought that would be helpful, and of course I am counting on your discretion. K.E. told me that I could confide in you and talk to you very frankly.
>
> I want to tell you the whole story from the very beginning. I think it started when I was in the seventh grade. I had a boyfriend who was always trying to get me to "do it" with him. I was really confused and afraid to touch him, but one day he made me do it anyway. I still look back on this as a horrible experience, and I think it was really traumatic for me. Even before I came to the university, when I was still in school, I had already started to masturbate. It was terrible—I found that I had to do it practically every two or three days. After my experience with my boyfriend I lost interest in boys completely. They kept asking me out, but I didn't feel anything serious for any of them. Besides, they couldn't give me what I needed. If I stopped masturbating for three or four days, I became totally apathetic, irritable, even hysterical—and

then I would have to start masturbating again. I always did it just before I went to sleep, because I'd have to rub myself for a long time before I got any pleasure out of it. Perhaps this was harmful to my health, because I got very anxious and began to think that I was seriously ill. I tried to distract myself by listening to jazz (which I really love), reading, and studying, but it was no use.

But the really horrible thing happened when I came to the university and one night I stayed over with one of my girlfriends. Since then my whole life has been turned upside down. I feel more and more terrified every day, even though I try to smile and still behave the same way I used to with my friends, so that no one realizes what's going on. I find men disgusting, I hate them, but I have very strong feelings about my girlfriend. I have stopped masturbating, but is that really worth the price?

The hardest thing for me to bear is that I've started to love my friend the way other women love men, to be jealous of her. There are other lesbians in our class, and if she left me for someone else, I don't know what I'd do. I can't live without her. Help me, please tell me what I ought to do.

Sincerely,
N.V.

Leningrad
March 3, 1971

This young woman was convinced that masturbation had not only ruined her health but turned her into a pervert as well. You might think that this sort of thinking could only be found in a convent, and a medieval convent at that, but in fact it is not at all exceptional by Soviet standards. This can be explained readily enough when we recall the sort of education that young people are offered in the Soviet Union; it is equally significant that this young woman lived in terror of being found out and summarily expelled from the university, as is the sordid brutality of her first sexual experience, which may have been ultimately responsible for the fact that she became a lesbian.

Chapter 17
Hermaphrodites and Transsexuals

> I want to be a man, and I anxiously await the day when scientific procedures for castration and the transplantation of male organs and glands are discovered.

This was written during the twenties by a young woman Komsomol in response to a sociological questionnaire, and it has all the flavor of that astonishing era when everyone supposed not only that the world was going to change but that human nature itself could be manipulated to suit their wishes.

But the dream of this young revolutionary has yet to be realized, and today in the Soviet Union a woman who "wants to be a man" (or vice versa) will search in vain for a surgeon or a clinic that will accommodate this desire. The only operations of this kind are performed by ordinary surgeons in hospitals and for strictly medical reasons, that is, to correct some congenital ambivalence in an individual's sexual development. Clearly then, a request for a sex change operation for purely psychological reasons (or to satisfy some homosexual caprice, to look at it from the viewpoint of official Soviet medicine) would be categorically refused.

Although abnormal sexual underdevelopment is very common (particularly among boys) in the Soviet Union, true hermaphroditism, in which the individual has the physical characteristics of both sexes, is extremely rare. At least in my own practice I have only encountered a few isolated cases, though these are still quite interesting for the insight they provide into the conditions under which medicine is practiced in the Soviet Union.

Here is one such case. The patient was a twenty-two year old student with well-developed breasts, a prominent clitoris, rudimentary testicles, a narrow vaginal opening, and a vestigial uterus. With the exception of the testicles (which were nonfunctioning) and the hypertrophied clitoris, all her sexual characteristics were female. Nonetheless she came to my office dressed in men's clothes; she complained that she could not grow a beard or a mustache, and she was involved with a young woman, whom she intended to marry. For more than a year she had been having sexual relations with her fiancée, making use of her clitoris in lieu of a penis. But for all of that she thought that nothing could be better than to be a man, and she wanted to become one, entirely.

I tried to persuade her that in the circumstances it would be much simpler for her to become a woman; all that would be necessary would be to remove the testicles surgically and to administer hormone treatments in sufficient quantities. But she was adamant, and since the choice in such cases is entirely up to the patient, the doctor is obliged to carry out the patient's wishes, however unreasonable they might be. The first step was a mastectomy, followed by hormone treatments, with the idea of further stimulating the development of the clitoris and perhaps even causing the testicles to begin functioning normally. After they finished school, though, my patient and her (his) fiancée left Vinnitsa, so I have no idea how this story turned out.

This patient's sexual ambivalence was congenital, but hermaphroditism may also be the result of unexpected physiological changes that overtake the individual in later life. I treated a woman who menstruated and lactated normally and was sexually attracted to men; her only unusual physical characteristic was her abnormally developed clitoris. She was married at sixteen, gave birth to a daughter at eighteen, and continued to have a normal sex life. But when she was thirty-three, she stopped menstruating, her voice deepened, her bodily contours became less rounded and more angular, her clitoris was transformed into a penis, and she began to feel sexually attracted to women. When her daughter got married, she left her husband and moved to another city, where she began a new life as a man—she wore men's clothes, shaved every day, even took to smoking a pipe. Then she became involved with a thirty-three year old woman and actually fathered a child. At this point the future course of her life was settled, even though she was still technically a married woman.

In every case that I have come across, sexually ambivalent individuals have always wanted to "become" a man, and I have never heard of an exception to this rule. This is perhaps a sign of the fact that the position of women in Soviet society continues to be inferior to that of men. In fact, male transvestites are rarely encountered in the Soviet Union; Soviet transvestites are almost always women who try very hard to cultivate as mannish an appearance as possible.

At any rate, the problems of intersexuality (hermaphroditism) are given short shrift by official Soviet medicine; they may try to resolve them as expediently as possible, but this is not really a subject that anyone takes much interest in, except for those who are directly affected by it, and not always even then. I recall an incident that took place in a research institute in Akademgorodsk in 1964. It was noticed that the latest issue of a student wall newspaper had drawn a particularly large crowd of readers. The attraction was an article by a biology student which advanced the rather fanciful hypothesis that human beings were originally hermaphrodites, neither men nor women; instead of his theory's being discussed and refuted in the normal course of things, the author was summoned to a special meeting of the Party committee, at which he was expected to engage in a thorough bout of self-criticism. Then the committee ordered every copy of the newspaper to be torn down and destroyed, as if this were a case of genuine sacrilege.

As I mentioned earlier, though, true hermaphroditism is exceptional, although the related problem of sexual underdevelopment is extremely common. Eunuchoidism is the more extreme form of hormonal deficiency, and women may suffer from a comparable disorder as well, though this is less common. Its victims generally grow to be extremely tall, the result of an overproduction of certain growth hormones.

Katya M., a woman from the village of Goroi near Vinnitsa, was my patient for twenty years. When I first saw her in 1954, she was eighteen years old, tall and thin, and extremely frail for her height. In addition, her breasts were scarcely developed at all, her uterus was no larger than a plum, and she had still not started menstruating. After two years of hormone therapy, all these sexual abnormalities had corrected themselves, though I continued to prescribe regular treatments.

Eunuchoidism must be detected early on if it is to be treated successfully. And this often involves a much more pervasive problem, since preventative medicine in the Soviet Union is severely handicapped by the fact that parents never see their children's naked bodies after they reach a certain age. And sex is such a taboo subject that both parents and children may not dare to discuss it, even if they are confronted with such a serious problem as this. Add to this an inexcusable ignorance of the elementary facts of human biology, and the result may be one of those absurd and almost incredible cases in which a young man of twenty who is about to get married finally becomes aware that his sexual organs are as undeveloped as a two year old's.

I have treated hundreds of cases like this. One of them, a young peasant called Stepan Baida, was produced as a "witness" at my trial. When he first came to see me, at seventeen, he exhibited the sexual development of a three year old; his penis was less than an inch long. But after eighteen months of hormone therapy, he "became a man" at last. My success with this patient prompted this playful tribute from a woman colleague when I presented his case before the Vinnitsa scientific society: "On behalf of all women, I would like to express our gratitude—now we have one more man among us."

In 1970, I treated a nineteen year old student from Uzbekistan, called Abdurahman Abdurashidov, one of a group of a hundred Uzbek students who had been sent to Vinnitsa as part of the government's campaign of Russification in the Central Asian republics (as I mentioned earlier, the runaway birthrate and Islamic nationalist sentiment in Central Asia are a constant source of anxiety in Moscow). At any rate, the medical committee of the local army recruiting center had referred this young man's case to me, since he was obviously suffering from some endocrine disorder: his penis was the size of a newborn baby's, and he had almost no body hair and a high-pitched voice, like a woman's. His gratitude and relief after a difficult but ultimately successful course of treatment were unbounded—particularly, as he explained, because he would no longer have to endure the taunts of a neighbor woman in his village who was constantly reproaching his mother for having given birth to "a girl." In fact, he was determined to return to his village and prove to this woman's daughters that he was indeed a man.

This young man's mother was an Uzbek peasant woman who had had no idea of what medical science could do to help her son. But this sort of ignorance is certainly not confined to Uzbekistan. One of the most glaring instances that I have come across concerned a man I shall call P., who worked in the cigarette factory in Vinnitsa. He was forty-five when he first came to the clinic, begging me to "make him a man." When he was a teenager he had been involved platonically with a girl in his class. His girlfriend had later moved to Vladivostok, gotten married, and had two children. Some thirty years later, after her husband had died and her two daughters had left home, she returned to Vinnitsa to track down her first love.

She had always supposed that it was for her sake that P. had never married. In fact, he was a eunuch—he had been born without testicles, his penis was the size of a five year old's, he had almost no facial or body hair, and so forth. Clearly, the prospects were not very encouraging. Even so, the hormone treatments stimulated the development of his penis (corresponding to that of a normal fourteen year old boy), and he was able to marry his childhood sweetheart after all, since he could have erections and regular sexual relations, as long as he returned to the clinic for his hormone injections three times a month.

I have only cited his case to underscore the point I made earlier about the pitiful state of preventative medicine in the Soviet Union. This man had reached the age of forty-five, and in all that time neither P. himself, his family, nor any of the doctors who had previously examined him had even had the slightest suspicion that his problem might respond to medical treatment.

On the other hand, it was not uncommon for a patient to approach me with a similar request, entirely frivolous in his case, that I "give him a shot" that would increase the size of his penis. When these requests became annoyingly persistent, I would give the patient an injection of vitamins to ease his mind and to get him out of my office. He would leave secure in the belief that his manly parts (which were perfectly normal in every respect) would finally command the respect that they deserved, and in fact many patients reported back to me that the results of the treatment had been most encouraging. This, of course, is simply another manifestation of the "virility complex" which I discussed in a previous chapter. Also, patients sometimes came to me with the request that I "give them a mustache and a beard." Once again, this had nothing to do with any kind of hormonal disorder, but simply a sparse growth of facial hair, which is especially common among Russian men, presumably because so many Russians are of Tatar descent.

I will end this chapter with an account of a truly extraordinary case. In 1968, a patient by the name of Karpenko came to my office with the same request, that I "give him a mustache and a beard." He was dressed as a man, and his hair was cut short, but when I looked at his passport, I discovered that Karpenko's first name and patronymic was "Anna Petrovich" (I should explain that *Petrovich* is a male patronymic, and that a woman whose father's name was Pëtr would invariably be called Anna Petrovna). Karpenko explained the origin of this hybrid entry in his passport: the document had been drawn up by a policeman in a very isolated district, and the brave fellow had attempted to reconcile the evidence of Karpenko's birth certificate (Anna) with the evidence of his own eyes (Petrovich).

When I examined Anna Petrovich Karpenko, I discovered that he, or rather she, was actually a woman, although her breasts were underdeveloped and her clitoris was enormous. She informed me that she had a wife, with whom she had "normal" sexual relations, using her abnormally developed clitoris as a substitute for a penis. And I in turn informed her that since she was biologically a woman, under no circumstances would I give her a beard and a mustache, which provoked a great deal of indignation on the part of Anna Petrovich.

I had a second, and even more preposterous encounter with her five years later, in 1973. She came to my office with a request from the Department of Social Security that I verify her sex once and for all; this ambiguity could no longer be tolerated since women are entitled to draw retirement benefits at fifty-five, whereas men have to wait until they are sixty. "Very good," I said facetiously, "I've decided that you were right after all—I'll put down that you're a man."

"Absolutely not!" Karpenko cried. "Out of the question! I insist you tell them that I'm a woman."

IV
FROM THE DACHA TO THE GULAG

SO FAR I have tried to define Soviet sexuality almost entirely in terms of the common characteristics of the species *Homo sovieticus*, the average Soviet citizen. But now is the time to examine the many exceptions that test the rule, the many classes and peoples who inhabit the various regions of the Soviet Union, from the deserts and warm plains of the south to the perpetual frosts of Siberia. Many still follow traditional ways of life, to which the culture of European Russia is totally alien. There are those who live in luxury that would be the envy of a sultan from the Arabian Nights, and others who live in wretchedness that is equally unimaginable. Each has a different way of living, and I would like to give a brief sketch of these differences and the ways in which they affect the sexual attitudes and behavior of the Soviet people.

CHAPTER 18
Sex and Nationality

ONE HUNDRED ninety-four separate nationalities were recognized by the Soviet census of 1926, 108 nationalities in 1959, and almost 100 in the last census in 1970. The 1970 census of the 241 million inhabitants of the USSR * gave this population breakdown (in millions) for the principal nationalities, based on linguistic criteria:

Russians	129
Ukrainians	40.7
Uzbeks	9.2
Byelorussians	9
Tatars	6
Kazakhs	5.3
Azerbaijanis	4.4
Armenians	3.5
Georgians	3.2
Moldavians	2.7
Lithuanians	2.6
Tadzhiks	2

* The current population of the USSR is estimated at 261 million.

Jews	2
Germans	1.8
Chuvashes	1.7
Turkmens	1.5
Latvians	1.4
Kirgiz	1.4
Mordvinians	1.3
Bashkirs	1.2
Poles	1.1
Estonians	1

As may already be clear, the term *nationality* has a very specific meaning in the Soviet Union, and the word is used quite differently than it is in Western countries. The law prescribes that the entry in a Soviet citizen's internal passport should read *Ukrainian, Uzbek,* or whatever it might be, not *Soviet,* so that *nationality* refers not to one's country of origin but to one's ethnic heritage. The preservation of these ethnic distinctions is supposed to foster the separate and independent development of each national minority, but in reality it has become a way of practicing discrimination and exercising social control. Whatever a citizen's religion or individual feelings may be, he cannot choose his nationality—except for the children of "mixed" marriages, who are allowed to choose either their mother's or their father's nationality at the time they are issued their passports. Naturally, there are various administrative shortcuts available to those who have money or influence, and it may be worth paying to have the word *Russian* inscribed on the fifth line of your passport, since Russians enjoy certain rights and privileges which Uzbeks, Ukrainians, Armenians, and the rest are denied. (It is important to remember that the vast territories that are ruled from Moscow contain over 110 million inhabitants of non-Russian origin.)

I will certainly not attempt in these few pages to give a complete account of the sexual practices of all of the principal national minorities. A study of this magnitude would be well beyond my competence. I would simply like to present certain observations which bear on the general problem of nationality in the Soviet Union.

First, it is clear that the total number of different nationalities is constantly decreasing. There are two principal reasons for this—the regime's policy of Russification, and intermarriage. According to the 1970 census, 13 percent of Soviet families were of mixed national origins (20 percent in the cities). The tribal peoples of the north are steadily dwindling away. The intermarriage rate among Jews, Ukrainians, and Byelorussians continues to increase. Among Central Asian peoples it is usually the men who take Russian wives; the young women generally remain subject to the authority of their fathers, who tend to have a more traditional attitude toward marriage. Also, when a man marries a Russian woman, this is regarded as a means of social advancement, a promotion, which does no injury to national pride, whereas a young woman who married a Russian would be "lost" to her people forever.

But the survival of the national minorities is also imperilled by the fact that the children of mixed marriages have the right to choose their nationality, and if they are at all inclined to step up a rung on the social ladder—even if they are barely conscious of the workings of this unacknowledged caste system—they will choose to be Russians.

But I have already mentioned several powerful factors which contribute to the vitality of some (although not all) of the national minorities. I am thinking primarily of the astonishing fertility of the peoples of the Caucasus and Central Asia; the table below gives a clear picture of the remarkable contrast with the birthrates in the Slavic and Baltic republics. (Bear in mind that the average birthrate for the entire USSR, according to the 1970 census, was 17.4 per thousand of the population.)

RSFSR	14.6
Latvia	14.5
Estonia	15.8
Ukraine	15.2
Byelorussia	16.2
Lithuania	17.6
Georgia	19.2
Moldavia	19.4
Kirgizia	30.5
Uzbekistan	33.5
Tadzhikstan	34.7
Turkmenia	35.2

Thus the hegemony of the ethnic Russians is obviously threatened, so much so that when the revision of the Soviet constitution was being discussed in 1977, it was proposed that any Soviet citizen who spoke Russian and had adopted Russian culture could voluntarily take on Russian nationality as well. Anyone who could be readily assimilated into the Russian majority would be actively encouraged to do so.

But, with the reawakening of nationalism in the past few years, assimilation may no longer seem like such an attractive prospect to many Soviet citizens. Today it often happens that children of a mixed marriage will choose to remain in the non-Russian minority, even if it is not in their material interest to do so. This new form of political protest is a source of constant perplexity to Soviet bureaucrats, who are literally incapable of understanding why a young man or woman with a Jewish father and a Russian mother could possibly choose Jewish nationality.

One of my patients once told me of the astonishment and the sincere compassion that was expressed by a police official when he learned of her decision:

> What you're doing is crazy; your father's Ukrainian, and you're still taking on Jewish nationality, like your mother. Don't you understand what you're doing? You're only putting this burden on yourself, and I advise you very strongly not to do anything so foolish. . . .

Nevertheless, such things are being done more and more often. To be Jewish is not just to choose one's nationality but to speak out in protest against the regime. And as far as the regime itself is concerned, though it ordinarily does everything in its power to assure the cultural homogeneity of the population and to erase all such national differences, it still sometimes stoops to conquer by promoting national and even racial antagonisms. This is particularly true in the case of anti-Semitism, which in the Soviet Union is not just popular prejudice but official policy as well.

Still, if we look at the divorce statistics for mixed marriages in the Soviet Union, we see that, though they are very high, they are still no higher than the national average. The reason for this is that, independent of all considerations of power politics, the uniformity of Soviet society does tend to minimize cultural differences. In Tsarist times the deficiencies of a sprawling decentralized bureaucracy at least preserved the benefits of cultural diversity. Today the great city and the tiny village, the capital and the remote frontier, all read essentially the same newspapers and listen to the same broadcasts, and all of them are controlled and censored by the state. Different ways of thinking and behaving, even different personality types, seem to blend together imperceptibly. Communism has created the prototype of the obedient conformist, the punctilious human robot with no will of its own, perfectly conditioned to a double standard of public propriety and private violence. And all of the general characteristics which I have ascribed to Soviet sexuality—puritanism and repression, sexual ignorance, sadism, the cult of violence, impotence, and all the rest—may be observed in Dushanbei, the capital of Tadzhikstan, in Tiflis in Georgia, in Minsk in Byelorussia. Thus we would be wrong to seek for the causes of all this in some hereditary defect in the national character of any one people rather than in the policies and the fundamental outlook of a particular form of government.

But even though not every Soviet citizen is an obedient cog in the machinery of the state and, as we have seen, the state still cannot exercise its authority over all forms of sexual behavior, this does not prevent it from trying whenever possible. For example, when the Soviet Union was still well disposed toward China, any young woman who married a Chinese would receive a kind of dowry from the state, though, of course, today such a marriage would be denounced as a betrayal of the Party. But this simply reflects a major shift in the political line; sometimes the sequence of events is less coherent. For example, fifteen years ago it became fashionable for young women to marry African students, since Africa was just beginning to figure prominently in Soviet foreign policy. Then, for the first time, black children were being born in the Soviet Union, and racism, equally virulent among the leadership and the people themselves, finally prevailed over international friendship and cooperation. These days an African's student's life is very difficult in the Soviet Union. An affair between an African man and a Russian woman is likely to lead to threats, beatings, even murder; white racism is incomparably more violent in the Soviet Union than anywhere else in Europe.

I would still say, then, that as far as sexual behavior is concerned, there are certain cultural differences that have resisted the control of the state, just as there are certain spheres of human existence in which words, thoughts, and emotions have escaped the drive toward conformity and standardization which is so typical of Soviet society.

Among the Chukchi * and the Ossets,† for example, traditional hospitality dictated that a host offer his wife or his daughter to a

* Eastern Siberian people whose culture is very similar to that of the Eskimos of North America. [Translators' note]

† Iranian people of the Caucasus, thought to be descended from the ancient Scythians. [Translators' note]

guest. This custom has evolved into a form of prostitution; today a Chukchi may rent out an apartment with a woman thrown in as an extra, which allows him to ask for a higher rent from the prospective tenant.

But nowhere is this sort of blending of tradition and innovation more apparent than in Central Asia. The position of women is much the same as in other Muslim countries, and women in Turkmenia, for example, still devote their days to their traditional occupation of weaving carpets, even though they may be working in state-sponsored workshops. In this part of the world, the birth of a girl baby is still considered to be a great misfortune for the family.

In Tashkent, the capital of Uzbekistan, most of the Uzbek population speak Russian, even among themselves. Twenty years ago it was difficult to coax them into leaving their yurts and moving into modern apartments; today there are complaints about the housing shortage. But as in the other Muslim republics, polygamy has not entirely disappeared; I once visited the household of an old Kirgiz who lived in the village of Aigurek, near Frunze, with his three wives; another polygamist of my acquaintance was a Kazakh from the Taldy-Kurgansk region, who also had three wives.

In 1966, the magazine *Young Communist* was scandalized by the discovery that the custom of *kalym*, the payment of the bride price, still had not been abandoned, even in the cities, nor have such other venerable customs as abducting one's chosen bride by force and selling young girls to the highest bidder.

Under Tsarist law men could marry when they reached eighteen, women at age sixteen; in deference to the traditions of the peoples of the Caucasus, the legal age was reduced to sixteen and thirteen respectively. Early Soviet legislation fixed the minimum age at eighteen for both sexes, again with the exception of the Caucasian republics of Armenia and Azerbaijan, and the Ukraine and Moldavia, where women were legally permitted to marry at sixteen.

The penal codes of the Armenian, Georgian, Azerbaijanian, Turkmen, and Uzbek republics still prescribe criminal penalties for the purchase or abduction of women, as well as for compelling a woman to marry against her will; the fact that these articles are still in force certainly suggests that these traditional marriage customs have not been forgotten.

Among the Gilyaks, an Eastern Siberian tribal people, children of both sexes remained completely subject to paternal authority. A father would purchase a wife for his son, and the marriage would be arranged without anyone's asking the consent of either the bride or the groom. If the son's new wife tried to run away, her husband was expected to tie her to his sled, whip up his dog team, and drag her across the snow until she was dead. According to Kurganov, in *Women and Communism*, this traditional code was still very much in force as late as the 1930s.

I once treated a young woman who had left her home in the Caucasus for the Ukraine. In 1965, this woman's daughter had turned down a proposal of marriage from a young Abkhazian.* Faithful to the traditions of his ancestors, the disappointed suitor carried her off by force, tied her hands, and raped her, on the assumption that this would leave her with no choice but to accept his proposal. Much to his surprise, however, she simply turned him over to the police.

Even those traditions that still survive are clearly slated for extinction. But the essential world view of the cultures that give rise to these traditions—always much less susceptible to change—is likely to remain vigorously alive for a good many years. I have already discussed the ambiguous position of women in Soviet society, and certainly Muslim women have even farther to go before they will achieve that "liberation" which the authorities claim to have assured long ago. Obviously it is not my intention to pass judgment or to lament for a vanished past; I simply would like to observe that the kind of social change which has been fostered by the regime has tended to make people abandon the outward signs of their cultural identity without seriously changing "the way they really are." People can only really change if they are free to change themselves. Thus the current situation of the national minorities is a sort of uneasy compromise between the diversity of traditional Russia and the cultural homogeneity which is steadily being imposed by the new Soviet society.

At this point it would probably be appropriate to mention some of the prejudices and ethnic stereotypes that have been concocted by Russian chauvinism. Ukrainians, for example, are given the derisive nickname *Khokholy* ("topknots," a reference to the traditional hair style of the Ukrainian Cossacks) and are commonly supposed to be rather simple-minded and sentimental. The figure of the Jewish in-

* People of the Western Caucasus, celebrated for their longevity. [Translators' note]

tellectual, though, inspires genuine hatred rather than mere condescension, as much hatred as the Russians are capable of feeling for anyone.

The "typical" Armenian (including the unfortunate Mikoyan) is said to be a pederast, though it is not my impression that homosexuality is any more common in Armenia than in Russia. The people of the Baltic countries are considered to be rather cold fish, if only because they tend to treat their Soviet occupiers with a certain reserve. Jewish men are said to be tireless sexual performers, and there are still Russian women who are eager to experience the unaccustomed thrill of sleeping with a man who has been circumcised, and so much the better if he's an intellectual as well. (Actually, the majority of Jewish parents today no longer circumcise their sons.) Georgians have the reputation of being lecherous and boorish—not that Russian men are particularly distinguished for their delicacy or sensitivity in sexual matters, as I think has been amply demonstrated in previous chapters. I should also not fail to mention that, according to the Russian sexual mythology, Uzbeks never bathe, Tatar women always shave their pubic hair, and Moldavians are all syphilitic (although I have also come across whole villages in Russia that were entirely riddled with syphilis).

I would not have brought up these preposterous ethnic slurs if they were not so deeply ingrained in the popular Russian mind, and I think that because the Soviet ethos is so cold and remote, the official ideology so lacking in credibility, this only means that these prejudices are likely to survive for a very long time. And, after all, the stereotype most actively promulgated in Russia is the idealized image of the Russian man and woman of official art and literature, in all their purity and beauty, towering over all these lesser breeds and subject peoples, resplendent in the shameless propagandistic glow of Russian chauvinism.

Chapter 19
The Masses

I WOULD LIKE to return to certain aspects of Soviet sexuality which are directly affected by the living conditions of the "toiling masses," to use a well worn Soviet cliché—farmers, factory workers, and clerical workers. My real purpose in writing this book has been to describe the sexual behavior of the ordinary people who make up the vast majority of the Soviet population.

The poverty of the Soviet people, which is unfortunately no secret to anyone, cannot help but have an impact on sexual behavior. I have already shown how malnutrition, protein deficiency in particular, may lead to sexual dysfunction, and also how the housing shortage has only aggravated the problem of divorce. This is only symptomatic of a larger problem which I would like to discuss in some detail.

At present 40 percent of the families in Moscow do not have private bathrooms, which are still considered a luxury in provincial towns. In communal apartments in the large cities, several families may have to use the same bathtub; there are still communal apartments in Odessa where families—grandparents, parents, and children—are billeted five to a room.

It is all too obvious that there is little opportunity to have a real marriage or a real family life in such cramped quarters. We should also take it into account that the great majority of citydwellers are recent migrants from the countryside. Even families who came to the city during the thirties have still not really put down roots, by which I mean that they have found nothing to replace the way of life they lost when they were driven from the land. After the calculated destruction of their thousand-year-old peasant culture, these refugees of Stalin's forced collectivization policies were ill-prepared to adapt to the life that awaited them in the cities.

Certainly very few of them were accustomed to living in separate rooms. The peasant isba had only one room, which was shared by the entire family. A married couple would not even have their own bed; everyone slept around the stove, on wooden benches, or on the dirt floor, in a small, familiar world of their own. However, the communal apartment (which the authorities only began to phase out in the Khrushchev era) was partitioned into as many as ten tiny cubicles, and thus lacked both the isba's capacity to shelter an entire family in comfortable intimacy and the convenience and practicability of a bourgeois apartment. The peasant's new quarters were clearly not designed for a long winter's evening with the entire family gathered around the stove (to say nothing of ready access to the farmyard and the field!). The communal apartment, in theory at least, was well suited to a small family (a married couple with their children) and an individual style of life (every family in a room of their own). But in practice this meant that the family found itself in the midst of a crowd of strangers, but still isolated in a small, enclosed space. Of course such problems have been encountered in every country that has experienced rapid urbanization. But in the Soviet Union its effects were particularly traumatic, both because of the extreme brutality of the policies that brought about this forced migration to the cities and the inability of the cities to assimilate these new inhabitants. Quite the contrary, it was this massive influx of population from the countryside that changed the character of the cities.

The primary drawback of this new way of life, as far as sexuality is concerned, is the lack of privacy. Setting aside the obvious problems involved with communal living (or extramarital sex, for that matter), even a married couple who have a modern apartment of their own may still have to sleep in the same room with their children. This can make married life "constant torture," as a patient of mine once described it, for the couple themselves, and may also have unfortunate psychological consequences for their children. One of my patients was a twenty-one year old medical student from Vinnitsa; she told me that when she was seven, she had woken up suddenly in the middle of the night and seen her parents making love. Naturally she had no idea of what was actually going on, but she became so terrified that it was several months before the memory of the incident ceased to trouble her. Shortly thereafter she started masturbating habitually, a habit she was unable to break herself of, even after her marriage.

Student residences are even less hospitable to young lovers, married or otherwise, who insist on privacy. Some married students can carry on quite happily behind a bookcase or a folding screen, though a patient of mine, a young student, Lida T., had to be treated for nervous depression after a married couple moved into her room.

And even the tenants of the newer "Khrushchev apartments" can hardly feel that their privacy is secure. The interior walls are far from being soundproof, and a couple with no children who do not have their parents living with them have to consider the neighbors all the same. Their lovemaking may not be especially vocal, but they still may be greeted with icy stares, since sex, even when sanctioned by marriage, is not entirely respectable. All this may seem trivial, I know, at least to anyone who has never slept on a Russian box-mattress that groans loudly at every tremor from above.

What is to be done? A couple who prefers to make love in their own apartment may have to resort to subterfuge to avoid waking the children or scandalizing the neighbors. For example, they may wait until everyone within earshot has finally gone to sleep and then make love on the floor—tolerable perhaps as an occasional diversion but not as an invariable routine.

I knew a couple who got around this problem by hurrying home from work at lunch hour (not as obvious a strategem as it might seem if you recall that Russians almost never make love in the daytime). One day they decided to take a trip to the Black Sea resort of Alder, where they ended up sharing a communal tent, with another couple and their children on the other side of the cloth partition. This setback obliged them to spend the night on the beach, but one night while they were walking along the beach in search of a secluded spot, they were attacked by some twenty teenage hoodlums, members of a local gang who had terrorized even the police. The husband was knocked unconscious; his wife was raped.

But making love in the open air is not always fraught with such danger, and it may be the most practical solution to the problem—even if other arrangements have to be made during the long Russian winter. Also, though young lovers in the villages feel free to wander out to the woods and fields, the young Muscovite couple may feel that they are above that sort of thing, and the less status-conscious among them will find the parks already carpeted with bodies and the benches full of bloody-minded old pensioners who will send up the hue and cry at the sight of the chastest kiss.

Lovers often prefer to wait until dark; others may find the cemetery more congenial, and I recall that the old cemetery in Vinnitsa was extremely lively at night.

Most adventurous couples have come up with all sorts of novel solutions in the perpetual search for privacy. A Soviet taxicab is not only a mobile brothel but the functional equivalent of a motel room, as long as the couple slips the driver a bottle of vodka and agrees to pay the meter. Students in Moscow have discovered a more elaborate variation on this: two couples pool their resources and book all four berths in a compartment on the night train to Leningrad—a day's excursion plus two nights on the rails for the price of a round-trip ticket. Another possibility is the amusement park, such as Moscow's Gorky Park, where the Soviet equivalent of the ferris wheel and the cable-car ride can offer a few minutes of solitude, forty or fifty feet above the ground. I recall an incident that took place in the Park of Culture in Vinnitsa: a young music student named Alla and her boyfriend decided to take a ride on the ferris wheel, since they assumed they would be perfectly safe at an altitude of one-hundred fifty feet. However, no sooner had she taken her dress off than it was carried away by the wind, and they were both picked up by the police a few moments after they reached the ground.

We have already seen why a hotel room is out of the question; lovers might prevail upon their friends to lend them their apartments for an hour or two, but even then a hurried rendezvous in the average Soviet apartment certainly falls far short of the erotic ideal.

And if the search for privacy seems hopeless, this naturally suggests the possibility of group sex, particularly when two, three, or four couples have spent a stimulating evening together, drinking vodka, and then decide to spend the night in the same apartment. A patient of mine once took his girlfriend on a vacation trip to the Caucasus. At night they found themselves in the same tent with twenty-three other couples, making love or simply trying to sleep. When he awoke, his girlfriend was still asleep, on someone else's cot.

In a great many cities there have been reports of sexual orgies, with the participants publicly denounced by name. In Vinnitsa, for example, a self-styled "association" of twenty young men and woman convened regularly until their last meeting was interrupted by the police. It is in the Arctic settlements, though, that both alcoholism and group sex are especially prevalent. Norilsk, which lies above the Arctic circle, is notorious both for the rigors of the climate and the monotony of daily existence. Besides vodka, the inhabitants' main source of amusement are partner-swapping games like Norilsk Roulette, in which the women arrange themselves in a circle and get down in the "crayfish" position. The men work their way gradually around the circle; the player that describes the widest arc wins.

Lumberjacks in the Siberian logging camps, who may go for months without seeing a woman, find solace in vodka and choral singing, and especially in a form of mixed entertainment called the Choir, which involves both of these, plus a prostitute who is paid a considerable sum to take on fifty men or so in the course of a convivial evening. This sort of thing is fairly common not just in Siberia but in any closed, isolated male community, such as the oceanographic station at Gelenzhik in the Krasnodar region,* whose inhabitants are more or less permanently restricted to base because they are allegedly engaged in top secret scientific research.

I would like to return to the question of the differences between the urban and the rural ways of life today, particularly as they affect Soviet sexual behavior, though when I speak of the rural way of life, I should mention that this includes some thirty-seven hundred small provincial cities in which the quality and the style of life is essentially the same as in the countryside.

The problems of housing and the search for privacy are certainly not critical—the communal isba is still the center of peasant family life, but young lovers have woods and fields all around them. To be sure, there are deviant sexual practices which are universally associated with life on the farm, although this is a subject that is rarely mentioned in the Soviet Union. The penal code prescribes a penalty of up to two years' imprisonment for "cruelty to animals," and I met a young man in prison who had been sentenced under this article for copulating with a goat. I also recall that in a village not far from Vinnitsa a young man of otherwise impeccable habits was accused of

* Between the western slopes of the Caucasus and the Black Sea in the southern RSFSR. [Translators' note]

copulating with heifers. Because of his excellent work record, however, he got off with a suspended sentence.

Obviously all this is secondary to the essential question: can we really say that there is more sexual freedom in the countryside than in the cities? Certainly this is consistent with the historical evidence we have already examined, and with the popular opinion (which may not be openly expressed) that the Russian peasant enjoys more freedom and is healthier and closer to nature than the citydweller.

There are certain facts that appear to bear this out. For example, in 1957 the divorce rate in rural villages was only one twentieth of what it was in the cities (though admittedly the picture may have changed since then). Should we conclude that the peasant family has not been "corrupted by civilization," or at least not as much? More to the point, it seems that sex has not yet become a taboo subject, as it has in the cities. For example, we might consider the folksong form called *chastushki,* humorous four-line verses sung or improvised by a soloist and then picked up by the chorus. Even though every manifestation of "people's art" is zealously collected and documented in the Soviet Union, most of these *chastushki* (though still a vigorous part of peasant folklore) are too obscene to be published. Here are two fairly typical examples:

When I go by mother-in-law's,
I step up, bold as brass,
And dangle my cock through the window,
Turn 'round and show off my ass.
Ai-ee-*ya!* [falsetto shrieks and yelps]

What a shit my husband is,
He hasn't fucked me these ten years,
I'll run out to the fields and cry,
"I want to fuck, my little dears."
Ai-ee-*ya!*

The fact that sex can still be the subject of ribald humor and satire, even on this unsophisticated level, is undoubtedly a healthy sign; the all-night drinking parties at which they are intended to be sung are quite a different matter though. Alcoholism and drunkenness are even more pronounced a problem in the country than in the cities. Country people get together to sing *chastushki* and drink enormous quantities of vodka or *samogon'* (the fiery homemade brandy that is especially popular in the Ukraine). In my experience, such an evening of vodka and song is more likely to turn into a riot than a sexual bacchanal.

Thus the picture of bucolic harmony and simplicity that I suggested earlier needs to be modified, at least in certain respects. The idyllic visions of the Slavophiles and the Russian nationalists are always suspect insofar as they try to idealize the traditional way of life of the Russian countryside. But at least at one time it was possible to speak of a genuine peasant culture, with its own manners and customs, and its oral literature. Today the Russian countryside has the melancholy aspect of an abandoned battlefield, a landscape ravaged by war, though not so much as a result of World War II as of the war the Soviet state waged against its rural citizens—the civil war, the period of collectivization in particular—which literally destroyed the peasant culture in its most vital forms. Today the collective farmer in his village is as rootless and alienated as the rural migrant in the city, and thus we are presented with the paradox of a society with a substantial rural population (forty-four percent according to the 1970 census) in which the peasants who have remained on the land, as well as the victims of forced urbanization, have been both uprooted and culturally dislocated. In this sense, at least, the regime has succeeded in one of its principal objectives—to eliminate the social disparities between urban and rural life.

Thus we should not try to make too much of *chastushki* and the like. Though the peasant may live closer to nature, the material and social conditions of his life may still be more oppressive and brutalizing than anything the citydweller will ever experience.

First, there is the problem of loneliness, especially as it affects women. In 1970 there were only 824 men for every 1000 women in the rural districts of the RSFSR (as against 843 in the cities). In the countryside this means not only that a woman may not be able to find a husband, and thus will have to account her life a failure, it also means more work for women on the collective farms, in addition to their domestic chores. It is often said in the USSR, and with good reason, that the entire burden of collective farming falls on the shoulders of women.

Life is still very hard in the country. Until fairly recently peasants received virtually no cash payment for their labor. And once more—as he was in the eighteenth century—the peasant is still effectively bound to the land, since the introduction of the internal passport system (which only began in rural districts in 1975) has made it impossible for him to leave his village freely.

I know that the word *slave* may seem too harsh to many of my readers, but I think the following story will illustrate my point.

In the autumn of 1945, a few months after the end of the war, near-famine conditions still prevailed in the cities, though the countryside had largely been spared. An enormous labor force would be required to restore production in the coal mines of the Donets Basin in the Ukraine, though there were few who were willing to go down into the mines for the pitiful wages that were being offered. The Soviet planners decided to organize a temporary draft of peasant labor to reopen the Donbass mines. This was certainly not an unprecedented step, since the regime had long since learned to rely on the peasantry for reserve manpower; usually the labor incentives involved were no more than thinly disguised tactics of coercion. The peasants, the young women in particular, were terrified that they would end up being transferred to the Donbass, since all sorts of stories were circulating about the backbreaking labor and the wretched living conditions that awaited them there.

This story was told to me by one of my patients, a single woman who lived alone with her illegitimate son. The president of the collective farm in her village was a drunken skirt-chaser. She was called to his office one day, where he showed her a labor manifest with her name on it; she was one of the workers who was to be reassigned to the Donbass. "Make up your mind," he said to her. "Either you get down and make like a crayfish, or I'll call a cop and you'll be off to the coal mines." She chose the first alternative, and later gave birth to a child. Her son did not find out who his father was until he was already grown. After his natural son made two attempts on his life, the president of the collective farm finally fled to another region.

Even if this were only an exceptional case—and we shall see in the next chapter that such things are not at all exceptional—it could not have occurred at all if the country people had not been reduced to a state of virtual slavery, completely subject to the whims of petty village tyrants who still exercise total power over their lives.

Chapter 20
The Power Elite

When we consider the great and powerful men of this world—and especially of the shadow world of the Soviet Union—we are always tempted to read between the lines, to ferret out the spicy stories and the backstairs gossip that are not included in the authorized biography. But apart from the fact that these stories are usually of doubtful authenticity, they generally have little to tell us about the personality of the great man himself or of the sexual mores of the age and the country in which he lived.

The media in Western countries are sufficiently independent to be able to cast a harsh light on the peccadilloes of their political leaders from time to time. But the air of mystery that has always surrounded the private lives of the Soviet leadership makes one wonder if they were not engaged in top-secret scientific research in their off-duty hours. In fact, Lenin's platonic affair with Inessa Armand might just as well have been one of the less creditable episodes from the reign of Nero or Caligula judging from the guarded and secretive treatment the subject has received from Soviet historians. There has been some speculation to the effect that Lenin might have suffered from congenital syphilis (contracted by his father), which of course has been dutifully suppressed; I have even heard rumors of historians whose careers were ruined because they chanced upon one of these buried slanders while poking about in the archives.

In fact, we have seen that the subject of Lenin's sex life, assuming that it is of some intrinsic interest, is one that might be quickly exhausted by the conscientious researcher, and hardly compares with the private lives of the Borgias or Ivan the Terrible.

As for Stalin, it is sometimes assumed (perhaps through an unconscious association with his sixteenth-century predecessor) that the Kremlin was given over to continuous orgies and nameless debauchery during his reign, as in the days of Ivan himself. In fact, Stalin's private dissipations began and ended with vodka, and his sadistic cruelty was the source of purely mental rather than sexual pleasure—by all accounts this was the most refined aspect of his character. I tend to believe that, as with Lenin's fanaticism, Stalin's megalomania and paranoia were sufficient in themselves, and that neither of them had much time or energy left over for the pleasures of the flesh.

The career of Beria, on the other hand, has a great deal more to offer to devotees of backstairs gossip. Appointed NKVD chief in 1938, he planned to seize power on Stalin's death but was outmaneuvered by his rivals in the Politburo and shot in December 1953. Shortly thereafter a secret memorandum signed by Khrushchev was distributed to local Party organizations. For us this meant three hours of heavy reading, as I recall, and more than half of the memorandum was devoted to an account of Beria's sexual escapades. He was accused of having extorted sexual favors from numerous women, particularly actresses and ballerinas, and very young girls; a NKVD colonel called Sarkisov acted as his intermediary in these matters. Toward the end of his life he acquired a taste for young athletes and especially young redheads from the Svan region, the home of a Caucasian people who are notable for the strictness of their morals. In the course of the Party meetings that followed, all Party members were given to understand that one of their top leaders had in fact been nothing more than a vicious brigand and a pervert who had richly deserved to be shot.

The "case" against Beria brings up several interesting points. Though his sexual inclinations were not particularly original—there are certainly any number of men who have a secret weakness for actresses, ballerinas, or even redheaded Svans—the fact remains that Beria, for a time at least, possessed virtually unlimited power, and when it came to gratifying these banal sexual appetities, the entire apparatus of Stalin's secret police was effectively at his disposal. Abducting young girls (which is how Beria acquired his wife, Nina, when she was sixteen), retaining a high-ranking police officer as a pimp, and sending his subordinates off on raids like a Caucasian bandit chieftain—all this can serve quite well as the image of arbitrary Stalinist terror.

The way in which Beria was "unmasked," as they say in the Soviet Union, is also quite interesting. First, as we have already seen, accusing someone of sexual irregularities is still one of the most effective and damaging charges that can be brought, though in Beria's case, these were far from being the most serious of the crimes he committed as NKVD chief. Second, a Party leader is allowed to indulge in all manner of sexual escapades if he is careful to preserve appearances and keep his activities well hidden as long as he remains in power. At the moment of his disgrace, however, every incriminating detail of his private life will be used to condemn him, and the devoted leader of the people will be instantly transformed into a monster of wickedness and depravity. In addition, the fatal bolt always falls from above—by the direct agency or at least with the approval of his colleagues in the Party leadership. The reader will appreciate the difference between this and the more familiar Western brand of political scandal, which may bring about a politician's downfall but does not suddenly materialize, after the fact, to provide a pretext for his removal. And any political figure may be the target of such a scandal, however blameless his private life and however few his political enemies, since the accusation is not brought by the party in power but by another power altogether—the press.

I would like to develop this theme not just in terms of the private lives of a few top leaders but in the more general context of Soviet society. The Soviet elite, the privileged class, if you will, comprises no more than a (relative) handful of people, perhaps 500,000 in all. They enjoy a standard of living that is certainly luxurious, though not widely advertised, and all the perquisites of rank which the ordinary citizen is not even aware of—unlimited bank credit, sumptuous villas on the Black Sea or in any other choice location, exemption from the normal rationing restrictions, deluxe consumer goods which are only sold in special stores, and free access to the artifacts of Western culture: all of these things are not acquired with money but by means of influence. The upper stratum of the power elite includes marshals, admirals, the managers of large state enterprises, government ministers, presidents of the various Academies of Science, Lenin Prize winners, famous names in the arts including a few writers, regional Party secretaries and the Party secretaries of the union republics. I should stress the particular significance of this last category; the influence of these provincial magnates is widely felt, and the power wielded by the Party secretary within his domain is almost unlimited.

More than any other social group—and more than the privileged castes in any Western country—the Soviet elite are particularly shy of any kind of publicity where their private lives are concerned. Divorce, for example, can spell the end of an *apparatchik*'s * career, since "moral stability" is a prime criterion for social advancement. An ambitious bureaucrat would thus do well to hold on to his wife—even if they can no longer bear each other—and seek his personal happiness elsewhere, outside his "public" private life. Of course his amorous adventures cannot be kept entirely secret, since the secret police and the upper echelons of his department will still be aware of what he is up to. But this is the real secret of the bureaucrat's secret life. He can be as "dissolute" and "morally unstable" as he cares to in private, as long as he conforms in his outward, public demeanor. And once again, the Soviet official has one immense advantage over his Western counterpart: he has nothing to fear from the press or from public opinion.

Thus there are two factors—almost unlimited power in the exercise of their public responsibilities and this cloak of invisibility that shields them in the pursuit of their private pleasures—which are highly conducive to the sort of behavior that one associates more with an Ottoman pasha than a Soviet "builder of Communism." The prevailing cynicism of the Soviet elite is perhaps best illustrated by a facetious observation made by one of my patients, the manager of a large factory, who was impotent and had to come to my office for a hormone injection every three weeks if he expected to have any kind of sex life at all. As he put it, "Our faults are not all that serious, since we know quite well what they are. As for me, I've been practicing true communism for a long time now, since I've always subscribed to the motto, 'From each according to his abilities, to each according to his needs.' "

* A career bureaucrat, or Party hack. [Translators' note]

The possibility of maintaining a private, state-subsidized harem of secretaries, film starlets, and waitresses is certainly something that distinguishes the sexual perquisites of the Soviet elite (by several orders of magnitude) from the interoffice liaisons of the Western business executive. However, the point that I am making here is not that all Soviet officials are debauchees and degenerates, but that their privileged position makes it easier for them to lead the kind of life which the average Soviet citizen could not even dream of.

The Soviet privileged caste also enjoys an immunity from judicial prosecution—not absolutely perhaps, but certainly to a degree that is unknown in the West. I will just mention one example among many thousands of similar cases: a judge in Vinnitsa by the name of Chaikovsky tried to strangle his fiancee when he discovered that she was pregnant (he was already planning a more advantageous match with the daughter of a minister in the Byelorussian government). No criminal charges were brought against him. In fact, he was later promoted to the post of vice-president of the Supreme Court of the Ukraine, and today he sits in judgment in the ancient city of Kiev.

We have already seen how the ranks of Soviet officialdom, especially on the local level, were filled in the early twenties by opportunists and parvenus who generally behaved like petty tyrants of the worst stripe. Apart from the examples given earlier, I can also refer the reader to the archives of the city of Smolensk, which fell into the hands of the Germans during the war and are now to be found in the United States.*

In the chapter on prostitution I mentioned the private brothels which cater to the sexual appetites of the Soviet elite. During the Khrushchev era, for example, an enterprising fellow called Shegin had turned his private dacha outside Moscow into a retreat for top-level bureaucrats and other privileged paying guests, including artists, writers, and generals. Young actresses and women athletes were also encouraged to visit, as well as prostitutes and the wives of lesser officials who were eager to advance their husbands' careers. Shegin, as the organizer of these Babylonian rites, turned a considerable profit, but two of his clients who were caught *in flagrante* were instantly relieved of their posts—Alexandrov, propaganda chief of the Soviet Central Committee, and his deputy, Tsvetkov. Worse than that, Alexandrov was packed off to Central Asia to taste the bitter bread

* See Merle Fainsod, *Smolensk Under Soviet Rule*, Cambridge, Mass., 1958.

of exile (which is to say that he was awarded the chair of Marxist-Leninist studies at the University of Frunze in Kirgizia).

Of course, the power of the local Party chieftain and the petty officer is sufficient to accommodate every sexual taste. A Party official in Vinnitsa arranged for the son of one of my patients to be enrolled in the local kindergarten (ordinarily a very difficult feat), and since the boy's mother was a lesbian, her benefactor only asked in exchange that she and her lover put on a private demonstration of lesbian lovemaking for him in his villa. Another patient of mine worked as a custodian in a number of houses and rest homes that were reserved for vacationing officials; he told me that full-length mirrors were often built into the urinals in such places, "because the ones who are impotent still get a thrill out of watching themselves take a piss."

My teacher, Professor Chernyshevsky, once told me about a prostitute who was particularly sought after among the elite because she had four nipples, and in the Vinnitsa prison in 1974 I met two dwarves, father and daughter, named Berdishevsky, who were arrested for selling three gold coins on the black market. The elder Berdishevsky told me that "the bigshots" occasionally came to his house to pick up his daughter, who had gained a certain reputation as an erotic novelty. Her father had been quite pleased by this, since they always treated her to a hearty meal before they brought her home.

Occasionally, though, these escapades may infringe on the rights of other persons of privilege, at which point they are considered a serious affront to public decency. During the sixties Professor Van Rejwe, then serving as Moscow correspondent for a Dutch newspaper, and his wife were invited to a banquet in the city of Orel. The regional Party secretary, who was already tolerably drunk, apparently was quite taken with the professor's wife, and forgetting that she was a foreigner and the wife of a journalist besides, he began to paw at her; his crude flirtations almost resulted in a minor riot. In another, rather more serious incident the soccer star Streltsov was brought to trial for the rape of the daughter of a Soviet ambassador by the name of Yudin; had the victim's social credentials been less impressive, Streltsov might well have gone free or at least faced a lesser charge. In the cirçumstances, however, he had attacked a member of his own caste, which was unforgivable. Similarly in 1956, after Molotov's son and the son of the well-known writer Alexander Fadayev * raped and murdered the daughter of a famous artist, Fadayev himself committed suicide.

Even the luminaries of the Soviet Academies of Science are not necessarily above an occasional attempt at sexual extortion. Academician Grashchenkov, for example, obliged the female staff members in his research institute to satisfy him sexually if they expected to continue their scientific careers (though since he was impotent, this involved no more than fellatio). One of his assistants once slapped his face publicly at an institute staff meeting and announced that she would rather give up her career than go on serving as a "sexual doormat." Another notorious old roué was Academician Myasnikov, director of the Institute of Physical Therapy, a teaching hospital sponsored by the Soviet Academy of Medicine whose facilities are largely reserved for the Soviet elite. It was his custom to summon the more attractive students to his house to take their exams, and since a failing grade would mean withdrawal of their scholarships, most of them were forced to resign themselves to this arrangement.

I am not claiming that the powers and privileges of the Soviet elite are universally subject to such abuses as these, and, as in every country, there are a great many quiet family men among them. I have simply described the ways in which this kind of power is often abused, and the ways in which these men are almost tacitly encouraged to behave toward their subordinates.

At this point I would like to enlarge the scope of this inquiry by moving down a few rungs on the social ladder. Particularly in such a hierarchical society as the Soviet Union, the official who is tyrannized by his masters will always be strongly tempted to treat his subordinates—or anyone who does not actually outrank him in the hierarchy—as a slave, and so the contagion spreads throughout the entire system.

The sixty-nine year old manager of an enamelware factory in Khmelnik kept his harem of factory girls, most of whom were peasants from nearby villages, in hand by threatening them with dismissal, or at least reassignment to one of the more unpleasant jobs in the factory. A Vinnitsa factory manager confined his attentions to

* Popular novelist and an important figure in the Stalinist literary establishment. Alcoholism and his despondency over Stalin's posthumous disgrace may also have contributed to his suicide. [Translators' note]

his current secretary, and of course his office was outfitted with the traditional couch. He kept a supply of condoms in his office safe—which did not prevent his estranged wife and a disaffected former secretary from getting some of their own back by rubbing them all with garlic.

We have already seen the collective-farm president in the role of local satrap, which only confirms the general observation that even the smallest parcel of power can be corrupting. Several of my fellow inmates in the camp at Kharkov had been sentenced for killing men who attacked their wives or fiancees; one of their stories is relevant here. One day this man had heard a woman's scream coming from the milking sheds, where his wife worked. When he arrived on the scene, he discovered the president of the collective farm tearing off his wife's clothes. He stunned him with a blow of his fist, and kicked him to death. Curiously, the other milkmaids working close by had not taken any notice of what was happening; for them the incident was not in the least unusual. I recall a similar story, which took place in a village in the Kharkov region, of several women who castrated the president of their collective farm after his sexual depredations finally became too much to endure. They too were sentenced to the camps.

Incidents of this kind have even found their way into literature, which is indeed remarkable. There is an episode in *The Cathedral* by the Ukrainian writer Honchar, for example, in which a young girl is raped by the head of her collective-farm brigade. She is disgraced in the eyes of the other villagers and forced to leave the village when she can no longer bear her shame.

CHAPTER 21
The Camps

The classless society is divided into three classes:
Those who have already been in the camps.
Those who are there right now.
Those who'll be there soon.
—*Popular Soviet saying*

WE HAVE finally arrived at the most somber and painful subject in this book—the forced-labor camps, where all of the most disturbing aspects of Soviet sexuality are raised to the highest power. The life of the camps exposes with brutal clarity all of the hidden mechanisms of "prison sexuality," which, as I have already stressed on several occasions, can be observed in a diffuse and modified form in the Soviet population as a whole.

This is one aspect of camp life which the literature of the Gulag often passes over in silence and which thus remains almost completely unknown. One might argue that the authors of these *samizdat* accounts have set themselves a gigantic task in cataloguing all the horrors of the camps, but I believe that the explanation for their silence on this one subject is essentially psychological. The sexual taboos promulgated by the regime have finally won over the population, and even Soviet dissidents, however determined they might be not to conceal one bit of evidence, have held their tongues simply for the sake of decency.

Soviet labor camps are officially classified into four categories, according to the severity of discipline that prevails in a particular camp; thus there are general-regime (commonly known as soft-regime), reinforced-regime, strict-regime, and special-regime camps. I myself was sentenced to a reinforced-regime camp, and from May 1974 to March 1977 I was successively an inmate of the Vinnitsa prison, various transit prisons, and finally "corrective labor colony" ITK-12 at Kharkov. I have every reason to believe that the incidents I am about to describe might have taken place in any camp or prison in the Soviet Union, and certainly this impression was confirmed for me by fellow inmates who had served time in other camps.

When I arrived at ITK-12, I was immediately dispatched to the camp infirmary. As is the general rule in such places, the doctor's essential role was to "unmask malingerers" and send them back to work, even if these "malingerers" were clearly in need of medical attention. On top of that, the incompetence of the camp doctors was truly appalling. As hirelings of the KGB, they had sworn a somewhat different Hippocratic oath, and their first duty was to serve the regime and the camp administration, not to heal the sick. At any rate, my presence was a great comfort to them (in case they were ever actually obliged to treat a patient), though I left the infirmary a short time later after the camp authorities received orders that I was to be given the most arduous work assignment that was available (this "corrective labor colony" served in fact as a small armaments factory).

I still carried on a fairly active medical practice among my fellow inmates, since I was able to advise them on the best strategy to adopt when they went on sick call. For example, an inmate who had suffered an appendicitis attack was likely to be dismissed as a malingerer unless he started screaming bloody murder and insisted that they operate on him immediately (and continued to do so until they did). In general, abdominal disorders were blithely ignored by the camp doctors; in 1975, an inmate called Sorokin died of an ulcer simply because a doctor had refused to treat him. Apart from these "bootleg" consultations, though, I was occasionally sent for by the head of the infirmary to establish a diagnosis or to assist with some emergency procedure.

Passive Homosexuality

Homosexuality is extremely common in the camps, whether practiced "voluntarily" (by necessity) or involuntarily (by force). And of course the Soviet authorities even refuse to admit that this is the case. When I took this up on occasion with the camp commandant, or his adjutants, the guard officers or squad leaders, they replied as one man that homosexuality did not exist in this camp, or any other: "Homosexuality is punished by the full rigor of the law, the maximum penalty is five years,* and that's certainly no secret around here."

When I protested that certain inmates (of the "untouchable" caste whom I shall be discussing shortly) were being physically abused and systematically raped by other inmates, they all replied in chorus, like a battery of little propaganda loudspeakers: "And where did you ever get that idea? Soviet power would never tolerate such an assault on human dignity!" When KGB colonels arrived on inspection visits from Moscow, Kharkov, or Kiev, and I tried to point out to them that homosexuality was rampant and rape an everyday occurrence in ITK-12, I got the same response: "Rape? Homosexuality? You've got a very active imagination. Homosexuality is so severely punished in our country things like that could never happen!"

In fact, homosexuality is just as common in Soviet labor camps as it is in American prisons, and probably more so. And certainly if this were simply a matter of homosexual relations between consenting partners, this might give us something to think about, but it would not be a source of outrage and indignation. However, I only encountered one "genuine" homosexual in ITK-12 (a man called Gupalo) who was sexually attracted to other men before his arrest and imprisonment. On the other hand, there were no less than three hundred open or covert "homosexuals" (out of a total inmate population of fifteen hundred), that is, men who had been raped by other inmates or forcibly recruited into a sordid network of terror, intimidation, and slavery which again was controlled largely (though not exclusively) by their fellow inmates.

Here is a typical story from the annals of ITK-12. On April 9, 1976, at 10 A.M., a thirty-six year old inmate, Anatol Shalapukhin, threw himself in front of a truck that was leaving the work area with its cargo of air filters for tanks. Why? Shalapukhin had lost his left hand in an accident; he could not defend himself when a gang of

* Any homosexual act between adults may be punished by a term of five years' imprisonment; the maximum penalty of eight years (mentioned at the beginning of Part III) is reserved for cases of homosexual rape, or those in which the defendant takes advantage of his superior age or authority. [Translators' note]

"common laws" * forced a gag into his mouth, dragged him into the camp bathhouse, and raped him. Realizing that this was only the first of many outrages he was likely to endure, he killed himself.

In February 1977 a young worker from Kharkov by the name of Sivtsov was brutally sodomized by twelve inmates, not so much because he had a pleasant face and rounded buttocks (a powerful attraction for the camp rapist), but because he had been causing trouble for the camp authorities. Such incidents often took place with the active connivance of the camp authorities, and the guard officers and noncoms often tried to intimidate particularly unruly prisoners with threats like, "If you keep acting smart and mouthing off like this, we'll throw you in the hole and turn you into a faggot." Captain Zakharchenko was fond of using the camp argot expression "We're going to buggerize you [*opederastim tebya*]." At any rate, the procedure was simple enough—the recalcitrant inmate would be locked in a punishment cell with a homosexual rapist recruited from among the "common laws." But the humiliation and the horror of the rape itself was only the beginning of his punishment, since as soon as word of the incident spread around the camp (which is to say, almost immediately), the victim would find himself ostracized by the entire camp and instantly relegated to the ranks of the "untouchables."

In 1972 A., a twenty-six year old musician from Kharkov, applied for an emigration visa. He was informed that his visa had been granted, and he and his brother were requested to pick it up at the OVIR [Office of Visas and Registrations]. On the way they were accosted by two plainclothes agents who picked a fight with them in the street. The brothers were charged with "hooliganism" and aggravated assault, and both were sentenced to four years. In ITK-12 A. kept his dignity, refused to kowtow to the camp authorities, protested against the maltreatment of other inmates (one man, for example, was forced to strip naked in below thirty-degree weather during a "routine search"), and finally renounced his Soviet citizenship in writing. After subjecting him to various threats and harassments, the camp authorities decided to break him completely—this according to the testimony of the "common laws" themselves who had been selected for the task. A group of them dragged him into

* Inmates who have been sentenced for common-law crimes, such as robbery or murder, also generically known as "thieves" (*blatnye*), as distinct from "white-collar criminals" (*bytoviki*), and "politicals." [Translators' note]

the lavatory—a separate building on the camp perimeter. A. struggled desperately, and shouted out to the leader of the group, "I know who you are, Serge Kupenko! If you rape me, I'll kill myself—but not before I've written to my parents about what you've done to me, and that'll give you something to think about while you rot in this place for another fifteen years." The effect of this was not lost on Kupenko and the others, and A. was released unharmed.

The dissident Alexander Bolonkin has provided us with a *samizdat* account of his interrogation and imprisonment in the Siberian city of Ulan-Ude. The examining magistrates repeatedly threatened him with torture, rape, and even murder in order to obtain a confession. He received similar threats from his cellmate, a man called Oleichik, who told him he had been enlisted for this "special mission."

But as I have said, homosexual violence was a routine part of life in the camps, not just an extreme form of punishment. At night in the barracks we could hear screams that quickly died away as a gang of rapists threw a blanket over a fresh victim and smothered his face. There were usually five of them—four to hold the victim's arms and legs while the fifth raped him. An inmate who had been forcibly sodomized by other inmates was referred to as a "pederast," and the word itself was the deadliest of insults. In fact, an inmate once attacked a guard with an iron bar (and had fifteen years tacked onto his sentence for "recidivism") because he had called him a pederast. I once risked death myself, quite unwittingly, by stepping too close to this abyss of prejudice; I was explaining to a group of inmates that the word *pederast*, which literally means after all "a lover of young boys," should properly be used to refer to an active homosexual. At this, a look of horror came over the face of one of my companions, and he gravely advised me never to repeat what I had said, particularly in front of the "others" (that is, the "common laws," the ruling elite of the inmate population). The active homosexuals among them would take this not just as a slander but a mortal offense, which would have to be avenged in cold blood. Though it seems incredible, the homosexual rapist is not considered a homosexual at all; he is still a "normal," even respected member of the camp community, while his victim is treated as a subhuman creature, a denizen of the lowest circle of the camp inferno.

But at the same time that the victim of a homosexual rape is hated and despised by the entire camp, far be it for him to refuse to "stick out his ass," as the camp jargon has it. When I arrived at ITK-12 in April 1975, I was startled to see that one of the pederasts, a twenty-two year old called Gradov, was covered with bruises. I was informed that Gradov had repeatedly refused to cooperate with a gang of "common laws" who were intent on buggery, and each time he had been savagely beaten. One day he was brought to the infirmary, bleeding from the anus as the aftermath of a gang rape. I was often called on to treat such cases; the "common laws" never missed an opportunity to express their hatred for their victims, to "assert themselves" at their expense, by spitting in their faces, beating them, and literally trampling them underfoot.

Outcasts and Untouchables

I have referred to the victims of homosexual rape as the "untouchables" of the camp, and this is by no means a fanciful comparison. The total segregation of the pederasts is carried out by the inmates themselves. A camp barracks is a self-governing community, as far as its internal affairs are concerned; the prisoners have their own barracks chiefs and brigade chiefs and decide on the arrangement of their bunks, even on the placement of interior walls and partitions. As far as the camp authorities are concerned, these are purely practical decisions, best left to the inmates themselves, and they are well aware of the barracks caste system, and perfectly content to ignore it. Thus there is a particular section of each barracks set aside for the pederasts (in our camp they were particularly numerous in barracks number three), just as there are certain tables in the messhalls, seats in the latrine, and even basins in the washhouse that are reserved for them exclusively. They are also assigned to the dirtiest, most dangerous, and unhealthiest jobs. In ITK-12 they linked tank treads together on a sort of primitive assembly line, a task that was performed in a large open shed, exposed to the weather on all sides; an assignment to this kind of "corrective labor" in winter was a sentence to slow death from exposure.

The caste system was so firmly established that it almost never occurred to anyone to question it. The rape victim simply sought out his new bunk in the barracks, sat down to eat with the untouchables in the messhall, and fell in with their work detail in the morning. His life had been totally transformed overnight, and this should make it clearer why Captain Zakharchenko's threats of "buggerization" were not to be lightly defied. I know of one case, though, where the roles were reversed. A notorious sadistic noncom called Ivaniak (who has already made an appearance in our discussion of exhibitionism) was set upon one night and raped by a group of inmates. Shortly afterward he received his discharge; in the Soviet Union when a servant of the State is discovered to have abused his authority, the usual consequence is immediate promotion. But Ivaniak had fallen victim to the caste system; he was no longer a KGB man but a "pederast."

There is a third caste in camp society, apart from the "respectable" inmates and the untouchables. These are the "outcasts" (literally, *opustivchesya,* "deserted ones"), inmates who have had some sort of physical contact with a pederast (though I should specify *nonsexual* contact, since the active "common law" homosexual cannot be stripped of his patent of nobility). Even if this "contact" is inadvertent, an inmate who sits down next to a pederast, accepts a cigarette from him, or touches him is instantly and irrevocably degraded. Here we see the particular relevance of the term *untouchable,* since the pederast's defiling touch is sufficient to transform a "high-caste" inmate into an outcast; from that moment on he will only be permitted to associate with his fellow outcasts in the barracks and in the messhall.

Here again, the camp authorities are quick to take advantage of the strictures of the caste system. A troublesome character called Blashchuk needed to be taken down a peg or two, and accordingly three outcasts linked arms and charged into him full tilt; Blashchuk automatically became an outcast himself, and the three others finally received their food parcels, which had been held up by the authorities as an incentive for performing this small service.

I only recall a single case in which the pederasts made the system work to their advantage—in what was no less than a class uprising. The camp had received a barrel of marinated Norwegian sardines, and such treats were allocated on a strictly first-come, first-serve basis. But this time the pederasts had passed the word among themselves, and punching and kicking furiously, they stormed their way through to the head of the line. Once the pederasts had served themselves from the barrel, the rest of the inmates lost their appetite for sardines.

Since homosexual rape and the ostracism of "pederasts" is actively or tacitly encouraged by the authorities for their own purposes, when a pederast tries to protest against any of these abuses, he is invariably ignored. In January 1977 an inmate called Kosolapov was stabbed to death after he refused to "stick out his ass"; the incredible brutality of this crime itself was only equalled by the callous indifference of the camp authorities.

In the pretrial detention block of the Vinnitsa prison I met a gentle and obliging young man called Moroz from the village of Kalinovka. I saw him again on the day I arrived at ITK-12; he was sitting behind the flimsy partition that separated the untouchables from the other inmates in the messhall, obviously in a state of deep depression. An inmate called Kirilyuk, who had been his cellmate in the Kiev transit prison, told me what had happened. They had spent ten days in the transit prison; Moroz was seriously undernourished, and a group of "common laws" took it upon themselves to feed him. On the seventh day Kirilyuk was awakened by his friend's cries for help; he jumped out of his bunk and began to pound on the door for the guard. The rapists were laughing and shouting at Moroz, "What did you expect? You thought we were going to feed your face for a week for nothing?" When the duty officer peeked through the gloryhole, Kirilyuk begged him to do something, but he simply laughed. "Let 'em go ahead and fuck him if they want it all that bad."

The caste system is not the only form of homosexual exploitation in the camps. Some of the more attractive pederasts became the "punks" of the leading members of the criminal elite and so were better fed and better treated than the rest. There was also a homosexual prostitution ring, controlled by a bearlike young man of thirty called Volga, who owed his position as vice lord of ITK-12 to his enormous physical strength and cunning. The price for a session with one of Volga's protégés was a ruble, a can of food, or a pack of cigarettes; the more popular pederasts cost five rubles, even ten for those who were willing to engage in fellatio after being sodomized by the client.

The prostitutes were invariably called by women's names—Genechka, Svetochka—or even the sort of affectionate nicknames that are given to peasant girls, such as Yogodka ("Little Mulberry"). When an inmate suggested to his companions, "Let's go over to Volga's," Volga would appear and greet his customers, take payment in advance, and ask them to wait. "She'll be with you in a minute"—while he went off to find one of the pederasts from his stable. If the latter refused to comply (for example, if his rectum was still sore after servicing twelve customers the previous day), Volga did not resort to elaborate entreaties but would simply respond with a punch in the face and "Come on, then, hop to it!"

Volga's was not the only floating brothel in ITK-12, merely the most successful; the others were set up in barracks rooms (with a few blankets strung up to ensure the customers' privacy) or in the camp washhouse, which contained two large rooms, each provided with ten wash basins. One of these, known as the "fuckhouse" *(yebalnik)*,* was reserved exclusively for pederasts and their customers at certain times of the day. Venereal disease, particularly gonorrhea, was rife in our camp, and one might hear an inmate remark to his companion, "Watch out for that one—she's got the clap." But a pederast who had contracted gonorrhea would still be assured, "You'll be sticking it out for us again as soon as you've got rid of that dose!"

The prostitutes themselves were entitled to a share of the proceeds, with the rest being divided between the barracks slush fund and Volga himself, or one of his colleagues. Volga also enjoyed the customary pimp's privilege of unlimited sexual access to his protégés, and certainly none of them dared to refuse him. His authority in the camp was in many ways as great as any of the guards' (who often availed themselves of the same privileges, by the way).

And what are the effects of this system of sexual violence and exploitation on the victims themselves? Most passive homosexuals in the camps are stripped of every shred of human dignity; their faces are frozen masks that can only express pain, or the brutish insensitivity to pain that is their only protection. Some manage to adapt to their situation, and even seem to derive a certain pleasure from it, and others, more concerned with the material side of things, assume the air of hardened professionals—"I turned three tricks today."

In most cases the victims of the caste system will never enjoy a "normal" sexual life on the outside, though in my opinion this is not because they learn to derive any particular pleasure from being sodomized in the camps, but because they have been degraded and dehumanized, and they have internalized the camp society's view of them as pariahs and untouchables.

It also is true, as I mentioned in an earlier chapter, that a certain percentage of their tormentors, the rapists and active homosexuals of

* From *yebat'* ("fuck") + *umyvalnik* ("wash basin"). [Translators' note]

the camps, continue to engage in homosexual activities after their release. But essentially, for Volga and his cronies, homosexuality is simply the lesser of two evils (abstinence being the greater), a temporary distraction and a source of revenue and power. They speak openly, even boastfully of their homosexual exploits, though they will still sleep with a woman, given the chance. They feel that they have every right to satisfy their sexual needs as best they can, and the exploitation of the pederasts is only a way of passing the time until they regain their freedom.

As for the caste system itself, it is true that every closed community develops a rigid hierarchical structure. But the unwritten laws that govern the sexual life of the camps are truly remarkable, to say the least, for their scrupulous attention to detail, for their severity, and for their savagery. And we might well be tempted to see in this a microcosm of Soviet society. The way that underworld kingpins like Volga behave toward the pederasts and the outcasts is *(mutatis mutandis)* a bit like the way that the members of the Soviet elite behave toward their social inferiors—in either case, they regard them as so much human cattle. The rigid and closed caste system is equally typical of the Soviet elite, who maintain themselves in splendid isolation from their ordinary countrymen. Finally, that process by which the individual is transformed into an "outcast," instantly and without warning, is equally reminiscent of the way in which the ordinary Soviet citizen may suddenly be visited by all kinds of misfortunes, may be automatically deserted by his friends and associates, when the State begins to take a serious interest in his affairs. Whether he has become a dissident or requested to emigrate to Israel, he is and will always remain an outcast.

Political Prisoners

Theoretically there is no such thing in the USSR, so the title of "political" is purely honorary. The "politicals" are not really integrated into any particular group, and certainly their sexual activities are considerably less conspicuous than those of the "common laws." The authorities still make every effort to disperse the dissidents among the "common laws" in the barracks, but the two groups do not ordinarily have a great deal to do with each other. In fact, most of the "common laws" are barely literate, and they tend to respect the dissidents for their education. For example, as a doctor I was regarded as the camp oracle, and every day I was besieged with dozens of questions, ranging from "Who is Aphrodite?" to "How long is Soviet power going to last?" The "common laws' " respect for the dissidents as a group, as well as their acquired immunity against political propaganda, goes a long way toward frustrating the old Stalinist tactic of setting the two groups at each others' throats, and the "common laws" are less and less inclined to join the authorities in their crusade against anti-Soviet agitation.

To conclude this discussion of the caste system and homosexuality in the camps, I might mention that both have a long history in the Soviet Union. According to Valery Chalidze, in the early twenties inmates were already seducing young men, and their cast-off lovers would be despised by the entire community. Homosexuality was extremely widespread in the thirties and forties, and it began to take on the violent form that it has retained to the present day; now a young man would be "seduced" with a knife at his throat, and the fact that very young boys were being sentenced to the labor camps only aggravated these pathological trends.

Visitation Rights

And what about heterosexuality in the camps? In theory married inmates have the right to conjugal visits (assuming that their wives are not in the camps themselves), although in practice this depends on the camp disciplinary regime and the good graces of the camp authorities. In ITK-12 we were legally entitled to four visits a year, two of them very short, during which inmates could only see their wives "through the glass." (I should mention here that special visiting days were set aside for the pederasts on the first of every month, since it was naturally unthinkable that they should be allowed to mingle with the other inmates on such occasions.) There was also a building with eight small rooms that was provided for our two annual conjugal visits (remember that there were fifteen hundred of us, however). The conjugal visit was supposed to last from one to three days, but in reality only the camp stool pigeons were permitted to spend more than a single day with their wives. In strict-regime camps these conjugal visits were limited to one a year, and in special-regime camps they were not permitted at all.

The camp authorities generally made it as difficult as possible for inmates to receive visits from their wives, and permission was likely to be withheld on the slightest pretext. For example, an inmate's wife had divorced him (a petition for divorce is granted automatically when the spouse is sentenced to more than three years' imprisonment), but she still wanted to "help him out" by visiting him from time to time. Her request was turned down. Only inmates who are legally married are entitled to conjugal visits, and girlfriends, fianceés (and ex-wives) need not apply.

Naturally a number of highly implausible schemes have been devised to evade this regulation. For example, a highly sexed young man of twenty-two ended up in ITK-12 after he became involved in a brawl over a woman (his fiancée, in fact). His mother insisted that he be allowed to receive visits from his fiancée, and of course this was out of the question. Unwilling to see her only son suffer the agonies of sexual deprivation (this was no exaggeration in his case), she began to have sexual relations with him herself on family visiting days, and she proclaimed her sacrifice from the housetops, in order to shame the authorities.

But of course this system is more subject to abuse than to evasion. We have already encountered Serge Kupenko, the "common law" inmate who led the abortive assault on the musician A. On June 26, 1976, Kupenko received a visit from his brother. In the corridor he struck up a conversation with a forty-five year old woman, also visiting her brother, then waited until there was no one else in sight and produced a knife that he had stolen from the kitchen where the inmates' families prepare their meals. He forced his terrified captive into the room where his brother was waiting, and they both raped her. Kupenko was only twenty-three at the time, though he had already spent five years in ITK-12.

The wives of "politicals" in particular are subjected to all sorts of indignities by the guards, which is simply another way of discouraging conjugal visitation. The Ukrainian dissident writer Svetlichny gives a *samizdat* account of this practice:

> My wife came to visit me in September 1973; she was not merely searched, but completely stripped, forced to crouch down on the

> floor, and, in short, to submit to a whole series of extremely humiliating procedures. The wife of the political prisoner Antoniuk met with the same kind of treatment.

My wife was also subjected to this elaborate "body search," as are the wives of all political prisoners. Here again we see sadism and sexual aggression, this time on the part of the guards, as an assertion of personal authority, rape as an exercise in power. For example, the guards are in the habit of soliciting sexual favors from the inmates' wives in return for the "favor" of arranging a visit or expediting a food parcel (in other words, of allowing the inmates to enjoy their legal rights). One inmate stabbed his wife to death after a particularly sadistic guard informed him what the price of her visit had been.

In 1976, we learned that Captain Glyevoi (deputy commandant of ITK-12) and Major Pyatochenko had promised to perform these "favors" for an inmate's wife, but instead had driven her to an isolated spot on the outskirts of Kharkov, raped her, and abandoned her. A short time after this incident, Glyevoi was promoted to the rank of major.

Another inmate requested permission to attend his wife's funeral, or at least to be able to say his last farewells while she was laid out in her coffin. The authorities were inclined to be compassionate—the inmate was permitted to watch, without leaving the camp, while the funeral procession filed by on the road outside.

It is difficult to imagine the effects of sexual deprivation on those inmates who do not even have the right of conjugal visitation. A single example should suffice: one of the inmates, a bachelor, wrote to a woman friend and asked her to send him an unwashed pair of her underpants. The fragrance of this precious token sent him into masturbatory ecstasies every night, and since he made no attempt to conceal this practice from his fellow inmates, he was able to share this vicarious pleasure with them; the rental fee was a can of food or a piece of bread. Before long the garment became shopworn, and he began to receive complaints, so he was obliged to write off for another pair.

I have already mentioned the free women workers in the camps who prostitute themselves to the inmates. I recall one occasion on which two inmates came back seething and indignant after an encounter with one of the women who worked in the storeroom—she had collected fifty rubles in advance, before they could discover for themselves that she was having her menstrual period. One of her coworkers was married to a fireman who was impotent and extremely jealous. One day she started abusing him publicly, calling him a "pederast," and added, "I can't see why you don't want anyone to fuck me, since you can't do anything about it yourself."

Sadism and Self-Mutilation

It may appear that the sadistic brutality of the KGB is already too well documented to require any further illustration here. However, I believe it would be impossible to condemn these outrages too strongly, and I will simply mention two incidents from the annals of ITK-12. Our commandant, Major Proshchin, kept a straitjacket on hand in his office, so that the pleasures of administering a beating would not be marred by the slightest risk. I knew two inmates, Tolmachev and Semitsvetov, who were singled out for this treatment; Semitsvetov subsequently slashed his wrists. Ivaniak was not the only camp sadist who was called to account for his crimes. Just before I arrived at ITK-12, another noncom had been burned alive in the course of a short-lived uprising; several inmates were later shot in reprisal.

Self-mutilation is commonly practiced by camp inmates as a form of protest or perhaps merely for the sake of notoriety, though it is difficult to assign a definite psychological motive to such a desperate and terrible act. Admiral Nikolai Shcherbakov, a distinguished inmate of one of the camps in Mordvinia,* actually cut off both his ears (having first covered them with tatoos) and flung them into the faces of the camp chieftains. (This act of defiance almost proved fatal; when he cut off his right ear, the razor slipped and nicked an artery.) Several months later, when he was asked what had prompted him to do such a thing, he replied, "When I leave this place, I want everyone to see what they've done to us." An inmate of ITK-12 got hold of a padlock, pierced the skin of his scrotum with the bolt, and snapped it shut—the ultimate ritual act of self-mutilation. The in-

* Autonomous republic within the RSFSR, on the upper Volga.

mate, deprived of his freedom and of all contact with women, can no longer think of himself as a whole man.

Self-multilation need not be purely symbolic, however. Many inmates are seriously afraid that their sexual organs will "shrivel up" after many years of deprivation. (In the camps the Russian "virility complex" may result in some fairly startling aberrations. The inmate who, in fact, is losing his sexual appetite and rarely experiences an orgasm may fall prey to a kind of schizoid delusion that his penis is actually shrinking, dwindling away to nothing before his eyes.) An inmate who is anticipating a conjugal visit and is worried about "getting it all the way up" may try to compensate by inserting little balls of plastic (called "dumbbells") under his foreskin, which is intended to make his supposedly atrophied organ a more formidable instrument of pleasure. This practice is not recommended. The wife of an inmate called Studenny, who had used fairly sizable "dumbbells," died of traumatic shock after a conjugal visit.

Another form of self-mutilation in the camps is tattooing, which is executed in the classic manner with a steel pen and India ink. The favored drawing surfaces are the chest, the soles of the feet, the buttocks, and even the penis. Most tattoo designs are pornographic, full of self-loathing and disgust for the world at large. One inmate, a passive homosexual known as Valechka (diminutive of Valentina) managed a tattooed representation of a vagina encircling his anus.

"Anti-Soviet" tattoos, such as "Death to Communism!" may be more than a straightforward protest against the inhumanity of camp conditions; a particularly conspicuous tattoo of this kind will be worth a trip to the hospital (and a vacation from the work brigade) while the offending inscription is removed, sometimes even by means of skin grafts. This presumably was not the motive of the inmate who covered his chest with a tattooed replica of the emblem worn by Soviet athletic teams—CCCP.

"Autosexuality"

This is the term I would propose to describe a phenomenon that I was totally unaware of before my arrival in ITK-12. The "autosexual" experiences sexual pleasure by sodomizing himself—that is, he inserts his semierect penis into his anus, and by means of the rhythmic contraction of the anal sphincter, assisted by the voluntary flexing of the muscles of the buttocks and the groin, he gives himself an orgasm. (Photographs of autosexuals circulate among prison inmates as a popular form of pornography.)

The autosexual is not a hermaphrodite or a member of some intermediate "third sex." The autosexual is not attracted to either sex, but only to himself. In contrast to the practice of masturbation, in which the imagination is always stimulated by an erotic image or idea, the autosexual is only aroused by the sight of his own naked body; one of the inmates of ITK-12 could bring himself to orgasm simply by getting undressed. In his outward behavior the autosexual appears to be virtually autistic; he says very little, or nothing at all, and he rarely seeks out the company of his fellow inmates. He lives in absolute solitude but never seems to be affected by loneliness. In this enclosed world the individual is both the subject and the object of his own gratification, which suggests the terrifying image of a creature that takes pleasure in devouring itself.

The Women's Camps

Since I am much less qualified to discuss this subject, for obvious reasons, I will confine myself to a brief description of the social conditions in the women's camps. My information is drawn from *samizdat* literature and the testimony of my fellow inmates, one man in particular whose wife had served a four-year sentence and described her camp experiences when she came to visit him in ITK-12.

Originally men and women simply lived in separate barracks in the same camp. During the Stalinist period the proximity of the sexes was a constant source of trouble—rape, brawls and riots, and violence and debauchery of every kind. Today men and women are confined in separate camps, and the women's camps are far less numerous. In some past years, though, there were hundreds of thousands of women in the camps, according to Kurganov: the wives of "enemies of the people," inexperienced girls who had not yet learned to conceal their true opinions and had thus been denounced for anti-Soviet agitation, peasant women who had stolen a few grains of wheat from the fields, Orthodox and Roman Catholic nuns, members of fundamentalist religious sects.

We know today what horrors these women endured; the guards'

absolute power gave free rein to sexual extortion. It required great courage to refuse under the threat of the most exhausting work, the worst indignities the guards could devise, the threat of death itself. We have already seen that women inmates were treated as human breeding stock by the authorities; women who were already pregnant when they were arrested, or who became pregnant in the camps, had their children taken away from them after a year, to be raised "collectively" in a prison nursery.

For me, there was no more heartbreaking sight than the fresh convoys of women prisoners arriving in the transit prisons, the inmate's way-station between pretrial detention and the camps. These women had suddenly found themselves abandoned in a sordid, unfamiliar world and humiliated by the brutalities and obscenities of the guards. In the mornings they would be marched out of the cell-blocks to the latrines, where the stench and filth were indescribable; the guards stood by and watched until it was time to march them back to their cells.

Here is a *samizdat* account written by a woman inmate of an incident which took place in the transit prison in Novosibirsk. Before their departure for the camp a group of twenty women was taken to the showers. As soon as they had taken off their clothes and lined up under the showerheads, they were pelted with boiling water. They screamed and flattened themselves against the walls, and a moment later, the water was ice-cold, then boiling once again.

> I thought at first that something had gone wrong with the pipes, and I started to pound on the door with all my strength. I could hear them laughing through the door, and I was furious. "Open up this instant!" At that moment they adjusted the water temperature to normal; we calmed down, started to soap ourselves, and the water stopped completely. "Everybody out!" Everyone's hair was still full of soap, so the reaction to this was nothing short of hysterical. We insisted that they turn the water on. It came on, boiling, then ice-cold. We were all backed up against the walls, rubbing our eyes and screaming. Then the door opened. "Everybody out!" This time the water was shut off for good, and we went out into the corridor. The girls (most of them were very young), still screaming, were huddled around the door. The guards started herding us down the corridor. "Let's go—nobody's going to hurt you." We started to run, and in fact there were guards and prison employees lined up along the corridor, heckling us as we went by.

> As for me, I had learned long ago that these sessions in the shower room furnished the guards with an excellent opportunity for satisfying their voyeuristic impulses, and I had acquired the bad habit of taking a shower with my slip on. I had already read stories of such things in Solzhenitsyn, I had seen them on the screen in Romm's *Ordinary Fascism*, but I never thought that I would have the chance to witness a scene like this for myself.

As far as I know, there is no equivalent of "untouchability" in the women's camps. Lesbianism is very common, but the social groupings that it gives rise to are not really closed castes. Thus inmates will speak of the *zavodily* ("leaders"), the female counterparts of the gangleaders and the active homosexuals among the "common laws." The *skoblikhi* ("scratchers") are so called because they masturbate their partners among the *zavodily*. They are not a despised underclass like the pederasts; theirs is a lucrative profession, and they are highly esteemed by the entire camp. They are really more like courtesans than common prostitutes, and their lives are not even remotely comparable to the homosexual slavery of the pederasts in the men's camps. I even heard stories of a celebrated *skoblikha* who cut off one hand at the wrist, since she felt that her fingers only hindered her in the exercise of her profession.

In the special-regime camps lesbian "marriages" are quite common, and the division of labor between the two partners is very sharply defined—the "wife" takes care of all the housekeeping, the laundry, and so forth. In the men's special-regime camps a pederast may be adopted (or abducted) by an active homosexual to serve as his sexual and domestic servant.

Of course all this can provide only the palest reflection of the real sexual misery of the Soviet labor camps. Three-quarters of their inmates are men and women in the prime of life, but sexual deprivation, even the loss of their freedom are only the preconditions for their misery. The tension, humiliation, and unrelieved fear that rule their lives ultimately leave them psychologically disoriented and emotionally numb. Violent social aberrations and sexual deviations are allowed to flourish in the camps, though the authorities can scarcely have imagined what the consequences will be for Soviet society.

We may choose to see the camp as a perfect scale model of the

Soviet Union itself, a microcosm, but in fact we must not forget that it has swallowed up millions of lives, and even today, long after the age of Stalin, beneath the thin crust of our "normal" lives with our new "freedoms," we can still feel its ominous presence. We have seen how the camp serves as the breeding ground for all of the psychosexual disorders and forbidden practices of Soviet society—from impotence, frigidity, sadism, and necrophilia to homosexuality and adult masturbation.

But the one vice that is unknown in the camps is hypocrisy, and I was always struck by the candor and brutal frankness with which my fellow inmates discussed their sexual adventures, swapped stories of their "conquests," boasted of how they had raped a fellow inmate, savored the misadventures of a pederast, or relived the pleasure of having "worked a scam" on the guards or the other inmates. It was as if all the prudery, the taboos, and the inhibitions of Soviet society had been swept away with a single impatient gesture. In the Soviet Union there is no middle course. "Respectable" people have nothing to say about sex. But as soon as men and women fall under the ban of society, they no longer have anything to hide, just as they have nothing to lose.

If I have ended this book with these stark and disturbing images of the camps, it is not because I intended to build up to a crescendo of horrors. In fact, far from imagining a sort of wasteland on the fringes of Soviet society, I think of the labor camp as the nucleus of the Soviet system. In a pessimistic moment Chernyshevsky once called the Russians "a pathetic race—from the highest to the lowest, they are no more than slaves." In this, the prophet of revolution seems to have had the last word on contemporary Soviet society.

CONCLUSION
Revolution or Catastrophe?

WHEN WESTERNERS think of the Soviet Union, they may imagine tanks and missiles, or the Gulag and the KGB, or an exotic vision of gilded domes and painted isbas—or, in short, anything but sex. But when the Soviet people think of the West, they think of creature comforts and consumer goods, free speech and free elections, and especially of sex—sexual freedom and the sexual revolution, pornography and eroticism. In fact, whatever name we might care to give it, this is the West's principal fascination in Russian eyes.

If I may speak of the Soviet Union as a "pre-Freudian" society, then the West seems to have come to terms with the Freudian revolution, first in theory, and more recently in practice. Psychoanalytic jargon has filtered into the common language, and cultured Westerners have committed themselves to exploring both the individual unconscious mind and the collective unconscious. (There is a paradox here—simply asserting that the unconscious mind exists seems to imply that it can be brought under conscious control and somehow assimilated into our ordinary working life.) On a more elementary level, it seems that the "erotic boom" of the last decade is beginning to lose its momentum, as recent studies appear to suggest.

None of this is true of the USSR. The official ideology claims to be able to give a clear and definitive scientific explanation of the past, present, and future. Thus, there is no room in this scheme for the unconscious mind, and official Marxism is extremely cool toward Freudian theory. I hope that I have shown that it is this repudiation of sexuality itself more than the most brutal tactics of repression that is responsible for the proliferation of all the pathological phenomena that I have tried to describe in this book. The Soviet Eros is no more than the demon of Gulag sexuality which has taken refuge in the lower depths of Soviet society and the Soviet psyche.

Yet, the mere fact that sexuality has suffered such restraint for over fifty years may still have certain unexpected consequences. The categorical denial of the erotic has made Soviet society a perfect model of repression (this time in the Freudian sense), and we should not rule out the possibility of a violent resurgence of these long-suppressed impulses, in the form of either a genuine cultural revolution or a catastrophic social upheaval.

The experience of sixty years of Soviet power has significantly changed the character of the Soviet people. And just as a sane person who expects to survive in an asylum would do well at least to simulate madness, the Soviet people have been similarly compelled to adapt to the special circumstances of their lives by disfiguring themselves, by abasing themselves before the despots who have stripped them of their fundamental human rights.

The Soviet citizen has forgotten how to take the initiative, how to cope with change, since change is something that he is never required to deal with. He is incapable of taking the long-term view, of thinking logically, of visualizing his life in a way that will enable him to behave responsibly. At the same time he is starting to lose his memory, in a society that is so devoted to the constant effacement and revision of the past. With all the other aspects of his life in such disarray, sex often plays a very important role—with its alternate moods of excitement and despair, and its whole train of fantasies, guilt feelings, and perversions.

Soviet society also disarms its critics by eliminating the idea of responsibility. Everything is done in the name of the people, and it would be impossible to find an official statement of policy that was not humanistic, progressive, and well intentioned. The blemishes, the darker corners of Soviet life are denied, or they are explained away once again by invoking the Marxist higher laws—"Who can we possibly blame for all this, when history is inevitably determined?" There is no use raking over the past or worrying about the future in a society without guilt or conflict. In such a paradise only a madman could be a rebel or a malcontent. Thus the circle closes on itself, like a maze in which the path is never blocked, though it still leads nowhere.

I have already suggested the equation of dissidence and madness, though I am certainly not the first to point out that any manifestation of nonconformity, independence, and opposition is sincerely believed to be a kind of insanity, and thus it is perfectly logical that dissidents should be whisked off to a psychiatric hospital. On the other hand, I would be inclined to compare the mass psychology of the Soviet Union to a hypnotic stupor. Hypnosis is based on a willing suspension of disbelief, and the hypnotist can only succeed if his patient (or his victim) is willing to cooperate totally.

In the Soviet Union the population is lulled into a permanent somnambulistic torpor, through constant exposure to every possible medium of lying propaganda, and the Soviet citizen is expected to incorporate these lies into his everyday norms of behavior. Certainly we are all familiar with the hypnotic power of advertising slogans in the West, but nowhere is this power so relentless and singleminded as in the Soviet Union.

The Soviet citizen is anxious, disoriented, and he devotes all his energies to a hopeless struggle to improve the material conditions of his existence in a world in which everything is in short supply. To assure his survival, he tends to shrink into the crowd, or perhaps to clamber up to the heights of privilege and power, so that he will not only survive but flourish. But once again, there is a price for this form of security; the would-be *apparatchik* must prostrate himself before a new idol that is even more demanding and implacable than the first. The life of the ruling caste involves even more duplicity and self-conscious distortion than that of the ordinary citizen, and their intricate code of conduct has its own internal logic which, like the self-consistent logic of schizophrenia, may be difficult for the outsider to grasp. In addition, this code has certain emotional imperatives—the Soviet citizen who wants to play the role of the good Communist, the faithful militant, must throw himself into the part with enthusiasm—just as his repentence (if he should be in need of some political reeducation) is expected to be sincere.

There is a short story called "The Inhabited Island" by the Soviet science-fiction writers Boris and Arkady Strugatsky which depicts a planet on which everyone's thoughts and actions are controlled by an extremely powerful ray. The allegory is quite transparent, and on our own planet it is the Soviet educational system that tugs the helpless individual away from his family in childhood and propels him along throughout his life, since it is true that "you're never too old to learn something new." Political education, literature, radio and television are merely the separate components of this gigantic educational machine. The clearest evidence of this, though, is the Soviet official language—"the wooden language," as it is generally known—in which words lose their meaning and seem to be swallowed up in a babble of static and white noise which are simply the audible frequencies of the Strugatskys' hypnotic ray.

The effects of all this can be readily observed in the behavior of the Soviet citizen who is taking his first steps on foreign soil. In fact, the participants in the current "third wave" of emigration generally take six months or a year to emerge from their post-hypnotic trance. Since they are conditioned to respond involuntarily (and often uncomprehendingly) to external signals, their first months of freedom often prove to be an arduous period of adjustment. They are suddenly compelled to make decisions, to ask questions, to choose between contradictory opinions, and (the most urgent imperative) to struggle to make a living—quite a contrast with the secure, well-ordered life in a total institution.

As Orwell has pointed out, sexual repression is a necessary component of this system of mass hypnosis. Just as we once had the barbarous custom of castrating young boys to make them sing more sweetly, the totalitarian society has to extinguish the erotic element in men and women, to neutralize their basic sexual drives, before it can make them speak the "wooden language."

As I mentioned earlier, recent studies by Shere Hite and Masters and Johnson suggest that Americans may be less concerned about sex than they were a decade ago, presumably a reaction against the "sexual revolution" of the sixties. But asexuality in the USSR is a result of sexual repression and a loss of sexual appetite that threatens the cohesion of Soviet society and, in my opinion, perhaps even the survival of the Russian people themselves, once certain psychological and biological limits have been reached. I treated a number of patients who suffered from a form of narcolepsy and used to fall asleep while they were making love, even at the precise moment of climax.

Their lovemaking was a passionless and labored affair, and sometimes the "sleep" they (men and women alike) fell into so abruptly was actually closer to a state of catalepsy. Essentially the act itself required such an enormous expenditure of emotional energy that the stress became too great for them to bear. This was no longer "mass hypnosis," in the metaphorical sense, but a genuine hypnotic trance.

Terror has always been conducive to sexual hysteria; sexual drives are sublimated in a fixation on a political leader or symbol, as was the case in Nazi Germany, or during that outpouring of hysterical grief that followed the death of Stalin. But as soon as the idol was toppled from his pedestal, the Soviet people were abruptly awakened from their trance.

This marked the first appearance of what I called "the gap in the hedge," or less picturesquely, "the breakdown of official morality." Certainly the Stalinist terror was concentrated on many other targets besides sexuality, but it is true that the most elementary aspects of sexual freedom were considered to be as subversive and as potentially dangerous to the Soviet system as freedom of thought or artistic expression, or the free-market economy itself. And it was for this reason that a new generation began to acquire a taste for freedom which in turn presented the authorities with a whole raft of social problems: the instability of the "Communist family," divorce, premarital sex, the constantly increasing abortion rate (up to the current ratio of two abortions for every live birth in Moscow). The regime is rightly concerned about all this, and perhaps this is an instinctive reaction to what they perceive as a threat to the foundations of their authority and not simply as a test of their ability to monitor the private lives of their subjects or as an indication that the declining birthrate is likely to deplete their future workforce and undermine the socialist economy. In fact, the authorities are primarily concerned because they have recognized in these phenomena the first willful and unpredictable manifestations of freedom, even under the guise of mere anarchy and sexual license.

Lenin once remarked that if even the slightest concessions were made to free enterprise and the free market, if the peasants were allowed to work their land and market their produce in the absence of strict controls over agricultural production, then the restoration of capitalism would become inevitable. In the same spirit, even the slightest sexual vagary on the part of young people is necessarily intolerable, lest this example prove to be contagious. The revolt of youth, usually a naive and diffident affair, is simply an attempt to rediscover a free and natural kind of love (free in particular from ideological imperatives and moral taboos), and this in itself is a challenge to the system. In the West young people have launched an attack on conventionality, complacency, and materialism; the enemy is society itself. In the Soviet Union, the youth revolt envisages only that the individual should be able to assert himself in the face of the Soviet system. These expressions, sometimes even proclamations of sexual license among young people are an affirmation of free will in their own lives, as well as a way of combatting apathy and depersonalization. Sometimes the tactics of this revolt are both ingenuous and extremely revealing—young people may refuse to drink vodka before they make love, they may insist on making love in daylight rather than total darkness. Thus when certain Soviet sociologists try to attribute all this to the decline of traditional peasant morality, we should treat their claims with extreme caution. In the first place, the traditional peasant morality was still another casualty of collectivization in the early thirties. The current Soviet "sexual revolution" is not the result of forced urbanization but rather the manifestation of a search for natural and normal forms of sexual expression. One sector of the Soviet population is seeking to replace the official norms of sexual behavior with a new definition of sexuality and of sexual morality. So far these preliminary attempts have usually been characterized by cynicism and sexual license, but it is far from clear what forms they will take in the future. But one thing at least is certain: Sexuality is not the least explosive of the elemental forces that are undermining the present structure of Soviet society. And if the future can be read in the ravaged social landscape of the Soviet Union, then it seems to offer only two alternatives—either a revolutionary change in social attitudes and sexual mores, or a catastrophic political explosion.

Paris, January 1979

APPENDIX

1

The Harvest of Cocks

(AFANASYEV'S *Secret Russian Tales,* XXXI)

Collected by Alexander Afanasyev (1826–1871) in the Russian countryside in 1840 and 1950, first published anonymously in Geneva during the 1860s.

ONCE THERE were two peasants who went out to their fields in seedtime; they had just finished plowing, and were ready to sow their fields with rye. They met an old man on the road who stopped the first peasant and said, "Good day to you, young fellow!" "And to you, grandfather!" "What are you sowing then?" "Rye, grandfather." "Well then, God grant the grain grows high, and every stalk bows low at harvest!" Then the old man asked the second peasant, "And what are you sowing then?" "A nosy old fellow you are!" the peasant replied. "I'm sowing cocks, and what do you say to that?" "Just this—God grant that you shall reap what you sow!" The old man went on his way; the two peasants went off to sow their fields with rye, and harrowed it in, and went back home. And after the spring rains came, the first peasant's field was covered with lovely green sprigs of rye, and the second peasant's field was full of little red-headed cocks, so you couldn't set your foot down without treading on one or two. The two peasants went out to their fields; the first was as happy as an honest man can be, but the other was so dumbfounded he didn't know what saint to light a candle to. "I'll be damned if I know," he said to himself, "what to do with these blessed cocks!"

At harvest time they went back to their fields; the first man set about harvesting his field of rye, while the other just stood there, shaking his head and wondering what to do. The cocks stood a full yard tall, as thick as mushrooms and as red as field-poppies. Then he went off home and gathered up some knives and honed them down, and found some paper and binding twine, and went back to his field to bring in the harvest.

Every time he cut two cocks, he wrapped them up, and tied them tight, and put them in his cart. And when they were all stacked up in his cart, he went off to hawk them through the town. "You never know," he said to himself, "but that some fool of a woman might buy a pair." When he came to town, he started to cry his wares—"Who'll buy my cocks, my cocks? Co-ocks! Cocks for sale! Who'll buy my lovely cocks?" A lady heard his cries and called for her chambermaid. "Hurry off now and ask that *muzhik* what he has to sell!" The girl caught up with the peasant, and asked him, to which he replied, "Cocks, if it please you, miss." So she went back to find her mistress, but she didn't dare repeat what the peasant had said. "Speak up, you stupid girl. I won't bite you!" "Well, ma'am, the worthless scoundrel told me he was selling cocks." "Well, you're even a bigger fool than I took you for then. Run back as fast as you can and ask him what he wants for a pair of them!"

So the girl ran back to find the peasant once again. "My mistress wants to know, how much for a pair?" "A hundred rubles," he replied, "And I don't haggle." So her mistress sent her straight back with a hundred rubles. "And make sure," she said, "that you pick out two nice big fat ones!" The girl found the peasant and held out the money. "Very well, my man, my mistress wants two of your best." "She'll get nothing but the best from me," the peasant said, and the girl went home again with a pair of fine cocks. Her mistress was so delighted that she couldn't take her eyes off them, at least till it was time to set them to work.

She thought she knew how it was done, of course, but it was still no use; the cocks just stood there and wouldn't budge. "Do you mean," she said to the chambermaid, "that *muzhik* didn't even tell you how to make them go?" "No, ma'am." "Idiot! Go back and find out." She went out to find the peasant again. "Tell me, my brave fellow," she said, "those things you gave me, how do you make them go?" "Another hundred rubles and you might find out," the peasant replied. The girl went back to tell her mistress, and she handed over the money right away: "Even for two hundred, they're not that easy to come by." So as soon as the peasant got the second hundred rubles, he explained, "Whenever she wants some, all she has to do is say "Giddyap there!' "

So the lady stretched out on her bed, and hiked up her dress, and said, "Giddyap there!" And the cocks leapt up and set to work, and gave her all she wanted, and more besides. And then she remembered that she did not know how to make them stop, and she shouted for her chambermaid. "Hurry off and find that rascal of a peasant and make him tell you what I do to get them to leave me in peace!" So the girl went back to the peasant and asked, "My mistress wants them to leave her in peace. Otherwise she's not long for this world!" "A hundred rubles," the peasant said, "and I'll tell you what she wants to know." By the time she got back, her mistress was at the end of her tether for sure. "Wait," she said, "there's another hundred rubles in the drawer, all I have left—give it to that son of a bitch and get back here while there's still breath left in my body!" The peasant took the third hundred rubles and told the girl, "Just say 'Whoa back there!' when you want 'em to stand easy." This time when she got back, her mistress was already more dead than alive. "Whoa back there!" the girl shouted, and the two cocks did just that. Her mistress took a deep breath, and got to her feet, and locked them away in a drawer. And from that day on she lived a life of pleasure; whenever she felt the inclination, she'd fetch them out again, and whenever she'd had enough, she had only to shout "Whoa back there!"

But one day she went off to visit some friends of hers in another town and left the cocks behind by mistake. That night she started feeling very lonely, and could think of nothing but going straight back home. Her friends begged her to stay. "Impossible," she replied. "There's something I left at home—never mind what exactly—and I'll never be able to get to sleep without it." "No need to trouble yourself," her friends assured her. "We'll send the footman off right away. He's a very trustworthy fellow." She agreed at once, and they sent for the footman. "Ask for my chambermaid," she told him. "She'll know what it's about." And sure enough, as soon as the footman arrived, the maid came out with a carrying case with the two cocks inside it. He took the case, jumped back in the saddle, and made for home. When he came to an uphill stretch, his horse began to slow down. "Giddyap there!" he shouted, and at that the cocks leapt out of the case and made straight for his asshole! The footman broke out in a cold sweat. "What kind of deviltry is this then?" he said to himself. "And where did those blasted cocks come from?" But luckily for him, just then he reached the top of the hill, and his horse started to gallop down the other slope. "Whoa back there!" he cried, and the cocks scuttled back into their cases. When he arrived at his master's house, he handed over the cocks to their mistress. "No trouble, I hope," she said. "The devil fly away with those cocks!" he cried. "If it wasn't for my horse, I'd have been fucked within an inch of my life!"

2

*Luka Mudishchëv (abridged)**

Attributed to Ivan Barkov (1732–1768), "Luka Mudishchëv" has never been published in the Soviet Union except in samizdat.

Prologue

O Cunt, the mother of us all,
And man's untarnished prize,
With what eternal industry
Thou mak'st the nations rise!

Part I

In a pleasant square in Moscow
There lived the plump and pretty,
The fetching fairskinned widow
Of a burger of the city.

Her husband kept a counting house,
But soon, to say the least, her
Cunt had used up all his stock,
And so he predeceased her.

* The title might be very freely translated as "Well-hung Luke."

For she, like all the women,
Had got the Devil in her,
And what a devil of a cunt
To punish a poor sinner!

For though his cock insisted
There was no more virtue in it,
Her placket was implacable—
"You'll fuck me, sir, this minute!"

Soon worn out in her service
(Three hundred nights of passion!),
He went to seek that Blessed Land
Where fucking's out of fashion.

Her tears ran down like rivers
Of sorrow, pain, and dolor,
Though Petya, Sasha, Mishka,
They all tried to console her.

A green lad or a graybeard
(Or anyone) she'd suffer
To climb into the saddle
(I mean she let them stuff her).

Her cunt was champing at the bit
But a gelding's not a horse,
And ev'ry stallion proved a cob,
Or couldn't stay the course.

Their cocks were short and stubby,
Their balls were low and lax,
Instead of tight light drumskins
Hung down like empty sacks.

"A pox on empty gallantry,
I'd rather keep my honor!"
But why had Fate been pleased to play
This vexing trick upon her?

With cocks as limp as dishclouts,
Not half what they were once,
Where was the cock whose ardor
Was equal to her cunt's?

But the melancholy humors
That filled her endless nights
Were vanquished by a vision
Of how to set things right.

"I'll find an old procuress
Who keeps a knocking shop—
And she'll have my widow's portion
If she'll find me such a cock!"

[In Part II she enlists the help of a procuress, who arranges an assignation with Luka Mudishchëv.]

Part III

In a lonely wretched hovel
At the bottom of Gin Lane
Lived our lonely wretched hero,
Luka Mudishchëv by name.

Like ev'ry man among us,
He had his cross to bear.
His was all of twenty inches,
With an inch or so to spare.

The maid, the wife, the widow
The doxy and the duchess
All shrank from Luka's member—
It was too much of a muchness.

[The poem ends in tragedy. The widow is eviscerated, the procuress castrates Luka in a vain attempt to save her client, and Luka clubs her to death with his severed virility. The stage is littered with corpses as the curtain falls.]

3

*Translation of a Patent Application * Filed in the Soviet Union in 1972*

Union of Soviet Socialist Republics	APPLICATION FOR DESIGN PATENT	329698
	Previous application: 7/1/68 Preliminary patent granted: 7/1/69	A 61f 5/42
Committee on Inventions and Scientific Discoveries of the Council of Ministers of the USSR	(United Kingdom: Pat. app. no. 1344924/31-16; Pat. no. 31237/68.) Design specifications published 2/9/72, Bulletin No. 7 Date of publication of patent description: 4/12/72	618.17-71 (088 . 8)

Name of Applicant and Author of Patent Description	Biresvar Bisah (Indian)

* See Part II, Chapter 7, page 100.

A Device Intended To Enhance Female Sexual Response

The device described herein is intended to enhance female sexual response by means of vibrations which directly stimulate the erogenous zones.

The proposed device is unique in that it consists of a hollow conical bulb which is composed of an elastic material and the base of which may be provided (for example) with an elastic collar to which a clip may be affixed in order to connect the device to an electrical source of vibrations. The outer surface of the bulb is provided with protuberances which correspond to the most sensitive areas of the female sexual organs. This substantive design modification ensures that the device will fit securely around the base of the penis and that the exterior surface of the bulb will adhere firmly to the erogenous zones of the female sexual organs.

Figures 1 and 2 illustrate the hollow conical bulb (1) with a flexible diaphragm (2), the inner rim of which contains a U-shaped indentation (3). Adjacent to the outer rim of the flexible diaphragm is the base (4) in the form of an elastic collar. The lower rim of the base is provided with a protruding clip (5), which enables the device to be connected to an electrical power source (6) by means of a transmission system (7), which power source causes the device to vibrate. The outer surface (8) of the base of the conical bulb is provided with protuberances (9) which correspond to the most sensitive areas of the female sexual organs.

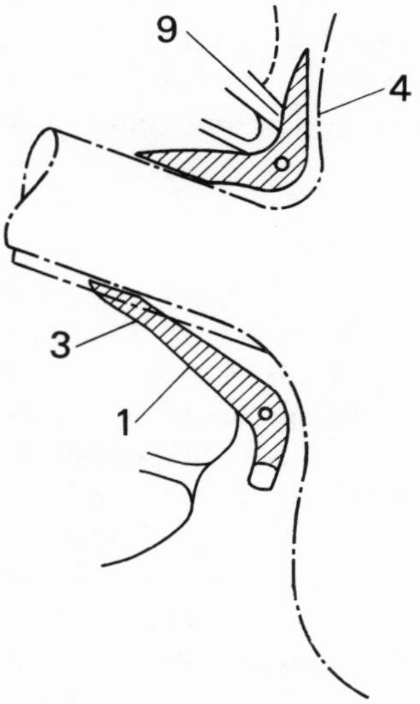

Figure 1

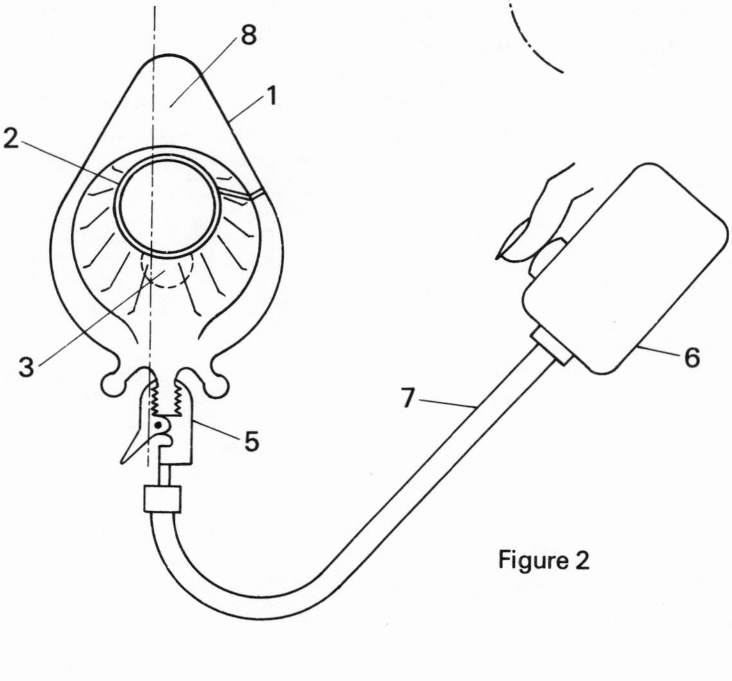

Figure 2

Before intercourse the male partner slips the device over his erect penis (the size and shape of the conical bulb may be selected by partners in accordance with the individual dimensions of their respective sexual organs). As soon as the penis is inserted into the vagina, the female partner switches on the external power source, causing the device to vibrate; the external power source may be switched off when erotic sensations have been aroused, whereupon sexual intercourse may proceed normally.

Purposes of the Invention

The unique design aspects of this device intended to enhance female sexual response by means of vibrations which directly stimulate the erogenous zones of the female sexual organs during intercourse are twofold: (1) An improved method of securing the device to the base of the penis and of ensuring the total adhesion of the outer surface of the device to the most sensitive areas of the female sexual organs, and thus facilitating the orgasmic response of the female partners is achieved by means of a hollow conical bulb composed of an elastic material whose base is outfitted with an elastic collar to which a protruding clip is affixed which permits the device to be connected to an external source of vibration; (2) The exterior surface of the base of the conical bulb is provided with protuberances which correspond in location to the most sensitive areas of the female sexual organs.

INDEX